Central America: Regional Integration and National Political Development

Westview Replica Editions

This book is a Westview Replica Edition. The concept of Replica Editions is a response to the crisis in academic and informational publishing. Library budgets for books have been severely curtailed; economic pressures on the university presses and the few private publishing companies primarily interested in scholarly manuscripts have severely limited the capacity of the industry to properly serve the academic and research communities. Many manuscripts dealing with important subjects, often representing the highest level of scholarship, are today not economically viable publishing projects. Or, if they are accepted for publication, they are often subject to lead times ranging from one to three years. Scholars are understandably frustrated when they realize that their first-class research cannot be published within a reasonable time frame, if at all.

Westview Replica Editions are our practical solution to the problem. The concept is simple. We accept a manuscript in camera-ready form and move it immediately into the production process. The responsibility for textual and copy editing lies with the author or sponsoring organization. If necessary we will advise the author on proper preparation of footnotes and bibliography. We prefer that the manuscript be typed according to our specifications, though it may be acceptable as typed for a dissertation or prepared in some other clearly organized and readable way. The end result is a book produced by lithography and bound in hard covers. Initial edition sizes range from 400 to 600 copies, and a number of recent Replicas are already in second printings. We include among Westview Replica Editions only works of outstanding scholarly quality or of great informational value, and we will continue to exercise our usual editorial standards and quality control.

Central America: Regional Integration and National Political Development

Royce Q. Shaw

This study challenges several widely held assumptions about Central American economic integration, arguing that the key to understanding the failure of the integration program lies in neither advanced economic nor regional integration theory, but in the domestic politics of the states involved. Thus, the author contends that the Common Market was not the cause of the balance-of-payments and balanced-growth crises in Central America; rather, domestic political forces were the major factor in the collapse of the market and the subsequent attempts at restructuring.

Professor Shaw disputes the standard interpretations of the role of the technocrats in the integration process and demonstrates that the domestic political elites played an important role throughout. He also challenges the assumption that economic integration is always a force for conciliation, pointing out that the Common Market aggravated some of the conflicts that led to war between El Salvador and Honduras in 1969. Nor are integration programs among less developed countries necessarily instruments of political and social change, according to this analysis; on the contrary, political elites used the Common Market to bypass the internal economic reforms necessary for national development.

This study incorporates new material--interview data and other primary source material--on events of the past eight years.

Royce Q. Shaw is assistant professor of political science at Newberry College. He holds a Ph.D. in political science from the University of Virginia.

Central America: Regional Integration and National Political Development

Royce Q. Shaw

Routledge
Taylor & Francis Group
LONDON AND NEW YORK

First published 1978 by Westview Press

Published 2018 by Routledge
52 Vanderbilt Avenue, New York, NY 10017
2 Park Square, Milton Park, Abingdon, Oxon OX14 4RN

Routledge is an imprint of the Taylor & Francis Group, an informa business

Library of Congress Catalog Card Number: 78-19664

ISBN 13: 978-0-367-01794-1 (hbk)
ISBN 13: 978-0-367-16781-3 (pbk)

Contents

Preface

The Central American regional integration movement has been the subject of widespread interest for almost two decades. In that period, more than a dozen major books and over one hundred articles have been written on various aspects of the integration movement. With few exceptions, observers have viewed the integration program from one of two perspectives. One group focuses on the narrow, essentially economic aspects of the integration program. The other group views the common market within the framework of regional integration theory. In both cases, the common market has been viewed outside the context of the Central American domestic political systems. While these two perspectives have yielded valuable insights and information, taken together they fail to answer adequately all of the important questions concerning the nature of the integration process and the reasons for its apparent "failure."

This study introduces a third focus: domestic politics and the role of the political leadership in the integration movement. The analysis is based on the premise that the key to understanding the failure of the integration program lies, not in advanced economic or regional integration theory, but in the domestic politics of the member states.

This study analyzes the major events and processes which compose the history of the integration movement and examines the roles and goals of the major actors. The object is to clarify a number of misconceptions about the nature and the process of economic integration in Central America. Specifically, the study challenges several of the most widely held assumptions concerning the Central American economic integration movement.

First, this study challenges the assumption

that the "external penetration" of the common market by the United States was a major cause of the common market's ultimate failure. According to "dependency theory," the common market failed because it was dominated by private United States capital investment; and United States private investors reaped the lion's share of the benefits of the common market. But dependency theory falls far short of explaining the failure of the integration movement. After examining the key decisions made by the Central American political elites regarding the growth and development of the common market, the study concludes that the Central American political elites were not dominated by external political actors.

Second, the analysis disproves the belief that the common market was the cause of the balanced growth and balance of payments issues and that these issues caused the common market to collapse. The study concludes that underlying domestic and regional political forces were the major factor in the collapse of the common market and subsequently have prevented the common market from being reconstructed.

Third, the analysis questions the thesis that economic integration, in its initial stages, is technical and apolitical, and that is the reason the integrationists were so successful in the early stages of the integration movement. This study demonstrates that the political elites participated actively in the early stages of the integration movement, because they saw that it promised substantial political payoffs.

Finally, this study explores the thesis that economic integration programs among less developed countries are an instrument of economic and social change. On the contrary, the analysis demonstrates that the political elites both supported and manipulated the economic integration program in order to reinforce the political and economic status quo. They used the common market to bypass the internal economic reforms necessary for national development.

1. The Origins of the Integration Movement

The ideal of political and economic union has existed in Central America since the post-independence disintegration of the former Captaincy General of Guatemala into the five sovereign units of Costa Rica, Honduras, El Salvador, Nicaragua, and Guatemala. Since then, there have been at least twenty-five unsuccessful attempts at unification. The last failure occurred in 1946 when Guatemala and El Salvador attempted to form a political union. The main reason for the failure of these early attempts at integration was (and perhaps still may be) the political climate in Central America. The series of short wars, strong isolationist dictators, and internal struggles for power paralyzed both internal and regional political and economic development in all of the countries except for Costa Rica.

The first successful steps toward the "reconstruction" of Central American unity were made in the decade of the 1950s, when the five Central American republics, with the guidance of the United Nations Economic Commission for Latin America (ECLA), launched a program of economic integration.

> Instead of superimposing the ultimate objectives of political federation upon several centrifugal systems, the attempt now was to add to them a real dimension of regional scope in the form of a series of common, newly created economic interests. Instead of a total movement toward immediate action, the sights were set upon a more limited, less inclusive target. The chances for union in the future were thus grounded on the consol-

idation of national markets and their gradual transformation and growth as a single economic unit.[1]

According to one integration official, this latest attempt at integration would have been added to the list of unsuccessful attempts to reunite the region, if it had not been for the post-war political changes which enlarged the political elites of most of the Central American countries.[2] Carlos Castillo, former Director of the Committee of Economic Cooperation and Executive Secretary of the General Treaty on Economic Integration, agrees:

> A new generation, more concerned with the realities of economic growth than with the niceties of diplomacy or the rhetorics of political union, had reached positions of power in the governments of the five countries. It was the vision of these men that enabled them to see far ahead and to conceive the economic integration program, in spite of the complacent mood encouraged by the high export prices prevailing at the time.[3]

This was the environment in Central America when the fourth session of the United Nations Economic Commission for Latin America met in Mexico in June 1951. The Central American delegations included three economic ministers who had been trained abroad; they considered themselves economists rather than politicians. They were concerned primarily about the external dependence of their economies on world commodity prices and the problems that the small size of their markets posed for industrial development. A resolution was adopted at the June ECLA session which called for the "gradual and progressive" integration of the Central American economies. The Central American governments agreed to "promote the integration of their economies and the expansion of markets by the exchange of their products, the coordination of their development programs and the establishment of enterprises in which all or some of the countries have an interest."[4] Both at the June ECLA session and at later gatherings, the ministers worked closely with the international civil servants of ECLA, with whom they thought they had a lot in common.[5]

This session had three consequences: it created the Committee for Economic Cooperation, the forum where the Ministers of Economy were to meet;

it entrusted ECLA's Secretariat with the task of outlining the program of economic integration; and it created a subregional office in Mexico City for Central America, Mexico, Panama, and part of the Caribbean. In this manner the institutional setting and the guidelines for the program of economic integration were established.

At the same time the Ministers of Foreign Affairs were working to establish a subregional organization within the framework of the United Nations and the Organization of American States. In October 1951, they signed the Charter of San Salvador to create the Organization of Central American States (ODECA). The foreign ministers thought they could approach political integration in spite of the failures of the past. This optimism had been created by the recent signing of the Bogota Charter of the Organization of American States, by the recent provisions of the San Francisco Charter, and by an underlying desire to operate under the techniques of modern international law.

> They seem to have believed that, guided by these modern legal instruments, they had taken a transcendental but realistic step beyond the symbolic and ineffectual attempts of the past. The language of their charter is gradualistic; the scope and level of the organization's authority are minimal, but its 'primordial objective' is to reconstruct the political unity of Central America.[6]

While the language of the Charter was gradualistic, it also was very general. ODECA's goals were: to strengthen the bonds that united them; to seek peaceful solutions for any conflict that might arise among them; and to search for joint solutions to their economic, social, and cultural development.[7] According to Isaac Cohen Orantes, an official of the Permanent Secretariat of the General Treaty on Central American Integration (SIECA) who helped prepare SIECA's "Decade Study" of Central American Integration in the 1970s, "The texts speak for themselves...the generality that characterizes the latter has been one of the major causes for ODECA's failure, while the technocrats' precision and more pragmatic goals have contributed to their relative success."[8]

One of the institutions established by the Charter of San Salvador was the Economic Council, which was subordinate to the Ministers of Foreign Affairs. The subordination of the Economic Council to the Foreign Ministers was in direct conflict with the goals of the Economic Ministers, who had set up the Committee for Economic Cooperation under ECLA's guidance in order to pursue their limited economic objectives. Foreseeing the result of their subordination to the "politicos," the "tecnicos" who were at the meeting of San Salvador as members of the national delegations immediately obtained the approval of a resolution which granted the Economic Council more independence than was originally proposed in the Charter, although the Economic Ministers were still technically under the supervision of the Foreign Ministers.[9]

The Central American technocrats wanted to free their activities from ODECA's attempts at political "reunification." Thus, they maintained the separability of the two committees. This was demonstrated graphically when the Ministers of Economy met in Tegucigalpa in August 1952. They actually held two separate meetings: they met for four days as members of ECLA's Committee for Economic Cooperation (CCE); after that meeting ended, they met for one day as members of ODECA's Economic Council. The Economic Ministers had completed all of their serious business in the CCE meeting, demonstrating their determination to protect their integration program from the politics of the region.[10]

Within a year the technocrats' fears were justified. At the very first meeting of the Ministers of Foreign Affairs in 1952, Nicaragua made the traditional appeal for immediate unification, which was unacceptable to the other delegations. At the second meeting in 1953, the government of El Salvador proposed to add to the agenda a discussion of the infiltration of Communism in the area. The Guatemalan government accused the other four countries of using ODECA to form a political-military pact against it and withdrew from the organization.[11]

The Foreign Ministers did not meet again until ideological homogeneity was restored to the area when the Guatemalan government was overthrown. When they met in Guatemala in 1955, one of the resolutions they adopted enlarged the functions of the Economic Council, giving it direct access to the governments in order to facilitate the accomplishment of its basic goals.[12]

But ODECA was racked by ideological confrontations, border disputes, and conflicts arising from disputes over the elections of its secretaries-general. It held only two regular meetings during the 1950s but was revived by other integration efforts in the 1960s. ODECA has been unsuccessful in making any progress toward its "primordial objective."

In spite of the political turmoil which characterized the 1950s, and in spite of ODECA's failures, the Economic Ministers met every year. Even though Guatemala had withdrawn from ODECA in April 1953, it sent a delegation to the second meeting of the Committee of Economic Cooperation in October 1953. This confirmed the technocrats' belief that ECLA furnished a "technical and noncontroversial setting for the program of economic cooperation."[13]

The record of the ECLA-guided tecnicos in the late 1950s is impressive, including: the Multilateral Treaty on Central American Free Trade; the Agreement on the Regime of Central American Integration Industries; the Central Bank for Economic Integration; the Central American School of Public Administration; the Central American Institute of Research and Technology; and agreements on uniform road codes and customs nomenclature.

The tecnicos' chief activity during the 1951-58 period was the preparation of a broad range of technical economic studies. These were principally the work of the ECLA regional office in Mexico City. Most observers agree that these technical studies played an indispensable role in translating the general idea of economic integration into a functioning reality.

The three basic legal instruments of the Common Market were signed between 1958 and 1960, although the last of them did not go into effect until 1961 and was not fully ratified until 1963. The first of these was the Multilateral Treaty on Central American Free Trade and Economic Integration, signed in 1958. It dealt primarily with removing tariff barriers among the member countries, but it was only a cautious first step because it covered only a small number of items that posed no special problems. Its major provision was that the member governments would periodically negotiate additions to the free trade list, looking eventually toward complete free trade within the region. In this respect, it was very similar to the treaty which established the Latin American Free Trade Association.

The second basic integration treaty, the Central American Agreement on Tariff Equalization, was signed in 1959. A complementary agreement to the 1958 treaty, this agreement took the important first step toward the establishment of uniform external tariffs for the Central American countries; it was also the preface to the subsequent virtual abolition of internal tariffs in Central America. The general approach was the rough averaging--with some upward movement--of the previous tariffs of the five individual countries. Uniform rates were agreed to on a substantial number of the more than 1,200 tariff categories, with some to go into effect immediately upon ratification and others to be instituted gradually over a five-year transition period.

Two important events preceded--and may have precipitated--the signing of the third of the basic agreements in December 1960, the General Treaty on Central American Economic Cooperation. A tripartite treaty of economic association among El Salvador, Honduras, and Guatemala was signed in January 1960. This agreement reflected the strong desire of these three countries to accelerate the pace of the integration program; it went well beyond the Multilateral Treaty of 1958 in that it called for immediate internal free trade in most goods. A number of factors, predominantly political in nature, limited this step to the three countries. A related development, which directly influenced the signing of both the Tripartite Treaty and the General Treaty, was the decision of the United States to extend special economic assistance to help solve the problems of transition if the Central American governments decided to establish a free trade area.

Against the background of these events, and following a period of intense negotiations, the most important of the integration instruments, the General Treaty on Central American Economic Cooperation, was signed by the five Ministers of Economy in December 1960. It was a bold agreement which reversed the approach of the 1958 treaty. While the 1958 treaty had agreed simply to free trade on a small list of uncontroversial items and left the vast majority for subsequent negotiations, the 1960 General Treaty called for immediate agreement on all items except those on a special schedule--less than ten percent of the total--and left this residue for future negotiations. Thus, the basic treaty provided for, almost within a single stroke, a firm agreement on a virtually complete free trade area. It was this decisive step that quickly transformed the integration movement from a slow and uncertain process into a definite reality.

The process of legislative ratification of the General Treaty continued for some time. Guatemala, Nicaragua, and El Salvador formally deposited their ratifications by June 1961, and the treaty immediately became operable for these three countries. Honduras deposited its ratification in April 1962, and Costa Rica did so in September 1963. Thus, while the Common Market formally became operational in June 1961, it did not become a complete five-member market until September 1963.

Between 1960 and 1968, some very real progress was made. The rate of growth for the entire region increased noticeably in the years following the ratification of the General Treaty. Intra-regional trade increased from 3.5 percent of the region's total trade in 1960 to more than 27 percent in 1968, the peak year in the relative importance of Common Market activity. The free flow of goods within the market stimulated output through specialization and economies of scale. Established Central American industries, suddenly able to produce for a regional rather than just a domestic market, expanded production. As the import substitution process--the domestic production of goods which were previously imported--moved from simple consumer manufactures to a wider range of production goods, new industries came into being. The improved growth opportunities of the area and the favorable attitudes toward foreign investors were instrumental in attracting a large inflow of private capital to the member states. Indeed, as a result of the erection of a common and relatively high tariff barrier, the integration movement provided foreign enterprises with a strong incentive to open branches or subsidiaries inside the market area to avoid import duties.[14]

As important as the new industries and the new jobs was the growing sense of identification with the integration movement among important segments of the population. The Central American Common Market, the showcase of Latin American regional integration, and probably the most successful integration experience outside of Europe, had become, if nothing else, a source of great local pride. A host of functional organizations had come into being, including a regional development bank, a regional tourist organization, a telecommunications organization, and an agro-industry organization. In addition, organizations not officially connected with the Common Market joined together businessmen and educators. As a result of the burgeoning contacts and the ensuing relationships, the mythology of Central Americanism began to take on new substance. Problems were faced and decisions were made in a regional context. Optimistic expectations about economic progress through economic integration became more prevalent. The process seemed both open-ended and irreversible. This attitude was due, in part, to the fact that the formative years of the Common Market had coincided with a period of rapidly increasing export earnings. With traditional exports doing well and industrial expansion under way, businessmen and government officials alike could afford to be very positive in their outlook.

By 1968, however, the bubble had burst. Some of the magic and some of the enthusiasm had disappeared, and political leaders began to see the market in perhaps a more jaundiced, but certainly a more realistic light. Beginning in 1965, prices of certain key export commodities started to fall, leading to a slowdown in economic growth and serious balance-of-payments and government revenue problems. Higher export earnings during the prosperous years effectively had hidden the fact that traditional sources of government income were being undermined while government expenditures and foreign exchange requirements were increasing. Industrialization was intensifying the demand for equipment and raw material imports, which put a great strain on foreign exchange reserves. Increased government interest in social and economic development programs was swelling government expenditures, while the rising volume of duty-free intraregional trade and fiscal incentives granted to attract industry were interfering with the growth of government revenues.

By 1968, therefore, the problem had grown too serious to ignore. The five member states signed an agreement, the San Jose Protocol, providing for a 30 percent tariff surcharge on imports from outside the region and allowing the levying of a regional sales tax on a number of nonessential items. The agreement, however, became a political football in Costa Rica and a bargaining lever in a minor feud between Honduras and El Salvador. The inability or the disinclination of these three countries to ratify the protocol prevented it from serving its function, and the balance-of-payments and budget problems continued unchecked.

Budgetary difficulties alone, however, were not responsible for the growing sense of frustration and disillusionment, particularly in Honduras and Nicaragua. The five member states had started the integration process at differing stages of economic development, and now they were becoming aware that they were also reaping the benefits in differing proportions. As a result, the Common Market began to polarize between those countries that were relatively satisfied with the Market as it existed and those that demanded its restructuring. The former enjoyed a favorable regional balance of trade and were concerned that they would find their economic development even further behind the others at the end of the decade than it had been at the beginning.

The countries that were less successful in attracting industry and less able to compete in intraregional trade began to point out some of the negative features of import substitution. They noted, for example, that Central American manufactures were not always very desirable. Consumers had grown accustomed to buying high-quality foreign goods at reasonable prices, and they were unhappy at having to subsidize inefficient Central American producers by purchasing items that combined high cost and low quality. It also was pointed out that some of the so-called Central American products were that in name only. A number of foreign firms were setting up plants within the Market area to gain tax advantages and tariff concessions. Only the final uncomplicated steps in the fabrication of a product were done locally before the item was labeled "made in Central America" and marketed. Thus, some of the "new" industries were providing relatively few jobs, introducing little new technology, and contributing only marginally to the industrialization process.

Although the flavor of sour grapes ran through much of the argument, the complaints had some basis in fact. The easy gains from import substitution were made quickly, and increased production was no longer merely a matter of utilizing the excess capacity of existing plants. Now modernization of traditional activities and production of increasingly complex goods were required. The ability of the various Central American states to provide or attract the needed technological skills, management capacity, and capital resources, therefore, became critical. Competition among the member states led to distortions in the placement of investment, duplication of factories, and the concession of exaggerated incentives to the detriment of government finances.

From the beginning the architects of integration had wrestled with the problem of whether to encourage investment in the poorer regions, where the investment was most needed, or in the more developed regions, where the returns would be greater. Business naturally opted for maximum profitability, but political considerations led to the adoption of the strategy of balanced development--an attempt to weight the scales somewhat in favor of the economic laggards by making it more attractive for industry to locate in the less developed areas. Thus, Honduras and Nicaragua were allowed to offer greater incentives to attract industry than were the other members, and they received a higher percentage of loans granted by the Central American Bank for Economic Integration (CABEI). Nevertheless, neither country was pleased with its economic progress.

Despite the growing realization that basic adjustments were necessary, little sense of urgency could be infused into the integration movement; and the member states seemed incapable of joint action to deal forthrightly with the emergent problems. In February 1969, the exasperated Nicaraguan President Somoza stage-managed the Common Market's first major crisis in an effort to shake the other member states out of their complacency and inactivity. Violating the free-trade provisions that lay at the heart of the Market, Somoza decreed a tax on certain imports from the other member states. This action prompted quick retaliation; but Nicaragua's firm stance ultimately succeeded in engendering some forward movement, particularly in winning ratification of a number of integration agreements that had long been stalled.

The most lasting significance of the crisis, however, was not that it reminded member states that existing agreements were being implemented imperfectly or not at all, but that for the first time it forced recognition of the need for structural changes in the integration movement. Somoza argued that if the Common Market were to play the dynamic role for which it had been designed, it could not rest on its laurels or merely tinker with a program devised for the 1960s. Instead, it was necessary to recast and update the integration mold to meet needs of the 1970s. Somoza's point was well taken, and the response was encouraging. The agreement reached in March 1969, which ended the Somoza-induced crisis, included a generalized plan of action to improve the functioning of the Common Market. The plan called for the establishment of a customs union, freer regional mobility of labor, creation of a regional capital market, formation of a monetary stabilization fund, regional administration of industrial incentives to attract industry, and implementation of a protocol on basic grains trade.

Before the new reforms could be effected, however, a new and more serious crisis shook the integration movement. War broke out between El Salvador and Honduras, the two members most closely tied by trade and commerce. Border disputes between El Salvador and Honduras had been occurring for many years. They had arisen, in part, from the population pressures in El Salvador leading to migration across the ill-defined border into Honduras. Many of the migrants were squatters, and their rights, status, and treatment were often in dispute. In the summer of 1969, armed conflict broke out with several days of fighting. As a result of the war, the operations of the Common Market were seriously disrupted. Honduras closed its portion of the Pan American Highway to the passage of Salvadoran goods, which cut off El Salvador from its Costa Rican and Nicaraguan markets. And the Economic and Executive Councils were unable to meet to continue day-to-day Common Market business or to help resolve the crisis.

Negotiations were resumed in mid-1970, and at the end of the year, a _modus operandi_ for the rehabilitating of the Common Market was announced. But El Salvador withheld its approval at the last minute. Faced again with a rising trade deficit, and furious with El Salvador for rejecting the _modus operandi_, Honduras imposed duties on Common Market imports beginning on December 31, 1970; this effectively withdrew Honduras from the Common Market.

Continued disagreement after the Honduras-El Salvador war of 1969 resulted in the _de facto_ creation of two four-country markets, with the three neutrals joining with El Salvador in one market and with Honduras in the other. In 1971, Guatemala, Nicaragua, Costa Rica, and El Salvador established a "Normalization Commission" to promote orderly trade and to take reform measures looking toward the eventual reconstitution of the five-country market. This four-country market continues to function in accordance with all Common Market regulations and institutions. Meanwhile, trade between the neutral three and Honduras was stringently reduced in 1971 and 1972 due to the December 1970 decree. By mid-1973, however, roughly equivalent trade agreements were in effect between Honduras and the neutral three. The agreements are designed to increase trade while assuring that the Honduran trade deficit remains within manageable bounds.

Integration officials renewed their efforts to obtain an agreement on the restructuring of the Common Market in late 1972, when they presented the Central American governments with a SIECA/ECLA twelve-volume study entitled "Integrated Central American Development During the Current Decade." Issued between October 1972 and March 1973, the "Decade Study"--as it is popularly referred to--proposed a program of action for the seventies which makes a strong plea for a much greater degree of integration in the future, including monetary integration, a customs union, tax reform, and co-ordination of national development policies. A High Level Committee was formed in mid-1973 to develop a work plan and priorities for restructuring, using the SIECA study as a guideline. The High Level Committee presented its tentative proposals in December 1974 in a preliminary draft of a document entitled "The Draft Treaty Creating the Central American Economic and Social Community." The final version of this Treaty was presented to the Central American governments in October 1975. However, negotiations on restructuring have not begun, because of the continued failure of Honduras and El Salvador to resolve their bilateral dispute.

Even though the Common Market may have had a positive effect on the economic development of Central America and of each member country, the manner in which the integration program was carried out led to its own downfall. After the Common Market got underway in 1962, the process of integration lost its initial drive and began to stagnate by 1966 or 1967. The "easy" phase of import substitution had been exhausted at the same time that foreign exchange earnings from primary exports had begun to decline. At the same time, a series of crises struck the Common Market. Honduras and Nicaragua complained that they were subsidizing the industrial development of their neighbors, because almost all of the industrial growth was concentrating in the more developed countries. Concurrently, Costa Rica began to experience serious balance of payments problems, and pointed to its participation in the Common Market as the cause. The regional institutions proved unable to deal effectively with these two issues: balanced growth and balance of payments problems.

Despite the series of crises which plagued the Common Market after 1966, most observers thought that these issues would ultimately be resolved and that the future success of the integration process would be enhanced by the successful resolution of these crises. Thus, most observers were surprised by the outbreak of hostilities between El Salvador and Honduras in July 1969 and the resulting paralysis of the Common Market institutions. It is only with hindsight that many observers have begun to see a pattern of events which, to most of them, suggests that the Common Market had been on the verge of collapse before the outbreak of the "Soccer War." The most important factors which, according to most observers, account for the demise of the Common Market are: the Soccer War and its aftermath; balance of payments crises; the issue of balanced growth; the lack of strong regional institutions; the absence of coordinated regional and national development policies; the exhaustion of the "easy" phase of import substitution; increased economic dependence; and the loss of political support.

Most of the observers of the Central American integration program look at the history of the integration movement from one of two perspectives. One group focuses on the narrow, essentially economic aspects of the integration program. To them, the issues of balanced growth, balance of payments crises, coordination of fiscal incentives programs, the coordination of regional and national development policies, and the mobility of capital and labor have technical economic solutions. To the members of this group, the issue of balanced growth has generally been accepted as the principal cause of the demise of the CACM and the principal stumbling block to the achievement of higher stages of regional economic integration in Central America. The other group of observers has an equally narrow focus. Members of this group view the CACM within the framework of regional integration theory. This group believes that the ECLA-backed techicos were able to gain the reluctant support of the Central American governing elites for the economic integration program because of the program's noncontroversiality and low cost. Moreover, they believe that this support increased as concrete benefits were forthcoming. According to the proponents of this belief, the integration program "failed" to progress to a higher level because the tecnicos were unable to develop a regional constituency and the strong regional institutions necessary to deal effectively with the crises which arose in the late 1960s.

In both of the above cases, the Common Market has been viewed outside the context of the national political systems. Therefore, neither approach has been very successful in determining the root causes of the apparent failure of regional integration in Central America. Each has analyzed the major causes of the demise of the integration program in too narrow a focus. The key to understanding the success or failure of the economic integration program lies, not in advanced economic or regional integration theory, but in the domestic politics of the member states.

This study is based on the premise that the Common Market must be analyzed within the context of the domestic political systems of which it is composed. Despite the apparently paralyzing weakness and instability of the Central American regimes, one must understand that the domestic political structures of these countries are evolving constantly. Each regime is concerned with the problems of system maintenance, staying in power, cooptation of marginal and emerging elites, and finding the resources necessary to run the country. The integration issue is part of the development challenge that these countries faced in the post-war period. This study seeks to understand both how and why the Central American political elites responded to the integration movement in the manner in which they did.

The thesis of this study is that, during the decade of the 1960s, the Central American governments continually used the Central American Common Market to further their own interests. They never intended to allow a separate regional authority to develop because it would clash with their domestic interests. The national governments utilized the Common Market to avoid the internal changes upon which the future of the integration movement depended.

The discussion begins with an examination of the impact of external catalysts on the integration movement. While the substantial influence of the philosophies and goals of both ECLA and the United

States are acknowledged, the discussion seeks to demonstrate that the goals and philosophies of the Central American political leadership are the key factors which determined the course which the integration movement took.

The argument moves next to a brief examination of the economic theory of regional integration and how the Central American leadership interpreted it as an ideology of the status quo. An analysis of the achievements and failures of the economic integration program demonstrates that, while the program was a failure from the point of view of economic theory, from the domestic political perspective, the program was very successful.

The investigation then attempts to probe the root causes of the crises that paralyzed the Common Market in the late 1960s and early 1970s. The analysis demonstrates that the Common Market was not the principal cause of the "balanced growth," "balance of payments," and "Soccer War" crises. The study will conclude with an analysis of post-1969 events with the intention of illuminating the long-term obstacles to regional integration in Central America.

NOTES

1. Carlos Castillo, Growth and Integration in Central America (New York: Praeger, 1966), p. 77.

2. Isaac Cohen Orantes, Regional Integration in Central America (Lexington, Mass.: D. C. Heath and Company, 1972), p. 14.

3. Castillo, p. 77.

4. U. N., Report of the Economic Commission for Latin America, Fourth Session (E/2021) (New York: 1951), p. 20.

5. Joseph Nye, "Regional Integration and the Less Developed Countries," International Conciliation, No. 562 (March, 1967), p. 18.

6. Philippe Schmitter, "Central American Integration: Spill-Over, Spill-Around, or Encapsulation?" Journal of Common Market Studies, Vol. 9 (September, 1970), p. 2.

7. Article 1, Charter of the Organization of American States, in Reuniones y Conferencias de Ministros de Relaciones Exteriores de Centroamerica, 1951-1967 (ODECA, Publicaciones de la

Secretaria General, n. d.

8. Cohen, p. 17.

9. Article 12, Charter of ODECA, pp. 14-26.

10. UN--ECLA, "Actos y documentos de la reunion del Comite de Cooperacion Economica del Istmo Centroamericano" (E/CN.12/AC.17/1-23), Tegucigalpa, Honduras, August 1952.

11. Cohen, pp. 16-18.

12. Ibid., p. 18.

13. Ibid.

14. For a detailed analysis of the beneficial impact of the CACM, see David McClelland, _The Central American Common Market_ (New York: Praeger, 1972).

2. The Role of the ECLA and the United States

ECLA's HEGEMONY, 1951-1959

It was natural for Central American economic officials to turn to ECLA for guidance and leadership in their efforts to initiate a program of economic integration. Since its founding in 1948, ECLA had played the predominant role in developing strategies for the economic development of Latin America, including the "ECLA Doctrine" of industrialization through import substitution, and its corollary, regional integration.[1] In addition, some of the founders of and major actors in the Central American integration process had worked for ECLA and other U. N. organizations.

Joseph Nye ties the early predominance of ECLA in the first stages of the Central American integration movement to the development of international organization after World War II. According to Pedro Abelardo Delgado, former Secretary General of SIECA, "It is impossible to think of Central American integration without the United Nations, not just for its direct role, but for the climate it created."[2] Historically, Central American integrationists have been sensitive to larger international trends. Moreover, some of the founders and key participants in the integration process have worked for international organizations and have derived from them both an intellectual focus and a source of political strength.[3]

A majority of Central American officials believe that Central American integration would not have taked place without ECLA's participation. According to one SIECA official, without the external influence of ECLA, the possibility of transforming the region from a situation of mutual exclusiveness to one of integration and simultaneously achieving each nation's goal of development could never have been considered.[4]

In a real sense, ECLA fostered economic integration in Central America:

> ...the elaboration of ideas, the promise and subsequent fulfillment of technical and financial support, the preparation of studies and reports by the Mexico office, and the goading and stimulating of committees and subcommittees by technocrats who stood above the conflicts of national interest, all made ECLA a crucial external factor in the 1950s.[5]

ECLA offered the Central American integrationists assistance in all aspects of the program. First, it had developed the "ECLA Doctrine" of regional integration; second, it provided the institutional setting; third, it provided leadership; and fourth, it secured the financial assistance required.

First, the ECLA Doctrine was the major factor in shaping Central American attitudes concerning the Common Market and economic growth. The doctrine of industrialization through import substitution had been developed with such states as Mexico, Argentina, and Brazil in mind, but it offered Central America an explanation of its economic difficulties and a prescription for economic development.[6] It had the psychological advantage of appearing to be an indigenous solution to Latin America's economic troubles. Furthermore, ECLA had amended its analysis to deal with the smaller Latin American countries. Since the smallness of the national markets prevented even the preliminary phases of import substitution, ECLA accompanied its proposals in Central America with a program of economic integration.

The development-oriented members of the Central American elites seized upon the ECLA doctrine as their only chance to modernize their economies. They were a generation of relatively young economists, most of them trained in the United States and Western Europe, who thought the main responsibility of government was to better the living conditions of the masses.[7] Their search for individual solutions for the economic ills of their respective countries had been unsuccessful, and they adopted ECLA's proposals after ECLA assured them that regional economic integration would complement rather than detract from their national development plans.

The second reason that ECLA dominated the early stages of Central American integration is that it provided an institutional framework which enabled the integrationists to pursue their development goals in a multilateral context which was outside the grasp of the political strife that had troubled Central America in the post-war years. The tecnicos, as governmental delegates to the annual plenary sessions, were able to establish contacts among themselves, with ECLA officials, and with officials of other international agencies. This core of officials eventually became known as the "integration mafia." It was in these meetings that ECLA was able to "sell" its program of economic integration to the tecnicos.[8] Furthermore, at the fourth plenary session of ECLA, the governmental delegations officially gave the Secretariat the responsibility of outlining the program to be followed. And finally, at this meeting the delegates established the Committee of Economic Cooperation with ECLA as their Secretariat. When the controversy arose between the Ministers of Foreign Affairs and the Ministers of Economy over the subordinate status of ODECA's Economic Council, the Ministers of Economy were able to sidestep the issue and disassociate themselves from the Foreign Ministers' attempt at political integration by making the Committee of Economic Cooperation, under ECLA's auspices, the primary institution of the integration movement.

The third aspect of ECLA's role in the early stages of the integration movement is that the Secretariat exercised the leadership necessary to keep the overly-ambitious tecnicos from going outside the framework of the program the Secretariat had established. While the tecnicos still appeared to be acting on the assumption that economic integration was the "practical formula" that "would again make us one,"[9] ECLA was determined to maintain the gradualistic and technical nature of the program. By requiring that integration take place gradually, ECLA kept the program noncontroversial and low in cost. By forcing the governmental delegates to keep their sights lowered, ECLA was able to make them concentrate on the technical studies and limited objectives the Secretariat had decided to pursue.

ECLA dominated the technical aspects of the beginning of the integration movement because it had the personnel and the financial backing to do the technical feasibility studies. A series of technical subcommittees was set up to deal with the studies proposed by ECLA. Subcommittees were established in the following areas: the unification of international trade statistics and tariff nomenclatures; industrial technology and research; electric power; transportation; technical training in industry and administration; and agriculture.[10] These subcommittee meetings, composed of government experts, became the channels of communication between the national governments and ECLA's Mexico office. Besides these subcommittee meetings and the meetings of the Committee of Economic Cooperation, ECLA encouraged the Ministers of Economy to set up two permanent institutions: the Central American School of Public Administration (ESAPAC), and the Central American Institute of Industrial Technology and Research (ICAITI).

Finally, ECLA ultimately controlled the early stages of the integration movement because it held the purse strings. The costs of almost all the studies and the experts to do them were financed by the United Nations Technical Assistance Administration (UN-TAA). In September 1952, the Technical Assistance Board created a group to handle the financial aspects of the integration program, consisting of the Technical Assistance Board, ECLA, FAO, UNESCO, ILO, and the World Bank. The Technical Assistance Board also appointed a permanent regional representative to supervise the program. All requests for financial assistance had to be sent to this regional representative after they had been drawn up by the Committee of Economic Cooperation and ratified by the national governments.[11] This enabled ECLA to maintain almost total control of the early stages of the integration movement.

The other important aspect of ECLA's tight grasp on the financial underpinnings of the integration movement is that it kept the costs to the national governments low. From 1952 to 1959, annual government contributions to the integration program were a mere $5,000. At the same time, the annual U. N. contribution increased steadily from $90,000 in 1952 to $300,000 in 1959. In addition, the U. N. supplied almost all the funds necessary to operate both ICAITI and ESAPAC.[12]

ECLA thought that by keeping the costs to the individual governments low, the gradualistic program of integration would be able to move forward virtually free of political interference. By stressing the technical nature of the integration program, the Secretariat thought that the integration movement could maintain a low profile. But ECLA soon discovered that it was mistaken; the governments proved to be a major obstacle, even in the early stages of the integration movement.

The first issue in which ECLA came into confrontation with the national governments was the question of the rational allocation of industries on a regional level. While one of ECLA's major objectives in Central America was the planned distribution of industrial activities, the governments were unable to agree with ECLA that this was of primary importance. The conflicting views that ECLA and the national governments held concerning the role of the state in the economy will be discussed in Chapter 3.

ECLA put forth the Integration Industries scheme as a parallel program of the tecnicos' desire to establish a free trade area. ECLA did not consider free trade as an end in itself; rather, the Secretariat considered the expansion of the market beneficial only insofar as it encouraged the establishment of new industries in the region. But while ECLA received general support for the free trade proposal, it could not get the member governments to agree to its far-reaching proposal for a planned distribution of industries. Although the governments signed the Regime of Integration Industries, the text was very different from ECLA's original proposal. All the Regime did was to outline the basic principles on which the distribution of industries was to take place, leaving to further treaties the thorny issues involved: the designation of the industrial plants to be distributed; the question of consumer protection; the participation of foreign capital; and the level of protection to be granted to each industry. The delegations who signed the protocol argued that "excessive regulation" would make it extremely difficult to enforce the clauses of the treaty when it was applied to concrete cases.[13]

The second issue which brought ECLA into conflict with the member governments was the question of ratification of the integration treaties. The governmental delegations to the meetings of the Committee of Economic Cooperation had signed all of the major treaties, but Honduras and Costa Rica had not ratified them. This meant that the integration process could progress no faster than the most reluctant members would allow.

ECLA had planned to reduce its participation in the integration program once the institutions created by the as yet unratified integration treaties began to function. The Secretariat planned to concentrate on general studies requested by the member governments. The refusal of the governments to ratify the treaties signified that the integration process was not becoming internalized; yet ECLA was unable to push the integration process forward on its own.

At the same time, in late 1959, the United Nations Technical Assistance Board had begun to deny some requests for assistance because of lack of funds; the evergrowing costs of the integration program had been almost totally borne by the U. N. The Secretariat suggested that the governmnets increase their financial support of the integration program, but they refused. It would have meant sacrificing national projects for the sake of regional ones, and this was unacceptable to them.[14]

> By 1959 the process was deadlocked, due mainly to the governments' lack of interest. For eight years these governments had been encouraged by ECLA to adopt and develop the regional program, but when ECLA started demanding higher levels of participation and sacrifices from them, such as increases in their financial contributions or the acceptance of free trade for a limited list of products, stagnation and disenchantment set in.[15]

Besides being unable to persuade the governments to become more deeply involved in the integration process, ECLA was losing the support of the local integrationists. First of all, the results of ECLA's leadership appeared too meager:

> The decisions arrived at...consisted mainly of a treaty in which it was agreed to sign further treaties....Some local tecnicos realized that the same painful process by which consensus had been obtained originally was going to be needed every time new measures were required.[16]

Secondly, many of the local integrationists had begun to resent ECLA's total dominance of the integration process; resentment arose not only because of ECLA's apparent failures but also because of the substantive differences in philosophy and goals between ECLA and local integrationists which were partially responsible for some bottlenecks. These differences, such as the issue of state intervention in the economy and the debate over the upgrading of the integration movement, will be discussed in later chapters.

ECLA: A Failure in Leadership?

Carlos Castillo, a high ECLA official from 1956 to 1966, defends ECLA's performance during the early stages of the integration movement. He argues that there were two phases in the early stages of the program. The first phase, from 1952 to 1957, "was one of incubation, examination, and confrontation of possibilities, assessment of possible consequences, and accumulation of limited experiences." The second phase, from 1958 to 1962, "was one of rapid progress and of far-reaching achievements."[17]

According to Castillo, the first phase served two purposes: it established the program as an ongoing endeavor; and it enabled the integrationists "to gain knowledge and sharpen the issues concerning the common market."[18]

> The first purpose required the development of an effective mechanism, including a close-knit group of government officials who could provide for continuity of effort and help create a regional point of view for approaching the problems involved. The Committee of Economic Cooperation (CCE) grew up to be that kind of a mechanism, and its Trade Subcommittee just that kind of a group. Stable in its composition over a period of years, the latter group contributed in no small way to the development of a regional point of view.[19]

Secondly, Castillo points to the concrete achievements of this early phase. They include: the establishment of the first regional institutions--the Central American School of Public Administration and the Industrial Research Institute; a series of major research studies--"the first ever to be attempted in these countries on a systematic basis"--on general development, transportation, agriculture, electric power, taxation, commercial policy, and industrial possibilities.[20] Thus,

Castillo finds ECLA's performance substantial in the early period, 1952 to 1957. ECLA created the major elements which eventually led to the establishment of a dynamic integration movement: "a cohesive group of government officials, a continuous flow of external technical assistance, a series of systemic studies, and an increasing experience with the problems of free trade."[21]

While Castillo admits that the accomplishments of the integrationists, under ECLA's guidance, in 1958 and 1959 left something to be desired, he defends their major achievements as the best that could have been realized under the circumstances. The member governments were preoccupied with the development for their individual economies and offered only lukewarm support for ECLA's integration program.[22]

The Multilateral Free Trade Treaty, Castillo stated, was "narrow in scope and slow in its procedures." The treaty called for the establishment of a free trade area within ten years, but it did not specify the mechanisms needed to reach this goal.

> A political decision to make the program for economic integration a genuine element of growth was lacking. Nevertheless, the Treaty was the first multinational instrument on economic policy created by the five countries. It was not a daring instrument, but then, daring decisions had all too often failed in the past. It did show the existence of a common ground, painstakingly built over a period of several years and broad enough to provide sufficient room for all to stand on. This Treaty thus turned out to be the point of departure for much of what took place afterward.[23]

Castillo does not believe that the impasse arrived at by the integration movement in 1958 was because of a failure in ECLA's program or leadership. In his analysis, ECLA accomplished as much as could be expected without embroiling the integration program in regional and national politics. While he admits that ECLA's major consideration became the avoidance of political "disturbances," he defends this because of the reluctance on the part of the member governments to support the integration movement.[24]

Castillo states that the other major reason for the stagnation of the integration program in 1958 was the inadequacy of financial support for the integration movement.[25] But in Cohen's analysis, merely increasing the financial support of ECLA's program would not have broken the impasse because of the substantive problems that had arisen as a result of the initial stages of ECLA's integration program.[26] The next period of the integration movement, 1959 to 1963, was to witness both a massive inflow of foreign financial assistance and a fundamental change in the scope and nature of the integration program.

THE ROLE OF THE UNITED STATES, 1959-1963

In the early 1950s, the United States was not in favor of the ECLA-inspired Central American integration program. The "Prebisch thesis," with its emphasis on state ownership, contained some very strong anti-private investment positions. The basic premise of the ECLA Doctrine was that the state must intervene against the market forces to aid in the creation of new industries in Latin America.[27] United States philosophy opposed the ECLA thesis; the United States favored private investment over government loans as the best means to develop a country. Unlike ECLA, the United States policy makers believed that industrialization would be a by-product of competition and other market forces.[28] John Moore Cabot, Eisenhower's Assistant Secretary of State for the American Republics, stated the current administration's version of the "trickle down effect": social development would come about gradually as a result of promoting foreign investment and private enterprise in Central America.[29]

But these theoretical concerns became secondary in importance in the mid-1950s, when the United States began to take a more pragmatic attitude toward development. With the ousting of the Arbenz regime in Guatemala in 1954, the United States began to see the alternatives in Central America as being between gradual reform and violent revolution. From 1955 to 1958, the United States gave Guatemala $80 million in bilateral assistance and supported a loan of $18 million from the World Bank.[30] The Cuban revolution and the establishment of the first Socialist republic in Latin America in 1959 made the United States even more concerned about the future of political and economic stability in Central America.

It was in light of these and similar events that the United States began to become more receptive to the question of regional integration as a tool for development and reform in Latin America. But its support of the integration proposals ECLA had made for Latin America was conditional: the ECLA thesis was in fundamental contradiction with the United States' expressed commitment to free trade and free enterprise.

In February 1959, the United States listed the conditions under which it would support integration in Latin America: (1)regional market arrangements should promote trade creation and increased productivity rather than concentrate on trade diversion; (2)there should be trade liberalization in all commodities; (3)the establishment of common external tariffs should not be higher than the former individual tariff barriers; and (4)there should be provisions for the eventual elimination of all barriers to intra-regional trade.

> The United States does not favor an arrangement that provides simply for regional preferences with little more than a vague hope of eventually creating a free trade regime....Regional trade arrangements should aim at increasing the degree of competition in the area...exclusive monopolistic privileges should not be given to particular industries. Not only is it believed that intra-regional competition will increase productivity and investment in the area, but that these conditions will also help to induce private investment.[31]

It was evident that the United States would not support the Regime of Integration Industries, which provided for the establishment of regional industries that would have exclusive rights to the expanded market for ten years. Furthermore, the United States was fundamentally opposed to the trade diversion effects of ECLA's program of import substitution. Moreover, there were several other aspects of ECLA's program of integration in Central America that the United States disagreed with, such as ECLA's insistence on regional planning aimed at promoting balanced growth, the high levels of protection, and the lack of a proposal to provide for free mobility of capital and labor.

In summary, it was evident that if the United States was going to assist financially the Central American integration movement, the program's main goals would have to be reordered and some of the original elements of the program would have to be abandoned. The focus of the integration program would have to change from encouraging industrialization through import substitution to widening the market.

This was the setting when President Lemus of El Salvador visited the United States in the spring of 1959. During the course of informal talks between Salvadorian officials and United States State Department officials, the United States indicated that it would be willing to do everything in its power to help create a "real" Common Market.[32]

> The establishment of an economically sound system for the integration of the economies of the Central American Republics and for a common market comprising those nations would be beneficial and would receive the support of El Salvador and the United States....This subject will receive continued study by the two governments with a view to taking action to carry on those sound plans already contemplated.[33]

The United States was willing to support integration on its own terms. In return, it would help break the impasse which the program had arrived at by extending large amounts of foreign aid, both multilateral and bilateral.

Later in the year, Washington sent a mission of two experts from the State Department's International Cooperation Administration--the precursor of the Agency for International Development (AID)--and the Vice President of the Export-Import Bank to determine what the United States could do to help the integration movement to advance. This mission resulted in the signing of the Tripartite Treaty by Guatemala, El Salvador, and Honduras in Guatemala in February 1960. The technical advisers from the International Cooperation Administration apparently were instrumental in getting the three governments to sign the Tripartite Treaty.[34] According to one participant, "U. S. support was necessary for this political tactic to work, both for the financial promises and to help us against pressure from ECLA when we broke their five-country integration plan."[35] One Nicaraguan official states that it was this promise of United States financial assistance that enticed the three northern countries to sign the Tripartite Treaty and Nicaragua and Costa Rica eventually to agree to its provisions, "despite the fact that from previous efforts we were not able to say that we had obtained a satisfactory experience justifying the acceleration of the process."[36]

With the signing of the Tripartite Treaty, the three countries had accelerated the pace of the integration program, but at the cost of excluding the ECLA Secretariat and Nicaragua and Costa Rica. The establishment of free trade was accelerated; and all Central American products, with a small list of exceptions, were included. This changed the major focus of the program from inward-looking industrialization to trade expansion. Although the issue of monetary stability had initially been made a part of the program in order to prevent dislocations among the participants, it was now included to meet the requirements of the United States.[37] The question of the free mobility of labor and capital also was included, as a completely new issue, to meet United States requirements. Finally, the United States' participation and financial backing enabled the Treaty to call for the creation of the Central American Bank of Economic Integration (CABEI), an institution which had been under consideration since the beginning of the integration movement in the early 1950s.

Nicaragua and Costa Rica probably had been excluded from the signing of the Tripartite Treaty for political reasons. Nicaragua had a territorial dispute with Honduras which had not yet been resolved by the International Court of Justice, and relations between the two countries had become embittered. Costa Rica, which always had looked with suspicion upon the integration program because it feared that the internal political problems of its neighbors would be transmitted to it, was in the hands of a very conservative government; the Echandi administration saw, in the issue of the Tripartite Treaty, an opportunity to divorce Costa Rica entirely from the integration program.[38]

ECLA's Mexico office reacted quickly to this attempt by the United States to supercede the Secretariat as the guiding light of the integration movement. It convoked an extraordinary meeting of the Committee of Economic Cooperation in San Jose, April 26-29, 1960. In this meeting, ECLA attempted to reconstruct the original five-country program and reinstitute some of the proposals which the

Tripartite Treaty had excluded. First, it advised Costa Rica and Nicaragua to adapt to the accelerated pace imposed by the three northern countries. Second, the Secretariat proposed that the five governments should agree on establishing a common market among themselves in five years, arriving at the same goal stated in the Tripartite Treaty. This would allow the application of the Regime of Integration Industries during this transition period, before the establishnent of free trade in the area, since free trade would eliminate the main stimulus to the Regime. Finally, ECLA did not attempt to set up a development fund competitive with the one called for in the Tripartite Treaty, since it had the financial backing of the United States.[39]

Costa Rica refused to participate in any accelerated program and withdrew. But ECLA succeeded in getting the other four countries to authorize it to draw up a new treaty, with the understanding that it would take into serious consideration the steps already taken by the three northern countries. In Managua in December 1960, the four countries signed the General Treaty of Central American Economic Cooperation, a protocol to the agreement of tariff equalization, and a treaty creating the Central American Bank of Economic Cooperation (CABEI).[40]

Thus, ECLA gained back some of the ground it had lost with the signing of the Tripartite Treaty. But the General Treaty closely resembled the Tripartite Treaty, and the United States was now the dominant force in the Central American integration movement. While it might appear that ECLA was responsible for inducing Nicaragua to sign the General Treaty, in reality it was the financial influence of the United States which caused both Nicaragua and Costa Rica eventually to subscribe to the accelerated integration program.[41]

Before the Managua meeting, the State Department had held a series of meetings with the Ministers of Economic Affairs and other high officials of Guatemala, El Salvador, Honduras, and Nicaragua. The United States stipulated that a member country had to sign the General Treaty before it could become eligible for CABEI loans. This induced Nicaragua to sign the Treaty with the others in December 1960. But Costa Rica still refused; it was not until 1963 that Costa Rica signed the Treaty. Even then, United States leverage through CABEI was largely responsible.[42]

The next major step that the United States

took was to institutionalize its influence and participation in the integration program. The United States had closely supervised the organization of CABEI through its regional economic advisor, who had been appointed simultaneously financial advisor to the Bank.[43] In early 1962, the advisor recommended that his "duties be amplified and taken over by a group of specialists."[44] In July 1962, the United States government responded by creating a Regional Office for Central America and Panama Affairs (ROCAP) of the Agency for International Development, with its headquarters in Guatemala City.

ROCAP's objectives were: (1)to strengthen regional institutions and their capabilities to formulate and execute regional development plans; (2)to promote coordination of national development, fiscal, monetary, investment, and trade policies; (3)to further the elimination of barriers to free movement in the region of goods, capital, and labor; (4)to increase private investment throughout the region; and (5)to reinforce bilateral US-AID missions efforts within each country to strengthen the national economies as future components of a viable regional community.[45]

ROCAP did not have any institutional ties to the United States embassies in the region, only to the countries' AID missions. This makes ROCAP appear to be "a functional office occupied with the more precise question of economic integration in Central America. It can be assumed that in ROCAP, the United States was trying to create an office similar to the one ECLA organized in Mexico City at the beginning of the program."[46]

The anticipated consequence of these actions by the United States was a diminution of ECLA's activities in the region. Only three meetings of the Committee of Economic Cooperation were held after ROCAP was established: July 1962, January 1963, and January 1966.[47] The meeting of July 1962 was the last significant meeting. The newly-elected Costa Rican government of Figueres had taken steps to join the accelerated phase of the integration movement. At the July 1962 meeting of the CCE in San Jose, Costa Rica adhered to the General Treaty, to the protocol creating the Central American Bank for Economic Integration, and the protocol calling for the equalization of import tariffs. By November 1962, Costa Rica had concluded negotiations concerning bilateral free trade and tariff equalization with the other four countries.[48]

Besides the infrequent meeting of the Committee

of Economic Cooperation, the meetings of the subcommittees also decreased in number and in importance. More significantly, ECLA's short-term activities decreased. As the Secretariat had planned, ECLA assumed a more analytical and consultative role on long-term problems, leaving the questions of decision-making and implementation to the local institutions. While almost 100 percent of the budget of ECLA's Mexico office had been devoted to Central American integration during the 1950s, by 1971, this percentage had declined to 60 percent.[49]

In March 1963, in a public and symbolic gesture of support for the integration program, President Kennedy met with the five Central American presidents and the president of Panama in Costa Rica. Together they issued the "Declaration of Central America," which confirmed the goals of the General Treaty, including: (1)the establishment of a customs union; (2)the establishment of a monetary union; (3)the regional coordination of fiscal, social, and economic policies; (4)reforms in the areas of agriculture, education, and public administration, as stated in the Charter of Punta del Este; and (5)their ultimate goal, the establishment of a common market.[50]

The text of the Declaration stated that the Central American presidents recognized the importance to economic development of a "vigorous and freely competitive private sector," and the importance of encouraging private investment and growth of private industry. In return for these commitments to integration and to "free enterprise," the United States agreed to make an immediate and substantial contribution to carry out regional development projects on the drawing boards of the various regional institutions.[51]

Furthermore, the presidents stated that, in order to carry out this program of economic and social reform, "it is essential to reinforce the measures to meet subversive aggression originating in the focal points of Communist agitation which Soviet imperialism may maintain in Cuba or in any other place in Latin America."[52] These measures included the supervision of travel to Cuba and the adoption of common security measures to deal with threats of subversion.[53]

Thus, President Kennedy's visit tied the United States' security interests in Central America to that region's future economic and social welfare. The program of economic integration became the instrument with which the United States hoped to arrest the influence of the Cuban revolution in the area. Central America was no longer "the backyard or forgotten part of the Hemisphere."[54]

The Magnitude of United States Financial Assistance to the Integration Movement

The major reason that the United States had such a strong influence on the nature of the integration program and the apparent speed with which it progressed was the large amount of financial assistance it committed to the program. While ECLA had spent approximately 10 million dollars in support of Central American integration between 1951 and 1963, by early 1963 the United States had already spent double that amount, or over $20 million.[55]

Of the $1.3 billion dollars in external assistance that the Central American governments received from 1961 to 1969, $1.037 billion, or 70 percent, was furnished by the United States.[56] For the Central American governments to have generated an equivalent amount of money, they would have had to increase domestic revenues by 31 percent or total export earnings by 20 percent.[57]

While the contributions of the Central American governments to the regional institutions increased over the meager $5,000 dollars per year that they had contributed during the 1950s, during the 1960s their annual contributions to all regional institutions amounted to 0.4 percent of their total public expenditures. What little they were willing to contribute was concentrated in the economic areas; even here their contributions were dwarfed by the contributions of the United States. "The relative demands of the regional activities...were almost insignificant, but still the governments failed to make their contributions on time. Perhaps this is an indication of the importance that the governments assigned to the regional institutions."[58]

The advances achieved in the "non-economic" areas, such as the social development programs supported by ODECA, were gained mainly because Washington wanted Central America to progress in all areas of integration rather than remain a strictly economic association. Thus, ODECA's subsidiary councils on Health, Education, Labor, and Defense provided the channels through which ROCAP could focus on improvements in these areas. While the Central American governments had little interest in these programs--each government contributed approximately $25 thousand annually--, in 1969 alone, Washington contributed $689 thousand to the ODECA-sponsored programs. Between 1961 and 1969, ROCAP spent between 15 and 20 percent of its funds in the form of grants to the "non-economic" programs of the integration movement.[59] The Central American governments were, at best, cautious about social development programs, but they were willing to take all forms of assistance Washington wanted to give them. This is especially true of ROCAP's assistance to the social development programs, since all of this assistance was in the form of grants. The Central American governments were unwilling to spend their own money on social improvements, let alone social reforms.[60]

Even in the strictly economic areas, the expansion of the scope of the programs and the institutions such as SIECA were made possible only through the increasing importance of external assistance. The member governments proved to be unwilling to take any step in the integration movement without the promise of financial assistance to mitigate their sacrifices. The main source of delay at almost every important step of the integration movement was the reluctance of the member governments to put into practice the measures they all had agreed upon previously in the General Treaty in 1960 and again in the "Declaration of the Presidents" in 1963.

The Central American governments did not fully realize the implications of the future obligations that the integration treaties entailed. They did not seem to take into account the conflict between the two prevailing theories about how the Central American economies were to be developed--those of ECLA and the United States--before they signed the treaties. They acted as if they had no development philosophy or commitment to the integration program.[61] In fact, their major concern throughout the period appears to have been the satisfaction of their mutually-exclusive national interests. At the time of the signing of the integration treaties, the sacrifices the member countries would be called upon to make in the future were greatly outweighed by United States assurances of large amounts of financial assistance. But as they were called upon to fulfill their obligations under the various treaties, they resisted. Instead of working to upgrade the common interest, each member sought to satisfy its own national interests. The integration process had become one in which the short-term benefits recieved from external financial assistance were more important than any long-term benefits which would theoretically be derived from the establishment of an economic community.

With the continuing increase in the inflow of external assistance and private foreign investment and the rapid growth of intra-regional trade, it appeared as if the integration program had been established as a going concern. Yet when the program was hit by a series of crises beginning in 1967, the regional institutions proved incapable of resolving them. With the crippling of the Common Market in 1969 by the war between El Salvador and Honduras, and by Honduras' subsequent withdrawal from the CACM, it was apparent that the degree of interdependence created by the Common Market had been a lot less than observers had thought.

Thus, like ECLA in the 1950s, the United States had failed to "internalize" the integration movement in Central America. In 1960, almost all of the participants in the integration program--the United States, ECLA, the local tecnicos, and the member governments--had thought of United States financial assistance as the missing variable; with the external financing of the integration movement guaranteed, the program would move forward quickly.[62] But external financing caused as many problems as it solved, and thus became one of the most controversial aspects of the program. On a practical level, the relatively massive amount of support was a windfall for the member governments, equal to 31 percent of their domestic revenues or 20 percent of their total export earnings. On the whole, the economies of the member countries appear to be in much better shape as a result of this rapid increase in external financial aid and investment.

On the other hand, some observers charge that the great amounts of external assistance prevented the "politicization" of the integration process by enabling the participants to avoid "high" costs. The regional institutions, by failing to develop any significant degree of authority, were unable to resolve the series of crises which crippled the Common Market. This has led Haas and Schmitter, writing about LAFTA, to conclude: "Only a crises which compels the members to fall back on their own collective resources can be expected to trigger the behavior patterns which will make the expansive hypothesis prevail."[63] The questions which this issue raises, such as the importance of crises in Central America, will be discussed in later chapters.

Dependence: "External Penetration" or "Reaching Out"?

In order to place the external influence of ECLA and the United States on the integration movement in its proper perspective, one must understand the historic role which foreign assistance has played in the development of the Latin American nation-state. Prior to the development of the export economy in the late nineteenth century, the Latin American nation-state had been virtually a "useless appendage." The leaders of the period desired to imitate the patterns of progress demonstrated by the advanced nations, but the liberal economic policies they devised evoked little response in the latifundia-dominated domestic economies.

> To make sense, the liberal, democratic Latin American nation-state had to be related to a network of private economic activity. Otherwise, its economic policies were futile, its form of organization meaningless. The Latin American nation-state and the international system of liberal economies discovered each other in the latter half of the nineteenth century, with striking results for each.[64]

This international economic system was based on the same foundation as the domestic exchange economies of the advanced nations: free trade, comparative advantage, a price system regulated by money values in a free market, and the unrestricted flow of capital between nations. The foreign capitalist would invest in Latin America to increase his profits; and the Latin American countries in turn would put their untapped resources to use, find their productivity enhanced, and take the first steps toward economic modernization. "This is the time," said the Venezuelan delegate to the Pan American Fiscal Conference in 1915, "in which North American capital must use the great opportunity presented to it for the industrial development of the Latin American nations."[65] To encourage foreign investment, the major economic function of the state became to grant concessions. The successful statesman was the man who could develop a a strategic combination of policies--land grants, tax and tariff exemptions, guarantees of political "stability"--which would draw such capital resources to his own nation. Diaz of Mexico, Gomez of Venezuela, Barrios of Guatemala, and many others, through a masterful manipulation of the resources at their disposal--the meager capabilities of the state--were able to attract a great deal of foreign investment to their countries.

The sectoral distribution of this foreign investment demonstrates that the political leaders had another important goal, in addition to attracting foreign investment for productive enterprise--the goal of enabling their countries to duplicate some of the physical characteristics of the modern nation-state through infrastructure development. According to Anderson's estimate, between one-half and two-thirds of the foreign capital received by Latin America between 1860 and 1930 was devoted to internal improvements of the type normally considered to be the economic function of the state.[66]

As the nation-state became integrated into the international economy, the gap between the modern sector and the traditional sectors widened. The modernizing elites--the bureaucrats and the new middle class which was formed by the emergence of a transactional economy--had become important participants in the political process. They demanded and received public policies which created for them an urban environment modeled after that of their Western counterparts. As the government continued to stress infrastructure and industrial development, the gap between the modern "enclave" and the traditional sectors widened.

Although there had been a moderate amount of externally-assisted infrasturcture development in Central America between 1930 and 1945--the period of tenure of the "Depression Dictators"--it was not until after World War II that the Central American countries aggressively sought the foreign assistance needed to develop their economies. The political process had been "frozen" for years, first because of the Depression and then because of the necessity for Hemispheric wartime solidarity. During this period, a new generation of political leaders had developed who were restless to enter the political arena. Influenced by the ideals of the war--the Four Freedoms, the establishment of the U. N., and the struggle for democracy--they had vague aspirations to rid themselves of their own archaic political and economic systems.

Because of the long reign of the Depression Dictators and the poverty of the region, the new leaders felt that they had a lot of "catching up" to do. To do this, they copied the development programs and institutions implemented by their larger Latin American neighbors years earlier. Like their neighbors to the south, they relied heavily on foreign financial assistance to pursue infrastructure development and begin the process of industrialization. Thus, says Anderson, they assiduously pursued the "historic" role of the Latin American nation-state of creating a package of inducements to generate private foreign investment, especially after 1956.[67]

Anderson suggests that the Central American governments concentrated on the modern sector--infrastructure and industrialization--because of the conservative orientation of the international lending agencies and the United States during the 1950s and 1960s. Differences in regime and development philosophy had little to do with the relative degree of success each country had in fulfilling its development aspirations. The conservative policies of the World Bank, the IBRD, and the Export-Import Bank, he says, discouraged policy experimentation.[68]

However, the conservative orientation of the Central American governments goes beyond the external influence of the international lending agencies and the United States. The best example is the reaction of the Central American governments to the Alliance for Progress in the early 1960s. The Alliance was a comprehensive design for development, including economic planning and agrarian and tax reform; financial assistance was made contingent on significant progress toward these goals. Central America responded with a multitude of new plans, projects, and proposals in order to obtain financial assistance; but there was no change in the pattern of political and economic transactions. All five countries established planning agencies, but not one country gave its planning agency any real authority. Costa Rica and Honduras passed agrarian reform laws with no intention of putting forth a full effort or commitment. The tax reform laws quickly passed in all five countries during this period went unimplemented.[69] Thus, the governments responded to United States pressure for reform with a set of symbolic actions designed to demonstrate good faith, but they never intended to pursue the development strategy advocated by the United States. These governments were able to manipulate the United States in order to obtain significant amounts of financial aid without losing control over the development process and without making any political sacrifices.

It is in this context that the Central American political leaders responded to the attempts of the United States to provide the financial assistance necessary to make the Common Market a going concern. The decision of the political elites to support the integration movement after 1958 represents an attempt to perpetuate the traditional linkages between the state and the external environment. The politicos saw in the integration program a chance to obtain a substantial increase in foreign assistance. Thus, they formally subscribed to all of the integration programs that the United States and the international lending agencies were willing to subsidize, but they were not willing to invest their own resources into most of the programs because they did not really support many of the stated goals of the integration program. Apart from the Common Market program itself, the major interest of the politicos was to obtain as much foreign assistance as possible in whatever program the donor was willing to spend its money. The Central American political elites saw the United States' support of the integration program as part of its Alliance for Progress strategy, and they responded to the integration program in the same way that they responded to the Alliance's calls for tax and agrarian reform. Thus, as with the Alliance for Progress, they often backed down from formal commitments they had made to the integration program.[70]

SUMMARY

It appears that the Central American integration movement did not evolve internally. Progress at every step of the integration program seemed to derive from external assistance or pressure. True, there was a group of development-oriented officials in each country who became marginal members of the political elite in the late 1940s. These techicos, mainly young economists trained abroad, started occupying key positions in the governments of almost all of the countries. These development-oriented elites brought to the attention of their governments the necessity of agricultural and industrial development, labor and social security legislation, and the need to eradicate illiteracy, poverty, and disease. But their common goals did not bring them together, because they perceived these goals in a purely national context.

> For the most part, the environment was not favorable to the success of integration. It is true that some favorable factors did exist in almost all of the countries, such as the 'developmentalism' that inspired the new ruling elites, but this condition was not complementary. On the contrary, it was mutually exclusive since it was perceived as a solution to the problems of each individual unit. Moreover, the heterogeneity caused by the political changes that brought the new elites to power was the most important source of conflict among the units, not a source of integration.[71]

ECLA proved to be the source that provided the link between the development goals of these marginal members of the political elite. The Secretariat evolved the program of economic development through regional integration, formed a pro-integration group of Central American economic officials, gave them an institutional framework which sheltered them from the political instability of the region, and provided all of the technical and financial assistance necessary to run the program.

When ECLA attempted to reduce its role in the integration program, the movement became deadlocked because the member governments were unwilling to increase their support of the program. They had allowed the tecnicos to "play at integration" because "the Central American and integration ideas were fashionable; we did not think it would amount to much; and it was important to keep the economists happy."[72] But they refused to support the program financially.

Thus, ECLA was unable to achieve its major goal, which was to enable the integration movement to develop an internal dynamism that would propel it forward under its own momentum. ECLA failed precisely because it expected a consensus among the Central American governments to evolve naturally and to lead to higher levels of economic integration, even though the Secretariat's basic premise was that political questions and even moderate sacrifices had to be avoided at all costs.

The United States succeeded in accelerating the integration movement because it virtually bribed the member governments to endorse the Tripartite Treaty and, subsequently, the General Treaty of Economic Integration. Moreover, further steps in the integration program were taken by the member governments only when the external financial assistance was available to mitigate their sacrifices. Any integration project that did not have United States financial backing was left on the planning table.

Like ECLA before it, the United States failed to achieve its major goal, with respect to the integration "process" of "internalizing" the integration movement.[73] Without such internalization, the program could not hope to achieve any of its long-term objectives, and the short-term payoffs proved to be no solution to the economic and social ills that plagued the region.

The financial assistance that the United States gave to the integration program pushed the Central American governments along the path of integration prematurely. While they were ready and eager for development assistance geared to strengthen their national economies, they were not willing or able to cope with an accelerated program of integration. On the other hand, ECLA's approach apparently was too slow to satisfy any of the development-oriented participants.

While the above conclusions appear to reinforce the general perception of the Central American integration movement as dependent on external assistance, they also obscure the more subtle and complex relationships which were taking place. If one looks at the same events from the domestic political perspective, one sees that it was not as much a case of "external penetration" by an "external catalyst"[74] as it was a case of "reaching out" by emerging political elites in an attempt to build a power base.[75]

First of all, the "historic" tradition of Central American political elites "reaching out" for external assistance must be qualified. In general, one can say that the new political groups were in search of a power capability with which to counter the power base of the traditional economic interests. The traditional interests were opposed to reforms of any kind, and they controlled the bulk of domestic capital. The new political elites allied themselves with foreign capital, then, because it provided them with a domestic power capability, without which development would be impossible. And their staying in office (maintaining political control) depended on fulfilling their development goals, because these were the demands being placed on them by the emerging middle sectors, including the bureaucracy, the military, the industrialists, and the commercial interests.

An even more graphic illustration of this emerging class conflict and the resulting manipulation of foreign assistance--"reaching outward"--to provide a domestic power capability is the rise of the industrialists--the "joven burguesia." The prime example is El Salvador, where, as demonstrated in later chapters,[76] the traditional oligarchy strongly resisted the attempts of the industrialists--allied with the military "reformers"--to modernize the country. While the government of El Salvador initially sought less foreign public assistance than its Central American neighbors, the industrialists actively allied themselves with foreign private capital to develop a domestic power capability in order to confront the traditional oligarchy.

Moreover, this emerging class conflict in El Salvador--the rise of the marginal industrial elite seeking political influence with a power capability based on external resources--demonstrates that El Salvador's reasons for exploiting the Common Market went beyond the generally accepted geopolitical "population pressure" argument. Allied with the military, the industrialists had attempted, especially during the Lemus regime between 1957 and 1960, to carry out some minor social reforms necessary to widen the internal market for domestically-produced consumer goods. The reaction of the traditional oligarchy was so violent that it eventually led to Lemus's downfall. Thus, the industrial elite, frustrated in its attempts to expand the internal market, sought to penetrate the markets of its neighbors, first through bilateral agreements and then through the Common Market. The Common Market and regional trade, then, provided this emerging elite with a growing domestic power capability. As regional trade became more important to the livelihood of the nation, the influence of the industrialists increased.

The third example of the "reaching out" of a marginal elite to use external resources to develop a domestic power capability is that of the tecnicos themselves. While the tecnicos--the "integration mafia," according to Nye[77]--are almost always treated as an "external influence" on the behavior of the politicos, they were primarily a marginal domestic political elite struggling to influence the development process of their countries. Thus, they initially used ECLA as a base of influence and refuge; their influence depended on the prestige and influence that ECLA was able to exert on the postwar development-conscious governments. As succeeding chapters will demonstrate, as the technicos assumed more importance in their own national economies--and thus became integrated into the political system--the influence of ECLA waned.[78]

NOTES

1. See discussion in Chapter 3.

2. Interview with Joseph Nye, September 28, 1966, in Nye, p. 51.

3. Ibid.

4. Cohen, p. 14.

5. Nye, p. 52. Emphasis added.

6. See Prebisch, "The Economic Development of Latin America and its Principle Problems," op. cit.

7. Cohen, p. 15.

8. Christopher Mitchell, "The Role of the Technocrat in Latin American Integration," Inter-American Economic Affairs, Vol. XXL, No. 1, Summer 1967, p.5.

9. Minister of Finance of Honduras, Closing speech at meeting of CCE, Tegucigalpa, Honduras, August 1952; in UN-ECLA, (E/CN.12/AC.17/IS57), August 1952.

10. UN-ECLA, "Breve Resena de las actividades de la CEPAL en Mexico desde su creacion en 1951 hasta Mayo de 1968," (CEPAL/Mex/68/11), April 1968, p.307.

11. Cohen, p. 22.

12. UN-ECLA, "Informe del represente regional de la Junta de Asistencia Tecnica de las Naciones Unidas para Centroamerica," (E/CN.12/CCE/330), January 1966.

13. UN-ECLA, "Informe del Comite de Cooperacion Economica del Istmo Centroamericano," (E/CN.12/CCE/103), June 1957, pp. 30-39.

14. Interview with E.L. Barber, U.S. State Department, AID, Washington, D.C., August 1975.

15. Cohen, p. 25.

16. Ibid., p. 24.

17. Castillo, p. 79.

18. Ibid., p. 80.

19. Ibid.

20. Ibid., p. 81.

21. Ibid.

22. Ibid., pp. 88-89.

23. Ibid., p. 89.

24. Ibid.

25. Ibid.

26. Cohen, pp. 24-25.

27. Raul Prebisch, "Commercial Policy in the Underdeveloped Countries," American Economic Review, Papers and Proceedings (May 1959); see also U.N., The Economic Development of Latin America and its Principle Problems (1950).

28. Spruille Braden, "Private Enterprise in the Development of the Americas," State Department Bulletin, XV (September 22, 1946), p. 539.

29. New York Times, October 10, 1953, p. 7.

30. John McCamant, Development Assistance in Central America (New York: Praeger, 1968), pp.25-33.

31. United States Congress, Senate Committee on Foreign Relations,"United States and Latin American Policies Affecting Their Economic Relations" (Washington, D.C.: Government Printing Office, 1960).

32. ROCAP, "A Report on Central America's Common Market and its Economic Integration Movement," (Guatemala, 1966), Section III, p. 1, mimeographed.

33. Council on Foreign Relations, Documents on American Foreign Relations: 1959, Paul Zinner, ed. (New York: Harper and Row, 1960), pp. 508-512.

34. David Landry, "United States Interests in Central America-- A Case Study of Policies Toward Economic Integration and Development from 1952 to 1968," (Notre Dame, 1972), unpublished dissertation, p. 85. The Tripartite Treaty issue is a prime example of the manner in which many integration theorists have misinterpreted a number of the important events in the history of the integration movement. According to Cochrane (p. 67) and Nye (p.29), the Tripartite Treaty represented a successful attempt

of the tecnicos from the three countries to accelerate the pace of the integration program. However, a careful reading of the historical record (Parker, p. 86) affords a radically different version of the events leading up to the signing of the Tripartite Treaty. According to E.L. Barber (interview, op. cit.), State Department representatives Isaiah Frank and Harry Turkell advised El Salvador and Honduras to sign a bilateral economic treaty of cooperation. In their analysis, Central America was not ready for multilateral economic cooperation. But Guatemala's Ydigoras objected for geopolitical reasons: a pact between El Salvador and Honduras would isolate Guatemala politically and economically from the rest of Central America. He insisted that Guatemala be a part of any such cooperative venture. Thus, the Tripartite Treaty was motivated as much by political as economic considerations. The role of the politicos in negotiating the Tripartite Treaty has been ignored by most observers.

35. Quoted in Nye, p. 53.

36. Francisco Lainez M.,"Discursos pronunciados en el Acto Inaugural del Primero Seminario Nacional sobre la integracion economica Centroamericana" (Managua: Banco Central, 1965), p. 13.

37. Cohen, p. 33.

38. James Calvin Billick, "Costa Rican Perspectives and the Central American Common Market" (University of Pittsburgh: 1969), unpublished dissertation.

39. UN-ECLA, "El programa de integracion economica de Centroamerica y el Tratado de Asociacion economica suscrito por El Salvador, Guatemala, y Honduras" (E/CN.12/CCE/212), May 1960.

40. Cohen, pp. 33-35.

41. Landry, pp. 84-103.

42. Ibid.; see also Billick, op. cit.

43. U.S. Congress, House, p. 24.

44. Ibid.

45. James Cochrane, "United States Attitudes Toward Central American Integration," Inter-American Economic Affairs, Vol. 18, No. 2 (Autumn 1964), p.89.

46. Cohen, p. 37.

47. Ibid., p. 69.

48. UN-ECLA, "Informe del Comite de Cooperacion

Economica del Istmo Centroamericano, 14 de diciembre de 1960 a 29 de enero de 1963," (E/CN.12/CCE/303/ Rev. 1), August 1963, pp. 47-73.

49. UN-ECLA, "Subside de la CEPAL en Mexico," (CEPAL/MEX/68/15/Rev. 1), November 1968, mimeo.

50. U.S. Department of State, "The Presidents' Meeting at San Jose," Department of State Bulletin, 48(April 8, 1963), pp. 515-517.

51. Ibid.; see also Landry, op. cit.

52. Ibid., p. 517.

53. Ibid.

54. Dean Rusk, in Department of State Bulletin, 48 (May 6, 1963), p. 639.

55. Carlos Castillo, "Growth and Integration in Central America " (University of Wisconsin, 1965), unpublished dissertation, p. 126.

56. U.S. Comptroller General, "Progress and Problems in United States Aid to the Economic Unification of Central America" (Washington, D.C.: U.S. Government Printing Office, 1970), p. 16.

57. Ibid.

58. Cohen, p. 75.

59. U.S. Comptroller General, op. cit.

60. Interviews with Barber and Lazar,op. cit.

61. The development philosophy of the Central American elites is the subject of the next chapter.

62. Interview with William Sowash, U.S. Department of State, July 11, 1975. At the time, Mr. Sowash was Deputy Chief of Mission at the American Embassy in Honduras. In the late 1960s, he was a high ROCAP official in Guatemala in charge of the coordination of projects with ODECA.

63.Ernst Haas and Philippe Schmitter, "Economics and Differential Patterns of Political Integration: Projections About Unity in Latin America," International Organization XVIII (Autumn 1964).

64. Anderson, p. 29.

65. Ibid., p. 31.

66. Ibid., p. 33.

67. Ibid., p. 355.

68. Ibid., pp. 337-347.

69. Gary Wynia, Politics and Planners (Madison: University of Wisconsin Press, 1972).

70. Interview with Irving Tragen, former head of ROCAP/Guatemala, Washington, D.C., December 1975.

71. Cohen, p. 11.

72. Former President of Costa Rica, quoted in Nye, p. 28.

73. Interview with Sowash, op. cit.

74. Nye, op. cit.

75. Anderson, pp. 87-114.

76. See discussion in Chapter 7.

77. Nye, op. cit.

78. As demonstrated in this chapter, the influence of ECLA began to wane as soon as the tecnicos established their own regional power base in the form of SIECA. But even SIECA's influence declined as the tecnicos became integrated into the national political and economic elite.

3. The Development Goals of the Central American Elites

THE CASE FOR REGIONAL INTEGRATION IN CENTRAL AMERICA

ECLA saw a special need for a program of regional economic integration in Central America several years before the establishment of the Latin American Free Trade Association (LAFTA). First of all, the Central American economies were so small that they could not efficiently begin the first "easy" stages of import substitution on the national level. A region-wide market was needed to encourage the establishment of light manufacturing industries on an economic scale. Without the growth of import substitution under a program of regional integration, the Central American economies were doomed to stagnation and continued dependence on foreign exchange earnings received from the export of primary products.

The second ECLA argument which supported Central American economic integration concerned the scarcity of capital and other resources available for development. To ECLA, coordinated national and regional economic development planning was the only possible way for Central America to utilize these resources effectively and avoid duplication and waste. While larger developing countries had a larger margin for error and inefficiency, the Central American economies could not afford the trial and error rationale behind the market mechanism. ECLA criticized those who "cherish the hope that the free play of economic forces will solve all problems, without any kind of planning." Competition had to be regulated by "impersonal intervention on the part of the State" in order to "guide, safeguard, and encourage individual action in economic life."[1]

Some observers believe that the United States objected to ECLA's program of import substitution in Central America mainly because it was a threat to U. S. private business interests in the area.[2] But the available evidence indicates that the United States was as much concerned about the welfare of the Central American economies as it was concerned about the welfare of U. S. companies (although the U. S. security interests discussed in Chapter 2 cannot be ignored). A typical expression of the position of the United States with regard to Central American integration was made by Senator Len B. Jordan:

> The issue is not whether we support or do not support economic integration; the important question is the nature and spirit of those groupings that are evolving. We should be concerned whether the world economy in the future is going to be characterized by healthy competition and allocation of resources largely through the market mechanism, or whether regulation, planning, and government operations will become the order of the day.[3]

The United States opposed ECLA's belief that the Central American governments must intervene against the market forces and provide artificial aids to foster new industries; rather, industrialization would be a by-product of competition and other market forces.

Moreover, the United States believed that the key to successful development in Central America lay, not in ECLA's plan to manage the scarce resources available, but in attracting large amounts of external assistance in the form of private foreign investment. The United States was afraid that excessive government interference would tend to discourage prospective investors, and the basis of industrialization would be political and not economic. On the other hand, ECLA was afraid that unrestrained private foreign investment would create serious problems, such as "unbalanced growth," duplication of industries, and massive repatriation of profits.[4]

THE CENTRAL AMERICAN ELITES' DEVELOPMENT GOALS

The basic goal of the members of the Central

American Common Market was rapid economic growth. The basis by which they measured the success of the economic integration program was the extent to which the Common Market helped to create the conditions for accelerated growth. With population increasing at the same rate as national income--over three percent per year--the national incomes of these countries had to grow between 6 and 6.5 percent per year if the goal of a 2.5 percent increase in annual per capita income set by the Alliance for Progress was to be met. ECLA saw "demand deficiency" for Central America's exports as the major obstacle to achieving this goal. An import substitution policy was determined to be the best remedy; production for the domestic market would have to be accelerated in order to attain satisfactory growth rates. A system of protective tariffs, leading to gradual industrialization of the region, would free Central America from external dependence on world demand conditions for its primary products. ECLA saw this as the only way Central America could achieve planned, sustained economic growth.[5]

But individual Central American countries could not achieve efficient industrialization and growth in isolation; a larger market was needed to permit the operation of large-scale modern industries. Without a common market, establishment of capital goods industries would be impossible. ECLA essentially wanted the area to regain the growth rate it had achieved during the ten post-war years.[6]

Although ECLA's portrayal of the obstacles to development of the Central American economies and their solution was inaccurate, the Central American elites eventually subscribed to the ECLA thesis because it offered them a concrete program of economic development. ECLA's generalizations about the common fate of all primary producing countries ignored some important differences among the Central American economies. ECLA's thesis is that, in these economies, the rate of growth is dependent on the terms of trade for their primary products. Yet this was not an accurate portrayal of the Central American economies after World War II. While the region did experience an intense period of prosperity due to an unprecedented improvement in the prices of its main exports in the world market, the countries were affected differently. While Costa Rica and Nicaragua exhibited very high rates of growth, in Guatemala and Honduras the rate of growth of their economies barely equalled the rate of population growth. Costa Rica, El Salvador, and

Guatemala had relatively well-developed export sectors; Honduras, in effect, had no national export sector--the bulk of its exports, bananas, was in the hands of well-known banana companies, and Nicaragua was just beginning to develop its export sector. Yet Nicaragua had the highest rate of growth, and Guatemala's relatively well-developed export sector could not help it take full advantage of the tripling of the price of coffee which occurred from 1945 to 1954.[7] Thus, it is misleading to say that the primary obstacle to economic development in the region during the 1950s was the dependence on primary exports, since Honduras and Nicaragua had yet to develop a national export sector. Nevertheless, after the prices of primary exports began to decline after 1955, many Central American economists and government officials began to adopt ECLA's arguments favoring a renewed effort at development through import substitution.

ECLA's call for industrialization through regional integration was not the only basis for the desire of the Central American elites to integrate their economies. In a way, the attempt at regional integration was also an outgrowth of the reformist efforts at economic development of the late 1940s and early 1950s. The post-war political changes in the region caused a broadening of the ruling elites and a new conception of the function of government. The region's last generation of personalistic caudillos--Ubico of Giatemala, Hernandez of El Salvador, Somoza of Nicaragua, Calderon of Costa Rica, and Carias of Honduras--had been concerned with the maintenance of political and economic stability. In this role, to the masses they were nothing more than the traditional symbols of authority; to members of the economic elite, they were the defenders of the export-oriented economic policy. But to a minority of young military officers and civilian political aspirants, they were tyrants who were incapable of managing the development issues raised by postwar prosperity and embryonic demands for economic and social reform.

These groups of young reformers came to power full of hopes and aspirations. In contrast to the negative role of the government under the "Depression dictators," the new members of the political elite thought that it was the responsibility of the government to overcome the poverty of the masses within a framework of democratic freedoms. But their development ideology could best be described as vague and eclectic. They had no coherent programs and policy proposals; rather, they borrowed from a variety of political and economic doctrines popular in Western Europe, Latin America, and the United States. Embarassed by Central America's economic and political backwardness, the new members of the political elite were determined, through imitation of their more advanced neighbors, to modernize their governmental machinery and economic policies.[8]

At the same time, however, the new members of the elite--whether supporters of the "controlled revolution" of El Salvador or the "practical Socialists" of Costa Rica--realized that the traditional elites, such as the landed oligarchy, were extremely powerful. Therefore, they virtually promised the economic elites that their privileged position would not be touched. The path of reform was not to be land tenure reform and income redistribution, but rather public works and industrialization. In Guatemala, when the revolutionary regime threatened the land-owners and the banana companies with agrarian reform, it was overthrown by the landed oligarchy and the army--with the support of the United States government. Thus, it became apparent that reform efforts would have to center in the industrial and related sectors.[9]

Despite the reformist aspirations of the new elites, because of political and economic realities, they essentially maintained a belief in what Anderson has called the "conventional" approach to development--defined as the elaboration of the existing modern sector.[10] They believed essentially in the free enterprise approach, where the traditional sector would be brought into the modern economy through the "trickle down" effect. Capital and technology were the keys to growth, because investment and productivity within the existing modern sector were at the center of the conceptual scheme. Social reform measures, such as minimum wage or agrarian reform, were justifiable only if they could contribute to the acceleration of productivity in the modern sector.

In the early 1950s, this conventional approach was less a development ideology than it was a technique of system maintenance, of preserving the political and economic status quo.

> Thus, the propositions of much of 'development economics' in the years since World War II--capital intensification, export diversification, and the like--were initially con-

ceived less as a format for change, and more as a set of adjustments essential to maintain the integrity and vitality of a conventional political economic system threatened by imbalances and disequilibria in balance of payments, commodity price fluctuations, and so on. In an important sense, that intricate set of economic propositions and policy recommendations that we identify with the early Prebisch or 'ECLA School' of analysis, was an ideology of development only by by-product, and a program of adjustment and system maintenance by original intent.[11]

Costa Rica, El Salvador, and Guatemala had begun to industrialize, not only because of the relative scarcity of imports during the war, but also because of the expansion of the internal markets, which was caused by the prosperity of the export sector. But the manufacturing sector remained small, accounting for only 10 percent of GDP in 1950. Because of the limitations of size of the domestic markets--and the desire to avoid the redistribution of income upon which a widening of these internal markets would be based--the further development of the industrial sector would require the establishment of a regional market.[12]

The Central American economic officials simultaneously began two separate but related attempts to widen the markets for their domestically produced industrial goods. In 1951, El Salvador began to negotiate a series of bilateral free trade treaties at the same time that ECLA's integration scheme began to take root. El Salvador was the leader of the "free trade" movement, on both the bilateral and regional levels, for geopolitical reasons. El Salvador faced increasing population pressures; it needed access to new markets for its manufactured products in order to finance the increasing amounts of foodstuffs it was forced to import.

Beginning in 1947, El Salvador signed bilateral agreements with Guatemala concerning the gradual removal of customs barriers, the elimination of restrictions on immigration, the unification of the two banking and monetary systems, and increased cooperation between the two educational systems. By 1953, El Salvador had signed limited free trade treaties with all four of its neighbors. Guatemala then responded with similar treaties with Honduras and Costa Rica by 1956. Other bilateral treaties were signed, but the six treaties mentioned above were the only ones that were of any significance. They were limited in scope and not very "free," but they contained (at least on paper) most of what was eventually achieved under the integration program. However, there were several limitations to the bilateral treaties which made regional free trade arrangements desirable. First, national industrial development laws were a big hurdle to free trade, because they created artificial cost differences. Secondly, differences in tariffs on raw materials imports made those countries which had the highest tariffs averse to free trade. This pointed to the need for equalization of tariffs, which could not be achieved in a bilateral context. In sum, these bilaterals could be called timid experiments which, nevertheless, provided the base for the CACM.[13]

The same men who fomented the bilateral treaties were behind the drive to establish a program of economic integration in Central America: Jorge Sol of El Salvador, Noriega of Guatemala, and Enrique Delgado of Nicaragua. They were all young men, educated outside Central America. These three tecnicos attended the fourth ECLA session in Mexico in June 1951; there they found that Honduras and Costa Rica, as well as ECLA, had similar sentiments about economic development, and they issued a joint declaration. This declaration called for everything which eventually was included in the 1960 General Treaty of Economic Integration.[14]

As indicated in Chapter 1, these tecnicos formed the Committee of Cooperation under ECLA's guidance. Unlike ODECA, it was informal and flexible; there were no political squabbles, because they considered the CEC a technical body which made recommendations and not policy. Many authors have stated that the key to the CEC's initial success was the modesty of its goals. But these observers ignore the great deal of trouble ECLA had in pressuring the economic officials of Guatemala, Nicaragua, and El Salvador to keep their sights low concerning the initial scope of free trade and of the integration movement in general. On the other hand, ECLA had to assure Honduras and Costa Rica that preferential treatment for the least developed members and a very cautious pace would characterize the movement. In his tour of the area, Prebisch had encountered private sector resistance in Costa Riac and government resistance in Honduras. The latter had been advised by foreign consultants to develop a stronger export economy before joining the Common Market.[15] Yet at the same time, there was a growing feeling among economic officials of all five countries that the postwar economic changes favored "unionism." The first meeting of the Presidents of the Central Banks, held in August 1952--at the same time as the first CEC meeting--had as its goal the testing of new theories in the monetary field. They intended to work toward unified monetary policies and a Central American payments compensation system. But ECLA was alarmed by the boldness of both the Ministers of Economy and the Presidents of the Central Banks. It restrained the tecnicos, stressing gradual and limited steps; total integration was to be achieved only in the distant future.[16]

ECLA placed its stress on the optimal placement of industries and a policy of reciprocity. Its two formal goals were the regional allocation of industry and limited free trade. In ECLA's thinking, free trade was not enough to insure a successful economic integration program; ECLA believed that more active participation through a regional industrial development policy was needed. Thus, the basic contradiction in ECLA's development strategy for Central America was apparent. On the issue of free trade, ECLA called for gradualness and restraint; yet ECLA called for concerted action at the highest level--coordinated industrial development planning--from the very beginning. ECLA was unable to reconcile its caveat concerning the avoidance of politicization of the integration program with the fact that the planning it advocated was highly political by nature.

Even those economic officials who were most in favor of ECLA's program of economic integration were not entirely satisfied with ECLA's "go slow" policy. However, they were not organized enough or clear enough on what they wanted from integration to go against ECLA or even to modify ECLA's program, so they signed the documents prepared by ECLA during the 1950s. Each Central American tecnico had different ideas about what the goals of Central American integration should be and how to attain them. Priorities differed from country to country and even from man to man. But they all agreed on ECLA's plan for new industries and the expansion of the old ones through the principle of reciprocity.[17]

There were major philosophical differences behind the "classical liberal" thinking of the bilateral treaties and the novel ECLA theory. While the "classical liberal" theory was based on free trade and market forces, ECLA's thesis was based on the argument that market forces without the interjection of planning would aggravate the imbalances among the member countries. It is interesting to note that, as mentioned above, the same group of men initiated the bilateral and multilateral treaties; they were able to integrate the two opposing philosophies into their eclectic, essentially pragmatic, development philosophy.[18]

All members of the private sector, amd most of the Central American governments, were suspicious of planning, however, because of its socialistic connotations. They thought of themselves as "classical liberals" who supported free trade.[19] Interviews conducted by Philippe Schmitter in the mid-1960s revealed considerable doctrinaire opposition to both comprehensive and sector planning on the part of both public officials and private interest groups and businessmen. Moreover, he found a substantial amount of criticism of ECLA's "excessively abstract" approach.[20] For this reason, says Fuentes, the bilateral treaties were of greater value than the integration program during the 1950s.[21] While Fuentes claims that this was due to the favorable climate created by the integration movement, the evidence indicates that the reverse may be true--that the integration movement was nurtured by the success of the bilateral treaties. In fact, it appears that the Central American economic elites in the late 1950s, including most industrialists and many government officials, were concerned primarily with the expansion of markets for already existing industries, because of their philosophical beliefs and the political pressures of certain influential economic groups, such as the industrialists. They did not want to wait for ECLA and the CEC to "catch up" to the goals embodied in the bilateral treaties. Thus, the 1960 Tripartite Treaty was a manifestation of the discontent of the Central American economic officials and industrialists with the philosophy of the ECLA-backed CEC program as embodied in the 1958 Treaty of Economic Association. In this sense, the Tripartite Treaty was a logical extension of the free-trade philosophy embodied in the bilateral treaties.

As demonstrated in Chapter 2, United States financial assistance was the catalyst behind the signing of the Tripartite Treaty by El Salvador, Guatemala, and Honduras and the signing of the General Treaty a year later by all five countries.

But this should not disguise the fact that the desire to accelerate the integration program originated in El Salvador, Honduras, and Guatemala, and not in the United States. According to Fuentes, the 1958 Multilateral Treaty was a step backward for all parties. Guatemala, Costa Rica, and Honduras had bilateral treaties (Guatemala-Honduras, Guatemala-Costa Rica) which permitted increasing the number of free trade items by simple exchange of notes of Chancery. Fuentes says that the Multilateral Treaty only served to formalize a few of the gains which had been made under the bilateral treaties. He adds that Guatemala, El Salvador, and Honduras did not appear to have much faith in the Multilateral Treaty, because between 1956 and 1958 they instituted new bilateral treaties among themselves. Thus, they were in no hurry to sign a treaty that was more trouble than it was worth. They obtained the same, or even greater, benefits from their bilateral treaties, yet they had more freedom to maneuver and negotiate.[22]

When the free trade list finally was established for the Multilateral Treaty, Costa Rica and Nicaragua had excluded virtually all of the important products in regional trade from the list, leaving mostly items of little importance. Honduras, El Salvador, and Guatemala, on the other hand, had left most of the important items on the free trade list. Thus, Costa Rica and Nicaragua were a serious obstacle to the accelerated growth of regional trade desired by the three Northern countries. Costa Rica and Nicaragua had rejected most items of importance on the list and had suggested a rigid machinery for expansion of the list. Therefore, while the Multilateral Treaty was important as a symbol, it was also a weak foundation upon which to build a common market.

Honduras, El Salvador, and Guatemala may well have relied on their bilateral arrangements for future development if it had not been for the financial assistance offered by the United States for the program of free trade expansion embodied in the Tripartite Treaty of 1960. It is important to point out that the Tripartite Treaty ignored the Multilateral Treaty's provision for planning and the Integration Industries scheme, not solely because of United States resistance, but primarily because of the goals of the Central American elites themselves. They were concerned primarily with accelerated growth of intra-regional free trade, and they had never fully subscribed to ECLA's program of industrial planning.

James Cochrane states that the Central American governments never completely accepted the Integration Industires scheme, and many still think it is unnecessary. Only ECLA has been a consistent champion of the scheme, while the Central American governments vascillated and changed their minds frequently. The three northern countries--Guatemala, El Salvador, and Honduras--had abandoned the Integration Industries scheme with the signing of the Tripartite Treaty because they thought they could develop industrially without it.[23]

ECLA managed to pressure the governments to accept the Protocol on Integration Industries after it reasserted itself and persuaded them to sign the General Treaty of Economic Integration in 1961. But the negotiators rewrote the Protocol to make it ambiguous, so that each government could interpret the Protocol. This was done simply to get the Protocol signed, in order to mollify ECLA. Even so, after the Integration Industries Protocol was signed, El Salvador and Guatemala publicly affirmed their dislike of the scheme because it required state control of certain industries; they both rejected "the monopolistic tendencies of the Regime."[24] Honduras, too, was a reluctant participant in the decision to make the scheme a part of the General Treaty. The Honduran representative to the Committee of Economic Cooperation stated that, although his government was joining in the decision, it would have preferred that the General Treaty make no mention of "integration industries."[25]

Why was the scheme retained if the Central American governments generally were opposed to it? Why would a particular government alternately strongly support and then suddenly strongly oppose the Integration Industires scheme? There are two reasons which stand out. First, ECLA strongly supported the scheme. The Central American governments have been reluctant to deliberately and needlessly offend the Secretariat, since it had been the major source of support and assistance for Central American economic integration during the decade of the 1950s. Thus, they retained the scheme in order to placate ECLA. But they did not commit their governments to anything; the provisions of the scheme could only be implemented by subsequent protocols to the agreement. The second major reason the scheme was retained was United States opposition to it. Rather than encouraging the Central American governments to reject the scheme, United States opposition had the opposite effect. All of the Central American governments rallied to give formal, public support to the scheme. As a result of external criticism, all five Central American governments insisted on retaining the scheme as a demonstration of independence and solidarity.[26]

In summary, the Central American elites supported ECLA's doctrine of industrialization through economic integration for two reasons. The primary reason was that they believed that ECLA's plan would lead to rapid and sustained economic growth. But the second reason, the desire to modernize their economies through industrialization, was also important. The Central American economists wanted to industrialize their economies for three reasons which were not necessarily complementary. First of all, they believed that ECLA's program of import substitution would help reduce the degree of external dependence of the Central American economies. Second, Central American support of the ECLA Doctrine was reinforced by the reformist efforts inspired by the postwar political and economic changes and the resistance of the landowners to change in the traditional sectors of the economy. And finally, the Central American elites tended to identify industrialization with development and modernity. Thus, their desire to industrialize their economies was not simply based on economic reasoning; equally important was their desire to duplicate the modern economic structure of the developed countries.

The Central American politicos responded to ECLA's development strategy because it concentrated on the modern sector; it specifically avoided the politically explosive issues of agrarian reform and income distribution--in short, the integration of the traditional sector into the modern economy. The integration program enabled the political leadership to pursue economic development while bolstering the economic and political status quo.

This perspective on the integration program and the emerging support of the politicos calls into serious question the standard interpretation of the role played by the tecnicos and the politicos in the integration process. It is generally held that the tecnicos were successful in initiating the integration movement because of its essentially technical and apolitical nature and the general lack of interest of the politicos. However, as discussed above and in Chapter 2, the politicos actively supported the integration movement specifically because of its political acceptability. The politicos were active participants in the integration process as soon as it began to demonstrate that it had potential for significant pay-offs. Thus, the integration program achieved its initial successes, not only because of the tecnicos' strategy of avoiding "politicization" of the movement, but also because the politicos played an active role in establishing the guidelines of the program and actively supported it. As future chapters will demonstrate, it is the role of the politicos in both domestic and regional politics that is the key to understanding the fate of regional integration in Central America.

CACM: SUCCESS OR FAILURE?

Most economists agree that the Central American economic integration program was not very successful in achieving its primary goal of rapid and sustained growth. At best, it fostered a moderate increase in the GDP growth rate. The Common Market also was not very successful in decreasing Central American dependence on primary exports through its import substitution program. However, the other major goal of the integration program was to stimulate industrialization at a low cost in terms of foregone income. The fact that there is little evidence of a negative CACM effect on income means that the Common Market was fairly successful in achieving this goal. The high rate of growth of manufacturing output fostered by the import substitution program and the widening of the market equalled the rate of GDP growth in Honduras and exceeded the growth rate in the other four countries between 1962 and 1968. This expansion of manufacturing output probably would have been more costly had it occurred autarkically with less specialization in production.[27]

If the economic achievements and failures of the Common Market are so straightforward, why did such a controversy arise in the late 1960s concerning the alleged "failures" of the integration program? The obvious answer is that each set of actors was judging the Common Market from a different perspective. United States officials, such as McClelland, analyzed the Common Market within the framework of orthodox economic theory. On the other hand, ECLA and SIECA officials based their observations on the ECLA Doctrine, a direct outgrowth of neo-orthodox thought. And finally, the political leadership of Central America, while essentially adherents of the orthodox theory, also had specific political objectives which they were attempting to use the Common Market to fulfill.

As indicated earlier, the fundamental difference between orthodox and neo-orthodox theory is that the former believes that the market mechanism will maximize economic efficiency and growth, while the latter believes that economic planning should be the instrument. Thus, from the perspective of orthodox theory, the greatest achievement of the Common Market was the expansion of free trade and the moderate amount of industrialization through import substitution. On the other hand, ECLA wanted coordinated industrial planning on a regional basis as the focus of the Common Market, and it interpreted the expansion of trade and the import substitution process in a very negative manner. The politicos saw the expansion of free trade, import substitution, and the increase in foreign investment and assistance as the greatest achievements of the integration program, and they were not concerned about the failure of economic planning.

Orthodox theorists viewed the $18 million in revenue lost due to the competing national fiscal incentives programs as being inefficient, but advocated no regional agreements to solve the matter. ECLA used the lost revenue as proof of the evils of competition and advocated a regional fiscal incentives agreement to prevent "unfair" competition. But the political leadership viewed the lost revenue as the price it had to pay for industrializing the Central American economies; to the Central American elites, industrialization was a goal which transcended cost-benefit analysis. The revenue loss was not large enough to force them to follow ECLA's advice and coordinate their fiscal incentives programs.

By "orthodox" standards, all five countries gained substantially from participating in a Common Market which focused on expanding free trade under the market mechanism. By ECLA's narrow standards, however,--measuring the growth of the five industrial sectors--this emphasis on free trade and the market mechanism resulted in the inequitable distribution of the benefits of the integration program. While all five governments initially appeared to be satisfied with the distribution of benefits, Honduras, Nicaragua, and Costa Rica began to complain that they needed preferential treatment in order to obtain an equitable share of benefits. As future chapters will show, however, these claims were politically motivated.

ECLA claimed that the uncontrolled import substitution which had taken place had caused a dramatic rise in consumer prices. But as McClelland's extensive study shows, this did not occur. Thus, the orthodox view that increased competition kept the prices down appears to be verified.

ECLA also claimed that the Integration Industries scheme would have been able to rationalize the industrialization process if the United States had not opposed it. However, not only did Chapter 2 demonstrate that the politicos themselves opposed the Integration Industries in principle, but also McClelland and Ramsett have demonstrated that the scheme was virtually unworkable in Central America--SIECA proved unable to perform any of the numerous tasks required to make the Integration Industries program a success. Once again, not only did the political leadership resist the scheme, but also those who were associated with these particular industries were hostile to it.[28]

By 1969, ECLA, SIECA, and those members who had become dissatisfied with their share of the benefits of the integration program had charged that the major problems confronting these economies--balanced growth and balance of payments problems--had been created by the current focus of the integration program. But, as the next two chapters demonstrate, these problems were caused by domestic political problems and were not the direct result of these countries' participation in the Common Market.

The final critique of the current focus of the Common Market was that it concentrated almost exclusively on the modern sector. Paradoxically, this charge is made by orthodox economists who want Central America to exploit its comparative advantage in agriculture. It is on this point that the politicos joined sides with ECLA. As indicated earlier, the politicos adopted the ECLA Doctrine of industrialization in order to avoid the explosive political issues which would have attended the integration of the traditional sector into the modern economy. Thus, they interpreted the ECLA Doctrine as essentially supporting the political status quo.

In sum, viewed from the orthodox economic perspective, at best the Common Market was moderately successful in achieving its twin goals of rapid and sustained economic growth and industrialization through the use of the market mechanism. On the other hand, from the perspective of neo-orthodox theory, the Common Market's focus on free trade expansion and competition aggravated the existing inequalities in the region and led to "distribution" crises in the late 1960s. However, from the perspective of the original political goals of the Central American political leadership, the Common Market enabled them both to accommodate the emerging marginal political elites--the tecnicos and the industrialists--and at the same time to improve the economic situation of their respective countries without upsetting the political status quo. Unfortunately, as the next three chapters will demonstrate, the objectives of some of the members underwent a dramatic change beginning in the mid-1960s; and this caused a radical reassessment of the value of the integration program.

NOTES

1. Prebisch, "Toward a Dynamic..."p. 92.

2. Landry, p. 63.

3. Senator Len Jordan, U.S. Congress, Joint Economic Committee, Hearings before the Sub-Committee on Inter-American Relations,"Latin American Development and Western Hemisphere Trade," 89th Congress, 2nd Session (Washington, D.C.: 1966), p. 8.

4. Interviews with Barber, Stern, and Lockard.

5. James Cochrane, The Politics of Regional Integration: The Central American Case (New Orlaens: Tulane University Press, 1969), Chapter II.

6. United Nations, "The Latin American Common Market," No. 59, II, G.4 (New York: 1969), p. 1.

7. Castillo, p. 48.

8. Anderson, op. cit.

9. Anderson, "Politics and Economic Development Policy in Central America," in Robert Tomasek, ed., Latin American Politics (New York: Anchor, 1966), pp. 544-565.

10. Ibid., pp. 163-173.

11. Ibid., pp. 166-167.

12. OAS, Secretary General, "Estudio economico de

America Latina, Parte 2: Algunos aspectos de la produccion y el comercio de America Central" (Washington, D.C.: 1964), pp. 342-358. mimeographed.

13. Alberto Fuentes Mohr, *La creacion de un mercado comun* (Buenos Aires: INTAL, 1974), pp. 38-54.

14. Ibid., pp. 59-62.

15. Interview with Barber.

16. Interviews with Lazar and Lockard.

17. Interviews; see also Fuentes, p. 71.

18. Gary Wynia, *Politics and Planners*, pp. 37-51.

19. Alberto Fuentes Mohr, "Observaciones sobre el desarrollo de la planificacion en Centroamerica," CIES, CIAP/116, September 14, 1964.

20. Philippe Schmitter, "Central American Integration," p. 18.

21. Fuentes, "Observaciones."

22. Fuentes, *La creacion*, pp. 122-123.

23. James Cochrane, "Central American Economic Integration: the Integration Industries Scheme," *Inter-American Economic Affairs*, Vol. 19, No. 2, (Autumn 1965), pp. 68-70.

24. Ibid., p. 143.

25. United Nations, ECLA, "Report of the Central American Economic Cooperation Committee," E/CN.12/552, E/CN.12/CEE/224 (June 1961), p. 7.

26. *SIECA Newsletter*, No. 34 (August 1964), p. 4.

27. The most authoritative analyses of the CACM's achievements are David McClelland, *The Central American Common Market* (New York: Praeger, 1972); Jeffrey Nugent, *Economic Integration in Central America* (Baltimore: Johns Hopkins Press, 1974); Eduardo Lizano and L.N. Wilmore, "Second Thoughts on Central America," *Journal of Common Market Studies*, Vol. 13, No. 3 (March 1975).

28. McClelland, op. cit.; also, see David Ramsett, *Regional Industrial Development in Central America* (New York: Praeger, 1969).

4. Balanced Growth

There is virtually unanimous agreement--among both economists and regional integration theorists--that the issue of "balanced growth" is the greatest obstacle to regional economic integration among the less developed countries.[1] Ernst Haas presents the balanced growth issue as his primary empirical generalization concerning integration efforts in the developing world. In the context of the general underdevelopment of a region, he says all national actors are sensitive to any negative changes in the patterns of their economic transactions. Because less developed countries are highly sensitive to the costs entailed by participation in an integration program, the controversial group of issues generally referred to as "balanced development" or "unequal benefits" emerges to threaten the process of integration.[2]

Generalizing from the same two case studies employed by Haas, Stuart Fagan concludes that

> ...in all common markets among underdeveloped countries, the operation of free market forces, when successful in stimulating growth in regional trade, import substitution, and increased investment, stimulates trading and investment patterns which, due to external economies, favor the traditional centers in the relatively more developed countries over the less developed members, even when initial differences in national levels of development are not severe.[3]

It is believed generally that the tendency for unregulated market forces in Central America to increase disparities among member countries, once perceived by the less developed members in the region, became the principal source of the series of political crises which began to plague the Common Market after 1964. On the one hand, Honduras and Nicaragua demanded preferential treatment because of their alleged less developed status. On the other hand, El Salvador and Guatemala, lacking the resources to fulfill their own national development goals, were reluctant to sacrifice the present benefits they were enjoying from integration for uncertain future ones.

However, the attempt to create a theory or a "pre-theory" about integration among less developed countries on such a narrow empirical base has led to two serious errors concerning the issue of balanced growth in the Central American Common Market. First of all, virtually all observers have concluded that the emergence of balanced growth as an issue of crisis proportions is almost automatic. The superficial observation of the fact that the issue of balanced growth created political crises in both the East African Common Market and the Central American Common Market cannot be accepted as sufficient evidence of automaticity or inevitability. A close examination of the political motivations behind the demands of Honduras and Nicaragua for preferential treatment reveals that the issue of balanced growth did not emerge automatically due to the relatively underdeveloped status of these two countries. In fact, this chapter will demonstrate that Honduras manipulated the issue of balanced growth to serve domestic political and economic ends. Moreover, the issue of balanced growth did not have to become magnified into crisis proportions and could have been avoided entirely--by both Honduras and Nicaragua.

The other error made by most observers is that they misuse the term "level of development" when analyzing the relative status of different members of a regional, economic arrangement. As the Fagan quotation above demonstrates, most observers believe that even very small differences in levels of development inexorably lead to distribution crises. Once again, this thesis is not supported if domestic political differences are taken into consideration. In the case of Honduras, for example, there is an underlying assumption that Honduras is at a lower stage of economic development than the other Common Market members and that preferential treatment will allow Honduras to "catch up." In reality, Honduras was at the same stage of economic development as its partners when the Common Market began operations, but peculiar domestic political problems prevented Honduras from reaping many of the benefits the Common Market had to offer. Nicaragua, for example, was in worse shape economically than Honduras in the early 1960s, yet by the early 1970s--and without preferential treatment--Nicaragua had developed an industrial sector as dynamic as any in the region. Once again, as this chapter will demonstrate, the crucial variable was the domestic political developments of the period.[4]

HONDURAS' DEMAND FOR PREFERENTIAL TREATMENT

As indicated earlier, during the negotiations for the Tripartite Treaty and later for the General Treaty, Honduras repeatedly stated that it was not in favor of the Integration Industries scheme and other measures designed to promote balanced industrial development which would interfere with free trade. In fact, prior to the ouster of the Liberal government of Villeda Morales in October 1963, there is absolutely no evidence which suggests that Honduran decision makers perceived the pattern of economic transactions in the Central American region to be especially unfavorable to Honduras.

The overthrow of the Villeda government in October 1963 set the stage for a dramatic shift in Honduras' perception of and policy toward the Common Market.[5] In contrast to the open support which the Villeda government had given to the integration program, the Lopez regime at first had no definite position on the Common Market. But within a few months of the October 1963 coup, one of the new economic officials began a vigorous campaign to persuade the government that Honduras was at a disadvantageous position in the Common Market. He also began to press the government to demand treaty revisions in Honduras' favor.

The economic official was Praxedes Martinez, Sub-Secretary of the Ministry of Economy and later Economic Adviser to the National Congress. As had his Tanganyikan counterpart a year earlier, Martinez had read Myrdal's 1957 study and had decided to apply Myrdal's "backwash" theory to the specific case of the Central American Common Market.[6] Thus, says Hansen, "elites involved in these integration schemes have been alerted to the problem even before it has arisen."[7] In neither of the two cases--upon which the empirical generalizations of integration theorists are based--did the issue of balanced growth or unequal benefits arise automatically as a result of perceived inequalities. Rather, the bargaining positions of both Tanganyika and Honduras were developed before their claims could be verified empirically. The timing of the Honduras demands was especially suspect, because the Common Market had only become fully operational in 1963--the year Costa Rica had ratified the General Treaty.

Martinez claimed that the Villeda government did not take into account Honduras' weaknesses relative to the other member states when it negotiated the General Treaty. Honduras could not compete favorably with its neighbors because of low industrial production, poor infractructure, low technical skills, and political instability. As a result, Honduras' regional trade balance had become unfavorable, its consumer prices were rising, the number of unemployed artisans was growing because of industrial competition from the other Common Market members; and the import substitution program was causing Honduras to lose fiscal revenues needed to support its national development programs. Honduras, he said, was so backward that it could not even satisfy the conditions to obtain integration industries which would help it industrialize. In short, Honduras was subsidizing the industrial development of the other member states. Martinez called for preferential treatment for Honduras: a grace period for the application of the uniform tariff, a protocol to the Common Fiscal Incentives Agreement (which had not yet been ratified) which would allow Honduras to provide extra benefits to firms in order to attract industry, and the creation of a development fund which would transfer capital to Honduras from the other members. Without this special treatment, Honduras would fall further behind its neighbors.[8]

In early 1964, Martinez made speeches to business groups, published magazine articles, and organized meetings of government officials in order to increase pressure on the government to adopt his views. After Martinez became economic adviser to the National Congress in 1965, the government found it increasingly difficult to obtain the passage of any integration agreement without a fight.

In December 1964, Martinez drafted an open letter to the new Minister of Economy, Manuel Acosta Bonilla, in which he repeated the claims and demands of his earlier publications. He added this threat: "We would seriously consider the declaration of a halt of a deposit of new integration instruments in those areas affecting the surrender of markets and fiscal losses."[9] Sparked by these efforts by Martinez, criticisms in the press of the country's disadvantageous position in the Common Market became more numerous. Rumors of Honduras' possible withdrawal from the Common Market spread throughout the region, causing President Lopez to deny the rumors and reiterate his country's support for the Common Market in his New Year's message of 1965. At the same time, however, he indicated that Honduras might require preferential treatment.[10]

Responding to the growing criticism of the Common Market, the new Minister of Economy began to develop a more aggressive policy toward the Common Market. In October 1965, he charged that inequality in levels of development between Honduras and its Common Market partners had been accentuated as a direct result of the formation of the Common Market. While Honduras was strongly in favor of remaining in the Common Market, it could not participate effectively without preferential treatment. As evidence of the alleged inequalities, Acosta Bonilla claimed that (1)the other countries enjoyed annual growth rates of up to 6 percent, in contrast to the Honduran average of 4 percent; (2)Honduras had the second highest population growth rate; and (3)the greater dynamism of the other economies had turned Honduras' "traditional" surplus in regional trade into a deficit.[11]

Many top Honduran economic officials, however, did not agree with Acosta Bonilla's tactic of portraying Honduras as backward in order to win concessions from its partners. Guillermo Bueso, a high official of the Central Bank of Honduras and the Minister of Economy under the Villeda administration, warned Acosta Bonilla that such a tactic might backfire and frighten away potential investors.[12] The head of the National Planning Council, Miguel Angel Rivera and Bueso both disagreed with the attempts of Martinez and Bonilla to blame Honduras' economic woes on its participation in the Common Market, but Bonilla disregarded their comments.[13]

The more aggressive Honduran policy was demonstrated in late 1965 when the Honduran representative at the Executive Council discussions of the terms of the Common Fiscal Incentives Agreement stated that the protocol would have unfavorable effects on Honduras. Then, in January 1966, Bonilla warned that Honduras would not deposit the protocol until it was revised in Honduras' favor:

> The government of Honduras believes that the ratification of this Convention would add to the unfavorable effects on the Honduran economy observed between 1958 and 1965, and certain clauses of the Convention would clearly retard and lessen the possibilities of the industrial growth on Honduras in the short, medium, and long terms.[14]

In August 1965, SIECA had rejected the charges made by Martinez and supported by Bonilla that Honduras needed preferential treatment in order to compete with the other Common Market members. But ECLA, in a report published in January 1966, came out in support of the new Honduran posture.[15] ECLA concluded that an imbalance in levels of industrial development and rates of growth unfavorable to Honduras continued to exist and recommended several measures designed to promote Honduran industrial development.[16]

Based on ECLA's suggestions--and spurred by the Honduran refusal to sign the original protocol--the Economic Council passed a resolution recommending several types of preferential treatment: (1)special studies should be carried out to determine which Integration Industries should go to Honduras; (2) CABEI should grant priority to Honduran projects; and (3)Honduras should be granted preferences in the concession of fiscal incentives. In return, Honduras would be required to ratify and deposit its outstanding integration agreements.[17] The ministers of economy accepted the Honduran interpretation of "balanced growth" as being balanced industrial development, but not because Honduras merited preferential treatment. Rather, they appear to have responded to what appeared to be an emerging crisis.[18]

Most of the recommendations were accepted by the member governments without controversy, except for the fiscal incentives protocol. This was actually the heart of the preferential treatment package, since the other steps would not help attract capital to Honduras--and this was the major goal. The first major clash over the fiscal incentives protocol took place at the April 1966 meeting of the Economic Council. SIECA presented Honduran proposals for the right to import raw materials and machinery for its industries exempt from tariffs, to grant tax exemptions for a period of time longer than that allowed for the other countries, and to apply a different, preferential system of industrial classification. All members rejected outright the first and third proposals, but they agreed to the second one. El Salvador proposed allowing Honduras a 20 percent differential on the import of raw materials, and the others agreed to it. But they could not agree on the starting date: Honduras wanted the proposal to become effective immediately, while the others wanted it to become effective beginning with the sixth year of the Common Fiscal Incentives Agreement.

After it had become clear that an impasse had been reached, the Economic Council asked SIECA to prepare a document in which it would set forth the two positions and then make a new proposal which took those conflicting positions into account. By June, each country had complicated the issue by presenting its own proposal for reform of the fiscal incentives agreement addressed to its own specific economic problems. None of Honduras' partners viewed the Honduran request for preferential treatment as legitimate; rather, they each viewed it as a Honduran attempt to solve its own domestic problems. Thus, the response of each country was to present a counter-proposal addressed to its own specific problem.[19]

To protest this lack of responsiveness, Honduras boycotted the meetings of the Economic and Executive Councils, bringing their operations to a halt. In light of this unprecedented "crisis," SIECA officials warned the other countries that they had better resolve this immediate problem--the granting of preferential treatment to Honduras--before they pressed for their own reforms of the fiscal incentives agreement. SIECA presented each government with a report which demonstrated that the costs to each government for the program of preferential treatment would be minimal.

In light of the crisis situation--and the SIECA report that such a program would be low cost--Guatemala and Costa Rica agreed to shelve their own proposals. Nicaragua refused to back down from its demand, however. Nicaragua intended to demand preferential treatment identical to that received by Honduras. Nicaraguan officials claimed that their country was qualified to receive preferential treatment as was Honduras, and that, therefore, they could not be expected to subsidize Honduran industrial development. The Salvadoran Minister of Economy flatly rejected the Nicaraguan request, and another stand-off developed. The Nicaraguan minister threatened Nicaraguan withdrawal from the

Common Market if its request for preferential treatment was not granted, and the Salvadoran minister threatened withdrawal if it was. The crisis was avoided when the Economic Council came up with a procedural solution: ECLA would study the relative position of Nicaragua in the Common Market--just as it had done for Honduras--and on the basis of that study, the CCE would make the necessary recommendations to the Economic Council. Nicaragua agreed to this procedure.[20]

The Protocol for Preferential Treatment for Honduras was signed by the Ministers of Economy in September 1966, but the other four countries--especially El Salvador--were reluctant to ratify and deposit it. Most deposits were made only under great political pressure. Even then, the agreement did not become legally effective until March 1969, and it never became operative. None of the governments or SIECA had accepted Honduras' demands as legitimate. Rather, they signed the protocol because it was the maximum economic price they were willing to pay to keep Honduras in the Common Market.

The Nicaraguan request for preferential treatment remained under ECLA study for years. ECLA never issued a report on the request because it realized that the other members strongly opposed granting Nicaragua preferential treatment. A reopening of the issue of balanced growth would have precipitated another crisis. It is important to note that, although its worsening trade deficit and upcoming elections had encouraged the Nicaraguan demands, Nicaragua never would have requested preferential treatment if Honduras had not done so.[21]

Nicaragua's demand for preferential treatment was even more politically inspired than the above events imply. Nicaraguan dissatisfaction with the Common Market had come to a head in the third quarter of 1966 because of the other members' complaints about the quality of Nicaraguan goods. Nicaragua was having a particularly difficult time with Honduras, which had banned Nicaraguan cosmetics and was threatening to ban Nicaraguan milk products.

The conflict between Honduras and Nicaragua was of long standing. As indicated in Chapter 2, Honduras and Nicaragua were involved in a bitter border dispute which had been resolved in Honduras' favor by the Hague in 1960. Since then, Honduras had been mistreating Nicaraguan citizens who owned property in the border area. The conflict spilled over into the Common Market, where both countries incorporated minor trade problems into their bilateral political dispute. Nicaragua retaliated against Honduras' ban on certain Nicaraguan goods by demanding preferential treatment equal to that received by Honduras.[22]

DOMESTIC OPPOSITION IN HONDURAS: THE RIVERA REPORT

As indicated earlier, a number of Honduras' top economic officials did not support the campaign to secure preferential treatment in the Common Market. Guillermo Bueso, President of the Central Bank and ex-Minister of Economy under Villeda, stated that a major cause of Honduras' economic crisis was the precipitous decline in public investment caused by the military takeover of October 1963.[23] Under Villeda, said Bueso, public investment had climbed to 30 million Lempiras per year ($15 million) by 1963. But under the Lopez government, public investment dropped sharply to 18 million Lempiras, and by 1966 it had only reached 23 million Lempiras--barely above the public investment figure for 1960.[24]

The above figures highlight a major difference between the Villeda and the Lopez administrations. Villeda, the "democratic reformer," had a broad-ranging national development program; but the takeover by Lopez--combined with Lopez's lack of concern for domestic and regional development--had caused at least a two or three year setback in Honduras' public investment program. Villeda had fostered a number of development projects--and had secured the capital needed to finance them--which were either abandoned by Lopez or delayed for three years or more.

Public disaffection with the apparent apathy of the Lopez regime toward the domestic economy had begun to surface around the same time that Martinez and Acosta Bonilla were developing their program designed to secure preferential treatment for Honduras in the Common Market. As exports began to decline and the private sector began to complain about the lack of government support for national development, Lopez met with Miguel Rivera, Executive Secretary of the prestigious Economic Planning Council, and asked him to prepare a detailed assessment of the major bottlenecks to economic development and the measures necessary to overcome them.

Lopez had expected Rivera's "full cooperation";

that is, he expected Rivera to issue a technical study designed to assist the regime's economic policies. In view of the recent crisis Honduras had engineered in the Common Market, Rivera's report was expected to support the Honduran demand for preferential treatment. Thus, when the Rivera Report was released in May 1967, it aroused a storm of controversy. Instead of producing a technical study, Rivera had written a scathing indictment of the Lopez regime's development policies.

The principal obstacles to Honduras' equitable participation in the Common Market, said Rivera, were not budgetary or financial but internal political and governmental problems: (1)the lack of a sustained effort on the part of all levels of public administration to foster a meaningful development program--especially the lack of leadership "at the highest level"; (2)the prevalence of political rather than professional criteria in selecting technical and administrative personnel; (3)the lack of feasibility studies for high priority development projects; (4)the slowness of administrative procedures in processing development projects, especially in contracting, procuring, and the controller's office; and (5)the slowness of administrative procedures in negotiating for and contracting loans, both with foreign parties and internal organizations.

As a result, said the Report, despite the abundance of financing, the government had been unable to complete the development projects which had been planned by the Villeda administration. In fact, despite that the years 1964, 1965, and 1966 were years of high growth rates, the absolute level of public investment had steadily declined. Moreover, the Lopez regime had left unspent $100 million of financial assistance from AID and the IDB.[25] And finally, the planning council report indicted the Ministers of Economy, Public Health, Education, and Public Works for not making all of the investments which were budgeted for them. Between 1965 and 1967, on the average, only one-third of the money budgeted for reforms and development projects was spent, due to administrative inefficiencies and corruption.[26]

However, said Rivera, the major reason that Honduras had been unsuccessful in implementing its development plans was the reluctance of Lopez to allow the concentration of government power required for coordinated development policy-making. But he did not place the blame on Lopez's shoulders;

rather, he stated that the President had been insulated from competing claims for greater policy-making authority by his chief political aide, Ricardo Zuniga, the Minister to the Presidency.[27] After he overthrew Villeda in 1963, the politically inexperienced Lopez had appointed Zuniga, an aggressive and ambitious Nationalist Party leader, as his personal secretary in order to secure the support of the Nationalist Party. Since then, Zuniga had been building his own political fiefdom; in asserting his own influence over national policy-making, he sheltered Lopez from the influence of tecnicos like Rivera who were seeking greater policy-making authority.[28]

The severity of the Rivera Report had been prompted by the political machinations of Zuniga. Rivera charged that Zuniga had become a one-man office that refused to delegate responsibility and authority. Zuniga had isolated Lopez from day-to-day power struggles in the government and had used his office for patronage in order to further his own political ends. Rivera offered Lopez a choice: either Zuniga or Rivera had to go. This was no choice for Lopez, since Zuniga was the architect and chief guarantor of the governing coalition of the Military and the Nationalist Party. In July 1967, therefore, Rivera was removed from office.

Zuniga denounced the Rivera Report as politically motivated and said it was not the economic report the President had requested. The report was a dual threat to Lopez. First, it challenged his economic policies, especially his attempt to pin the blame for Honduras' economic difficulties on external factors. Second and more important, the report called for administrative reforms which challenged the traditional power structure. The fulfillment of large development projects requires a centralization of power that is anathema to the parochialism and regional dispersion of power which characterize the Honduran political system. For this reason, Lopez resisted the intense pressure from tecnicos like Rivera and the international agencies to accelerate the development process, because his political survival depended on the careful management of the participation of numerous regional power contenders in the political process.[29]

The Rivera Report touched off a nationwide controversy. Workers' unions, campesino unions, the Liberal Party, and the private sector agreed with both economic and political charges Rivera had leveled against the Lopez regime. The workers and campesinos, who felt that they were not benefiting in any way from the Common Market, were upset over the regime's lack of concern for the national development projects which would be of direct benefit to them.

The private sector was upset because it felt that the government was not supporting its efforts to compete in the Common Market. The entrepreneurs of San Pedro Sula had responded to the stimulus of the Common Market, but they had been hampered by government lethargy. With the publication of the Rivera Report and the simultaneous drop in exports in 1967, the entrepreneurs pressured the government to move. At the same time, the Liberal Party added its voice to the growing discontent.

These various groups called an unprecedented meeting to discuss means to bring the government around to a development orientation, to develop a constructive attitude toward the Common Market, and to work toward national political and economic integration. Carlos Mutate, ex-head of the Planning Council, said that the fundamental obstacle to Honduran development was the disintegration of society and the profound distrust of government and the resulting lack of a national mentality or spirit. According to Mutate, national integration was a prerequisite for Honduras' successful integration into the Common Market.[30]

The government reacted harshly to what it interpreted to be a threat to political stability. Lopez arrested Liberal Party leaders and others active in the protest, calling them "nongaras"--a vulgar term for "communists." According to one observer, "the military branded these honorable men as communists and treated them like indicted criminals."[31]

Then even the Nationalist Party became alarmed over the growing controversy. The Economic Committee of Congress, citing Honduras' economic difficulties--especially its negative trade balance in the Common Market--called for the closer cooperation of the government with private enterprise. The committee stated that if the government did not begin to communicate with and work with the private sector more closely, Honduras would be at a great disadvantage with its Central American neighbors for many years.[32]

It is difficult to determine to what extent the increasing dissatisfaction with the Lopez regime's economic performance was due to the growing political opposition to the Lopez regime. At any rate, the issues of administrative reform and balanced growth soon became overshadowed by the events surrounding the March 1968 elections, the Salvadoran encroachment upon Honduran territory, and the events surrounding the implementation of the San Jose Protocol. However, the issue of balanced growth rose again shortly before the outbreak of the Soccer War. As detailed in Chapter 6, Lopez took advantage of the incidents with El Salvador in order to take the public's mind off of Honduras' internal political and economic problems. As tensions grew between Honduras and El Salvador, Honduras began to depict the current framework of the Common Market as a tool of Salvadoran economic imperialism. The growth of anti-Common Market sentiments in Honduras closely paralleled the growth of anti-Salvadoran feelings. By 1969, the balanced growth issue had become completely politicized.

CONCLUSIONS

The major obstacle to the equitable participation of Honduras in the Common Market was not the "backwash effects" of the current free trade arrangement. During the formative years of the Common Market, theorists had predicted that Nicaragua would have economic difficulties similar to those of Honduras and would thus require similar preferential treatment status. But an analysis of the two economies during the 1960-1966 period shows that, while the Honduran economy did not respond well to the Common Market, the Nicaraguan economy boomed. While Honduras' GDP grew at 5 percent annually for the period--compared to a 6 percent regional average--Nicaragua's GDP grew 9 percent annually for the period. Public investment grew 2 percent annually for Honduras and 24.8 percent annually for Nicaragua, while private investment grew at 8.7 percent annually for Honduras and 16.4 percent for Nicaragua. Finally, while the industrial sector grew at an annual rate of 7.8 percent for Honduras, the sector grew 14.1 percent per year for Nicaragua.[33] In short, the Honduran statistics are the worst for the region while the Nicaraguan statistics are the best.

The reason for such a great disparity in the response of the two countries to the Common Market was that the political elites of the two countries responded differently to the stimulus of the Common

Market. While the Honduran political elite seemed to be totally preoccupied with the maintenance of political power, the Somozas played a dual entrepreneurial and political role. The Somoza family tied its future to Nicaragua's economic growth and made the country's development synonymous with its own economic empire. Rather than base its wealth on the traditional latifundias, the Somoza family invested heavily in cotton and rice plantations, sugar refineries, a steel mill, a cement factory, the national airline, and so on. Many of their later investments were in industries geared toward the regional market.

> The young Somozas have learned that there are large profits in the development business, especially for those who control the political and economic competition. Yet the Somozas are not alone in these economic pursuits, for a favored minority of Nicaraguan agricultural entrepreneurs have attached themselves to this development enterprise. As long as the ambitions of this favored group have led to furthering the Somoza development effort rather than to competing with it, they have been welcome.[34]

While the economic impact of the Somozas' development orientation was not totally positive, it spelled the difference between growth and stagnation.[35]

Like their Nicaraguan counterparts, the young industrialists of San Pedro Sula responded to the stimulus of the Common Market; but they were hampered by Tegucigalpa's preoccupation with political intrigue. While the Nicaraguan government accelerated the pace of infrastructure development and passed industrial incentives laws, in Honduras tens of millions of dollars of financial assistance designated for infrastructure development went unspent because of the political orientation of the Lopez government. The national industrial incentives law, requested by the private sector to allow it to compete on more favorable terms for the establishment of new industries, languished in Congress.

The balanced growth issue did not arise inexorably, as Honduras, the least developed member of the Common Market, saw that it was not benefiting equitably from participation in the integration scheme. Rather, it emerged in Honduras after an abrupt political change and during the early stages of the Common Market. Martinez had based his analysis, not on large amounts of empirical data--

because it did not exist--but rather on the theoretical observations of Myrdal and the political crisis in the East African Common Market.

Acosta Bonilla, the new Minister of Economy, faced increasing criticism for failing to implement the national development programs engendered by Villeda. At the same time, he faced the impossibility of securing the domestic reforms necessary to implement Honduran national development programs and enforce the national industrial incentives law. Thus, Bonilla took advantage of the emerging balanced growth issue to seek an external solution--preferential treatment--as a substitute for the needed domestic reforms. The balanced growth issue also served to differentiate the Lopez regime's economic policies from those of Villeda, and Bonilla could blame the Villeda administration for some of Honduras' current economic problems.

ECLA manipulated the balanced growth issue and the Honduran request for preferential treatment to regain its leadership over the integration movement. SIECA had not been sympathetic to Honduras' demands, and the United States and the IDB were putting intense pressure on Lopez to introduce the reforms necessary to enable Honduras to spend the financial assistance it had received. ECLA took advantage of the situation by writing a report which supported Honduras' request for preferential treatment.

Lopez had experienced increasing political pressure, both internal and external, to reform the public administration and to support the private sector's attempts to industrialize the country. These pressures for domestic reform, however, challenged the traditional parochial and patronistic bases of presidential power. Lopez responded by attempting to direct public attention outward, first against the Common Market and then against El Salvador.

NOTES

1. Hansen, Central America, pp. 56-64, and "Regional Integration"; Joseph Nye, "Patterns and Catalysts in Regional Integration," in Nye, International Regionalism; Miguel Wionczek, "Requisites for Viable Integration," in Wionczek, ed., Latin American Economic Integration (New York: Praeger, 1966); Sidney Dell, "The Early Years of LAFTA," in Ibid.; Aaron Segal, "The Integration of Developing Countries," Journal of Common Market Studies, Vol.

5, No. 3 (March 1967); and Abdul Jalloh, "Neo-Functionalism and Regional Political Integration in Africa," Yale University , 1970, unpublished Ph.D. dissertation. For economists, see Lizano, La Crisis del proceso de integracion de Centroamerica, Series Economica y Estadistica No. 14, 1965; Myrdal, Rich Lands and Poor (New York: Harper and Row, 1957); W. Newlyn, "Gains and Losses in the East African Common Market," Yorkshire Bulletin, Vol. 17, 1965.

2. Ernst Haas, "The Study of Regional Integration: Somber Reflections on the Joy and Anguish of Pre-Theorizing," International Organization, Summer 1970

3. Fagan, p. 21. The two case studies are the East African Common Market and the Central American Common Market.

4. The political "levels of development" are the same also, but there are tremendous political differences.

5. For details of Honduran domestic political developments of this period, see Chapter 6.

6. Martinez was familiar with the political crises caused by the issue of balanced growth raised by Tanganyika in the East African Common Market the year before. For an analysis of the dubious nature of Tanganyika's claims, see Newlyn, op. cit.

7. Hansen, "Regional Integration," p. 259. This is one of the causes of "overpoliticization."

8. La Industria (Honduras), November 1964, pp.3-10

9. Asociacion Nacional de Industrias, Nota No.949, 1964, mimeo. Translated in Fagan, op. cit., p. 25.

10. U.S. Department of State, American Embassy, Honduras, "Economic Survey," Fourth Quarter, 1964.

11. El Dia (Tegucigalpa), October 25, 1965, p. 12. Acosta Bonilla's data was incorrect; Honduras' average GDP growth over the 1960-66 period was over 5 percent. Moreover, in response to the charge that Honduras was losing revenue as a result of its participation in the Common Market, Honduran central government revenues, as a percentage of GNP, increased steadily throughout the Common Market period. This percentage was second only to Costa Rica. Thus, neither Acosta Bonilla nor Martinez could back up their charges with sufficient empirical evidence. See State Cable, "Growth Trends," Tables A-9; B-3.

12. Interview with Bueso, in Fagan, p. 26.

13. Rafael Leiva Vivas, Un Pais en Honduras (Offset Calderon: Tegucigalpa, 1969), pp. 15, 46-47.

14. Quoted in Wardlaw, p. 90.

15. ECLA jumped at the chance to release a study favoring the Honduran position, especially after it had been rejected by SIECA.

16. "El crecimiento economico de Honduras y el desarrollo equilibrado en la integracion centroamericana," (CEPAL E/CN.12/762), p. 200.

17. CCE, Res. 141, SIECA, Carta Informativa, No. 52, pp. 16-17.

18. Fagan, p. 30, disagress. He feels that the Ministers of Economy had been persuaded by ECLA's and Honduras' arguments that Honduras merited preferential treatment.

19. For the series of specific proposals, see Fagan, pp. 33-34. The conclusions, however, are the author's, based on interview data.

20. Hansen, Central America, p. 47.

21. Based on interview data. This conclusion is supported by Fagan's findings, p. 34.

22. See Economist Intelligence Unit, August 1966, November 1966, May 1967, August 1967, for accounts of the Nicaragua-Honduras Common Market disputes.

23. See Chapter 6 for evidence of growing Honduran domestic political instability.

24. Leiva, p. 46.

25. Economist Intelligence Unit, November 1968.

26. Leiva, pp. 13-56.

27. El Pueblo (Tegucigalpa), July 12, 1967.

28. For details of Zuniga's role in the emerging political crisis in Honduras, see Chapter 6.

29. There are currently over 30 lieutenant colonels in the Junta, each with his own political fiefdom.

30. Leiva, pp. 51-56.

31. Ibid., p. 34.

32. Ibid., pp. 42-45. The same report recommended that, the Preferential Treaty notwithstanding, Honduras should demand more concessions from its Common Market partners in order to balance its

regional trade. But this was a recommendation to deal with the current economic crisis and not a contention that Honduras' participation in the Common Market was the cause of Honduras' economic difficulties.

33. State Department Cable, "Growth Trends."

34. Wynia, Politics and Planners, p. 20.

35. N.B. Jackson, The Adaptation of Technology in Nicaragua. University of Florida, unpublished Ph.D. dissertation. A detailed analysis of the negative influence of the Somoza family on Nicaraguan development. See also, Economist Intelligence Unit, August 1967, p. 12.

5. The San Jose Protocol

The balance of payments problem is the economic issue that, along with the balanced growth problem, has been interpreted by most observers to be the biggest threat to the continuation of the Common Market. Most analysts agree that the Common Market operated fairly smoothly until 1966 when all five countries apparently began to experience balance of payments deficits due to the decline in third-country exports, the decline in import revenues, and the increasing import bill due to the program of import substituting industrialization. In 1961, at the beginning of the Common Market period, there was a near balance on the current account for the region as a whole. But in 1966 and 1967, all five countries experienced record postwar deficits.

From the beginning of the integration movement, economic officials realized that unilateral actions in defense of the balance of payments would disrupt the integration program. Thus, they developed long-term revenue and balance of payments policies for the Common Market. In March 1963, the Central American Presidents agreed to establish a monetary union and common policy in fiscal, economic, and social matters, within the framework of the economic integration program. At this meeting, they agreed to the creation of the Central American Monetary Council, composed of the five Central Bank Presidents. In February 1964, the five Central Bank Presidents signed an "Agreement for the Establishment of Central American Monetary Union." In January 1968, the Monetary Council created the Monetary Stabilization Fund to coordinate Central American monetary policies. The Fund was to serve as an intermediate step toward eventual monetary union, including the creation of a Central American currency. At the same time, however, tumbling world prices for coffee, cotton, and bananas caused unilateral actions--such as Costa Rican imposition of a dual exchange rate in 1967--which threatened to disrupt the integration mechanisms. To forestall any further unilateral moves in defense of the balance of payments, the Economic Council and the Monetary Council met in joint session to consider a regional solution to the balance of payments "crisis." In June 1968, they presented "Emergency Measures in Defense of the Balance of Payments," which became well known as the San Jose Protocol. The San Jose Protocol, argued the economic officials, would be a partial interim solution to balance of payments problems while the long-range plans were being completed.[1]

The attempt to establish regional monetary policies and institutions has been applauded by economists and integration theorists, and they have interpreted the San Jose Protocol in light of these apparent regional goals. The San Jose Protocol was important because it apparently marked a change in the attitudes of the member governments toward regional cooperation. Until the emergence of balance of payments problems in every country, most of the members had resisted the calls for cooperation in monetary and fiscal policy. The signing of the San Jose Protocol allegedly symbolized the growing awareness on the part of the member governments that, since they had been unable to solve their balance of payments problems unilaterally, regional cooperation was the only answer. According to one observer, they used the crisis to redefine the scope of the integration process.[2]

The purpose of this chapter, however, is to demonstrate that the San Jose Protocol was not as momentous an event in the history of the integration movement as economists and integration theorists have contended. The economists and integration theorists have misinterpreted the significance of the San Jose Protocol because of the excessively narrow focus of their respective analyses. As indicated above, economists view the San Jose Protocol in relation to the formal economic agreements signed by regional and national economic officials; they virtually ignore the political aspects of the Protocol. Integration theorists have concentrated on the regional political maneuvering surrounding the Protocol, paying little attention to the domestic political issues involved. As in the preceding chapter, the key variable to understanding the significance of the regional controversy--in the present case the San Jose Protocol--lies in the domestic political situation in each country. This chapter will demonstrate that, contrary to what most observers believe, the Common Market members did not envision the San Jose Protocol as a regional solution to a common problem. Rather, each country had different economic and political problems which it had been unable or unwilling to solve unilaterally, and each country seized upon the San Jose Protocol as the most acceptable political solution to its domestic problems.

THE EMERGENCE OF THE BALANCE OF PAYMENTS ISSUE

The balance of payments issue emerged on the regional level in April 1965 at a joint meeting of the Economic Council and the Ministers of Finance, called for by SIECA.[3] To prevent their balance of payments situations from deteriorating any further, the ministers suggested a variety of measures which could be implemented at the regional level.[4] First, they supported the continued use of monetary, credit, and exchange measures by the Central Banks, but they suggested that the Banks coordinate their activities at the regional level. Second, they requested that SIECA and the Monetary Council study exchange regulations on capital movements in order to curtail capital flight abroad. Third, they requested that SIECA and the Monetary Council consider the advisability of imposing consumer taxes on nonessentials. Fourth, they requested that SIECA draft a protocol to provide for a more flexible system of tariff renegotiation for use as an instrument of development.

According to integration theorists, however, the most important long-run result of this meeting was that the two sets of ministers institutionalized their meeting and appointed SIECA as their Secretariat.[5] By their actions, states Fagan, the Ministers of Economy confirmed their right to deal with balance-of-payments and fiscal issues at the regional level, brought the Ministers of Finance into the integration nexus, and helped insure that a regional point of view and continuity of action would pervade future meetings.[6] Thus, it appeared as if the 1965 meeting had resulted in an important step forward for the regional integration movement.

Although the balance of payments situation continued to deteriorate during the year following the April 1965 meeting--especially for Costa Rica and

Guatemala--no regional action was taken. As indicated in the previous chapter, Honduras had created a crisis in the Common Market with its call for preferential treatment and its subsequent boycotting of regional meetings. In order to end the crisis, SIECA had persuaded the other countries--especially Costa Rica--to shelve their demands until after the Honduran-engineered crisis had been resolved.

In late 1966, however, the situation changed dramatically. The "balanced growth" crisis had been weathered, and the regional meetings had resumed. Even more significant, a new government had come to power in Costa Rica; and it found itself in the middle of what appeared to be a domestic economic crisis. Trejos, the new president, was a conservative economist who placed the blame for Costa Rica's growing trade deficits on the former Liberal government's liberal application of the national industrial development law. The industrialization which had taken place was dominated by assembly industries involving little value added. At the same time, revenues from tariffs had been undermined, and increased government expenditures on social and economic development programs had intensified Costa Rica's fiscal problems. The Orlich government's attempts to solve the fiscal crisis had aggravated the situation. The Orlich government had taken out several short-term loans, and the Trejos government now faced a situation in which amortization of these loans increased the drain on foreign exchange reserves. Moreover, the Orlich government had followed an expansionary monetary policy which had aggravated the country's balance of payments problems.[7]

While the above description was true, it was not a completely accurate description of the causes for Costa Rica's balance of payments "crisis" in 1966. The trade deficits of that year were chiefly a result of the disastrous effects on agricultural production of the Irazu volçano. However, Trejos could not make much political capital out of blaming an act of nature for Costa Rica's economic difficulties.

As the foreign exchange shortage became severe and the fiscal situation failed to improve, the International Monetary Fund pressured the Trejos government to come up with a new economic policy; the new government complied. First, it tightened credit conditions; second, for the first time in years, it proposed a balanced budget to the national legislature. The budget was to be balanced by new land, sales, and excise taxes. But the opposition-controlled National Assembly rejected the government's budget proposals. While there was some substantive philosophical debate over the conservative economic policy, a major reason for the rejection was political. The National Liberation Party wanted to embarrass Trejos for its own future political advantage. Despite that Costa Rica is the only country in Central America which allows free and democratic elections and peaceful and orderly presidential succession, the party out of power generally refuses to cooperate with the government on many of the most important issues. In this case, the opposition party was willing to allow the country's dangerous financial situation to worsen in order to gain a minor political advantage.

Unable to obtain the Assembly's approval of increased taxes and a balanced budget, the administration came up with an austerity program which could be implemented by presidential decree. The Central Bank devised a program to increase revenues and cut imports, including a multiple exchange system which discriminated against the import of nonessentials. The discriminatory multiple exchange system was to be effective until the Assembly authorized a bill permitting the Central Bank to levy foreign exchange surcharges. In January 1967, the government imposed the multiple exchange system by decree and introduced the surcharge bill to the Assembly. Both measures applied to imports from all countries, including Common Market members.

Common Market members and regional economic officials were quick to react to Costa Rica's moves. In a joint meeting of the Economic and Monetary Councils, the ministers condemned Costa Rica for interfering with free trade. They demanded that the old rates of exchange be used in the operations handled by the Central American Clearing House.[8] The ministers ordered Costa Rica to exempt Common Market members from its measures within forty-eight hours or leave the Common Market. Along with the ultimatum, however, they agreed that Costa Rica's balance-of-payments and fiscal problems should be dealt with at the regional level. The Monetary Council agreed to help Costa Rica obtain international financial assistance and to study possible means to coordinate the defense of the individual countries' balance of payments.[9]

A few days later, the Costa Rican government announced that it would comply with the Economic Council's demands and agreed to handle regional trade at the old exchange rates. Both the President of the Central Bank and the Minister of Economy protested that they had merely responded to Costa Rica's economic crisis and that they had no intention of interfering with free trade. However, the original decree's inclusion of regional trade was not an oversight. Central Bank officials drafted the plan in secret, expecting--and, in fact, desiring--a strong reaction from SIECA and the other Common Market members. According to one high Bank official, the government intentionally engineered the crisis in order to emphasize the seriousness of its fiscal and balance of payments problems and to establish some "rules of the game" for dealing with similar situations in the future. "We knew the game was lost beforehand."[10]

Costa Rica was not the only country willing to act unilaterally to solve its balance of payments and fiscal problems. A new government had come to power in Nicaragua in May 1967, headed by Anastasio Somoza. He immediately launched an austerity program designed to reduce luxury goods imports and increase fiscal revenues. Throughout the last half of 1967, Somoza repeatedly pressured the other member states to adopt a protocol which would increase the Central American tariff and impose consumption taxes on luxury items. Otherwise, he threatened, Nicaragua would be forced to act unilaterally to defend its balance of payments.

As the region's fiscal and balance of payments situation continued to deteriorate, the Economic Council called for a joint meeting with the Monetary Council and the Ministers of Finance in order to agree upon measures which would make it unnecessary for members to enact unilaterally policies similar to those imposed by Costa Rica in January. This first Tripartite meeting, held in November 1967, studied proposals by SIECA and the Monetary Council. The general consensus appeared to be that the traditional monetary and credit measures had proven ineffective, and therefore, regional action was necessary to support the balance of payments. Several ministers agreed with President Somoza of Nicaragua, who charged that the policy of import substitution had caused great fiscal sacrifices, and that to remedy this problem the policy of granting tariff exemptions to industrial firms importing raw materials should be revised.[11]

To avoid future crises such as the one engineered by Costa Rica in January, the delegates agreed with SIECA to institutionalize a system of consultation on exchange problems. They requested that the monetary council formulate by-laws to Article X of the General Treaty which would define those measures a state might take unilaterally, those requiring prior consultation, and those which could be adopted only through joint action. In order to make the prospect of prior consultation and joint action more attractive to the members, SIECA proposed the creation of a Monetary Stabilization Fund to help countries with short-term exchange difficulties.

Most of the delegates agreed with SIECA that Central Bank monetary policies had proven inadequate in relieving pressures on foreign exchange. They supported the SIECA proposal that, in order to cut imports and increase revenues, states facing balance of payments and fiscal problems should impose sales taxes on luxury items. The list of taxable items would be uniform throughout the region.

SIECA wanted this proposal accepted in order to put an end to the growing disparities in the national tax structures. Costa Rica and Honduras had already imposed consumption taxes on luxury items, and the situation threatened to escalate into another crisis if steps were not taken toward tax harmonization. The SIECA proposal was not controversial, and imposition and administration of the tax was to remain in national hands. Besides, it was felt that, if several countries applied the taxes, the aura of regional legitimacy would make it easier to impose the taxes in countries where there was domestic opposition.

Costa Rica once again attempted to introduce its proposal for the complete reform of the fiscal incentives program, including proposals to eliminate tariff exemptions on raw material and intermediate goods imports and to raise external tariffs to protect final products. Costa Rica insisted that its proposals would help alleviate balance of payments problems, stimulate industrial production, and eliminate unfair competition. But the proposals were not popular among the other delegates because they reopened the issue of balanced growth. However, they did encourage the delegates to urge the Common Market members to deposit the Common Fiscal Incentives Agreement and its Preferential Treatment Protocol, because they were concerned that the tariff exemptions were stimulating the rapid increase in imports and thus undermining their countries' balance of payments and fiscal situations.

In addition to the above proposals, the delegates recommended several actions to promote exports, and they agreed to study SIECA's proposals to establish a permanent and automatic mechanism for the funding of regional institutions. Finally, the delegates agreed to meet again in May 1968 to review the progress the countries had made in solving their balance of payments and fiscal problems.[12]

Meanwhile, the balance of payments and fiscal situation of the region continued to deteriorate. Final trade figures for 1967 revealed that Central American exports had risen 1.1 percent in the face of a 10.2 percent rise in imports. At the same time, government revenues had grown by less than one percent, while current costs had increased by 13.5 percent, resulting in a 10 percent decline in public investment.[13]

With no end in sight to these economic difficulties, the Presidents of Nicaragua, Honduras, and Costa Rica publicly called for new and more effective policies which would enable them to unilaterally correct their balance of payments deficits. Nicaragua in particular had threatened to introduce measures which would interfere with regional free trade.[14] In response to this perceived threat to the integration movement, the Economic Council and the Monetary Council held a second joint meeting in March 1968. They decided that immediate action at the regional level was necessary to forestall the anticipated unilateral actions. First, they proposed a new tax on third country imports to strengthen all five countries' balance of payments positions. Second, they recommended the imposition of the optional consumption tax on luxury items which they previously had agreed to at the Tripartite Meeting in November. Third, they requested that SIECA submit the proposals as a protocol to the second Tripartite Meeting to be held at the end of May.

SIECA prepared the Emergency Protocol to Defend the Balance of Payments, and after it had been approved by the five governments, submitted it to the second Tripartite meeting. The sole purpose of this meeting was to approve the final draft of the protocol which had been drafted chiefly by the Ministers of Economy. On June 1, the delegates recommended that their governments approve the emergency measures; and the Economic Council approved the Protocol.[15] The delegates believed that they had to act quickly to secure the approval of their respective governments, or the Common Market would disintegrate as a result of the unilateral measures certain members would have imposed in defense of their balance of payments.[16]

To make the emergency measures attractive to the member governments, the tecnicos made certain that the Protocol would involve no political costs. First of all, national executives were given the authority to grant exemptions from the third country import tax to firms in industries of particular importance to the economic development of the region and firms which would suffer greatly from its application. Second, national customs houses would be in charge of its administration. Third, the consumption tax on luxury items was optional.

The stress on national control guaranteed that the Protocol would be neither economically nor politically controversial. As Fagan has pointed out, both measures were traditional responses to fiscal and balance of payments difficulties which involved neither changes in the traditional economic structures in the region nor any surrender of national authority.[17]

In his sweeping criticism of the San Jose Protocol, Vincent Cable states that while it might help solve the relatively minor revenue problem, it could be more easily solved by raising income tax, tightening up on fiscal incentives for industry, introducing property taxes, or levying export taxes on surplus commodities. However, he says, as a revenue measure, the San Jose Protocol is another step in the wrong direction--away from direct taxation.[18]

THE FAILURE OF TAX REFORM

While direct taxation would have been a far more effective revenue measure, it was politically unacceptable to the national elites. The national political leaders responded favorably to the San Jose Protocol primarily because they wanted to avoid the real issue behind their growing fiscal losses--the explosive issue of fundamental tax reform. They were well aware that their fiscal problems were due, not to the Common Market, but to growing social services required by an exploding population, the failure of past tax reforms, inefficient revenue administration, and low productivity of the government sector. Thus, the San Jose Protocol was a political compromise, based on the continuing desire of the national political elites to manipulate the integration movement to enable them to avoid fundamental domestic reforms.

After the historic Alliance for Progress meeting at Punta del Este in 1962, Central American presidents faced a dilemma created by the Alliance for Progress demand for tax reform. On the one hand, virtually every sector of Central American society opposed tax reform: landed elites opposed land taxes and prevented their enforcement; commercial farmers threatened to withdraw from production if their taxes were increased; industrial firms were used to receiving tax incentives to invest and produce; and the salaried middle class vigorously opposed progressive income taxes, because they alone could not avoid paying them. On the other hand, after 1962 the international lending and development agencies and the United States tied future financial and technical assistance to meaningful tax reform. Refusal to implement tax reforms would have meant losing much of the needed external financial assistance. In every country, each president attempted to work out a strategy for coping with this tax reform dilemma. With the possible exception of Costa Rica, none were successful.

President Ydigoras of Guatemala was the first president to attempt to enact unpopular tax reforms in order to obtain Alliance for Progress assistance. His first tax reform bill was defeated by the opposition's majority in Congress in 1961. It was the eighth tax bill in ten years to be defeated by the combined opposition of the Association of Agriculturalists, the Chamber of Commerce, and the Association of Industries. Then, in the December 1961 congressional elections, Ydigoras' Redencion Party fraudulently increased its membership from twenty-five to fifty out of sixty-six seats. But the opposition to Ydigoras grew so violent after this fraudulent election that the military intervened and forced Ydigoras to concede to them the majority of his cabinet ministries. Thus, although he now controlled the Congress, the military controlled much of the executive.[19]

Facing increasing fiscal difficulties, Ydigoras attempted to use his new legislative majority to pass an income tax reform in November 1962. Guatemala's agricultural and commercial associations immediately denounced the government. They took out full-page newspaper advertisements stating that they would not pay the income tax or the emergency real estate and gasoline taxes. As the opposition to Ydigoras continued to grow, the military stepped in and removed him from office on March 3, 1963--with the full support of the opposition parties and the business and agricultural groups.

President Villeda of Honduras faced a situation very similar to that faced by Ydigoras when he attempted to implement major tax reform legislation. Villeda faced very strong opposition from both the Nationalist Party and the military. The Nationalist Party violently opposed his "democratic reformist" reform initiatives, while the military resented Villeda's creation of a Civil Guard designed to counter the Honduran army's influence in the countryside. Despite this vigorous opposition, Villeda pushed his tax reform bill through his Liberal Party-controlled Congress early in 1963. But the reforms were never implemented, because the military removed Villeda in a coup in October 1963 and rescinded his tax legislation. In the cases of both Ydigoras and Villeda, while the attempted tax reforms were not the primary cause of either president's downfall, they both proved to be catalysts which led directly to that downfall.

Tax reform met a similar fate in El Salvador, but under different circumstances. The leftist military-civilian junta which replaced President Lemus in October 1960 had promised free elections, land reforms, and tax reforms. But the junta was forcibly replaced in January 1961 by a more conservative military-civilian junta which claimed it had acted to stop the spread of communism which threatened to destroy El Salvador's democratic values. The first junta, however, had unleashed demands for reform among various sectors of the population which the new junta could not ignore. To satisfy some of these demands, Colonel Rivera, the head of the new junta, enacted an income tax reform and a new tax on reinvested profit. The landowning oligarchy and the businessmen strongly protested the new taxes, forcing Rivera to drastically reduce the new tax rates in order to maintain the support of the oligarchy for the new junta.[20] Rivera believed that, without the full and active support of the economic elites, the Salvadoran economy would not rapidly recover from the 1958 recession and the political difficulties of 1960 and 1961. The oligarchy believed that increased taxes would discourage national and foreign investment and place Salvadoran business at a disadvantage with its Common Market competition. Judging the support of the economic elites to be more important than his proposed social reforms and the tax reforms needed to fund them, by 1963 Rivera had obtained the support of the oligarchy by dropping most of his reform proposals.[21]

A second round of attempted tax reforms came in 1967 and 1968. Several events had taken place which made the outlook for successful attempts at tax reform more favorable. First, the international agencies intensified their insistence that future financial assistance would be tied to concrete progress on tax reform. Second, as described above, all five countries were complaining about the decline in import tax revenues resulting from the Common Market tariff reductions and the increasing import bill attributable to the program of import-substituting industrialization. The region, as a whole, had experienced chronic fiscal deficits every year of the 1960-1967 period: while expenditures were rising over 10 percent per year, revenues were increasing only 7.9 percent annually.[22]

President Mendez Montenegro of Guatemala was virtually forced to attempt new tax reforms in early 1968. The conservative Central Bank refused to expand credit to the public sector, and the international agencies were demanding tax reform as a precondition for additional assistance. Under the strong leadership of Finance Minister Alberto Fuentes Mohr, one of the most respected economists in Central America, the Guatemalan Congress enacted a five percent sales tax and a twenty percent tax on nonessential goods. For the first time, the new taxes were to be enforced at the wholesale level to make tax avoidance more difficult.

As soon as Mendez signed the tax bill, he was met with protests as vigorous as those which had been made against Ydigoras five years earlier by the conservative economic associations. The urban middle class argued that they would refuse to pay the new taxes until the enforcement of existing taxes was more consistent and equitable. Their case was supported by a U. N. study which had just been published in the Guatemalan press. According to this study of the tax rate of sixty-four countries, Guatemala placed sixty-third with the next-to-lowest tax rate, getting 7.7 percent of GNP.[23] The Guatemalan budget director was forced to admit that in Guatemala, taxes are generally paid only by those who cannot avoid them, like salaried workers.[24]

Under intense pressure from the economic interest groups--which threatened the very existence of the government--Mendez abandoned the tax reforms less than a month after their passage and forced the resignation of Finance Minister Fuentes, whose personal leadership of the tax reform fight had made him the chief target of the opposition.[25] To compensate for the revenue lost by the withdrawal of Mendez's tax reforms, the Congress was forced to reduce the salaries of public employees in order to balance the budget.[26]

Mendez's failure had a very debilitating impact on the attempt of El Salvador's President Sanchez to implement a new tax reform program. The Salvadoran oligarchy had closely monitored political events in Guatemala for decades. The military had created the authoritarian reform party PRUD in 1949 in order to prevent the movement to the left in El Salvador which had taken place in Guatemala. In late 1967, after a long debate in Congress, Sanchez secured the approval of his tax reform proposals. As was the case with Mendez, Sanchez immediately was faced with a strong outburst of opposition to his tax reform proposals. Seeing the politically insecure Mendez retract his tax proposals, Sanchez decided that he, too, should preserve his upper and middle class support by withdrawing his tax reforms in early 1968.[27]

Costa Rica was the only country in which the attempt at tax reform was at least partially successful. As indicated earlier, President Trejos had come to power in 1966 facing the gravest fiscal crisis in the region. This fiscal problem had been created by the extensive government programs in the fields of health, education, and social assistance which had produced dramatic increases in current expenditures and created large fiscal deficits after 1964. A conservative economist by training, Trejos would have preferred to reduce expenditures by imposing strict budgetary austerity. But he quickly became aware that this was politically impossible for two reasons: first, the opposition controlled the legislature; and second, half the budget went to hospitals, education, and other social services that received income set by law. Consequently, Trejos' only alternative was to increase taxes. Although his party did not control the legislature, Trejos naturally assumed that the liberal PLN majority would support the new taxes since most of the additional revenues would be used to support the social and economic programs they had traditionally supported and had, in fact, enacted in the first place. Thus, Trejos was surprised when his property and sales tax proposals became embroiled for months in a three-way struggle between himself, the Legislature, and the International Monetary Fund. As in Guatemala and El Salvador, the IMF had insisted on tax reforms as the prerequisite for the financial assistance that Costa Rica needed for 1967. Yet the Legislature rejected both tax proposals in order to gain a short-term political advantage by embarassing President Trejos. Finally, in July 1967, the Legislature gave in--not to Trejos, but to the increasing pressures from the IMF and the United States--and enacted the sales tax to help solve the country's growing fiscal problems.[28]

The enactment of the Costa Rican sales tax was one of the rare successes in tax reform in Central America during the 1960s. Except for the decline in import taxes caused by the regional tariff, the domestic tax structures in 1968 were virtually the same as they had been almost two decades earlier. The dominant oligarchies were able to block almost every attempted tax reform by threatening to withdraw their economic and political support from the Central American presidents if the reforms were implemented. Moreover, while the international agencies repeatedly threatened to curtail their assistance if the tax reforms were not forthcoming, they were often forced to disburse funds because of their long-range commitment to many development projects.

However, while the history of tax reform in Central America during the 1960s has been interpreted by most observers as an economic failure when viewed as a potential source of desperately needed revenues, it was viewed by the Central American presidents as a political success. The presidents were confronted with intense pressures to engender significant tax reforms by the international agencies and the tecnicos. At the same time, however, their very political survival was threatened by challenges from the upper and middle classes over the same issue. Yet when each battle ended, the president involved had usually managed to emerge with both his foreign financial support and his domestic political support generally intact.[29]

In every case, the president responded to pressure from his economic advisers and the international agencies by proposing ambitious tax reforms. And in every case, strong opposition from opposition parties and economic interest groups forced the president to withdraw or modify the new legislation. While the presidents practically were forced to implement tax reforms in order to convince the international agencies of their good intentions, they knew beforehand that they most probably would fail in their attempts to implement the reforms.[30]

What is striking about the above cases is that, despite that defeat was almost guaranteed, each president initiated an active and public reformist campaign which was met by equally public and forceful opposition. Gary Wynia attributes this new openness in Central American politics to the growth in popularity of reform politics since World War II. Before World War II, revenue policies were made covertly by the ruling elite. However, since then, the same policy decisions have been surrounded by public debate and controversy.[31]

There is, nevertheless, another reason for the presidential behavior described above. The presidents actually were not as weak and indecisive as many observers such as Nye have portrayed them to be. In the case of the attempts at tax reform, for example, the presidents actually manipulated the two opposing forces which they faced. Presidential goals were straightforward: to stay in power by maintaining the support of the economic elites and to retain as much of the foreign assistance as possible. The strategy they used to achieve those ends, in the face of intense pressures from the international agencies, was simple. By encouraging public battles over tax reform, which they were almost certain to lose, they usually convinced the international agencies that they were sincere in their reform attempts. In this manner, the oligarchy or some other combination of vested interests would emerge as a scapegoat; and the president's foreign support would remain relatively secure.[32]

THE FAILURE OF THE SAN JOSE PROTOCOL

Considering the failure of the individual governments to implement tax reforms and the opposition they faced when they unilaterally attempted to impose additional consumer taxes, most observers believed that the San Jose Protocol would be ratified quickly by the national legislatures and rapidly implemented throughout the region. The prestige of a regional agreement would enable even the countries where domestic opposition to increased taxes was strongest to implement the Protocol. Unfortunately, most observers had misjudged the domestic political climate of several of the member countries.

Economic officials had expected vocal opposition from the private sector, but they did not think that it would be serious enough to block passage of the Protocol by the national legislatures. Even so, during the formulation and negotiation of the emergency measures, neither the regional nor the national economic officials consulted the regional or national business groups. Representatives of the national business associations were pointedly excluded from the national delegations to the meetings at which discussion of the proposals took place, although they had been routinely appointed to such delegations in the past. In fact, the business groups and the general public were not informed in any detail about the emergency measures until national economic officials already had agreed informally on the measures to be taken.[33]

Most observers attempt to account for the political opposition which arose to prevent the San Jose Protocol from being ratified and implemented by claiming that those groups which opposed the Protocol did so because they either misunderstood the nature of the provisions of the Protocol itself or they were acting on outdated economic data. In both cases, observers have blamed these misunderstandings on the regional and national economic decision-makers' failure to include representatives of the business groups in the decision-making process.

Opposition to the San Jose Protocol, before its adoption was formally announced in June, was very limited. The only formal opposition came from FECAICA in May, when FECAICA sent a letter of protest to the Economic Council opposing all of the provisions entailed in the Emergency Measures. It warned that eliminating tariff exemptions would endanger infant industries and create the dangerous precedent that industrial incentives once granted could be withdrawn. Reviewing the proposed taxes, FECAICA charged that the principal reason for insufficient government revenues was the failure of the government to collect the taxes already in effect. Moreover, the additional taxes would undermine business confidence and cause private investment in the region to decline. Finally, FECAICA objected to the fact that SIECA, the Economic Council, and the national economic officials had not sought the advice of the business groups concerning the proposed measures.[35] FECAICA's criticisms were ignored, however; and the Protocol was approved without consulting any businessmen.

Nicaragua was the only country to ratify and deposit the San Jose Protocol quickly. The Nicaraguan Congress ratified the Protocol on June 15, two days after it was approved; and the Somoza government deposited it one month later. Unlike in the other four countries, in Nicaragua there was no effective political opposition to the regime in power. Under the authoritarian leadership of President Anastasio Somoza Debayle, domestic opposition had little influence on government decision-making.

Guatemala was the second country to approve the Protocol; but while the Congress ratified the Protocol on July 23, the government did not deposit it with ODECA. The industrial sector in Guatemala opposed the Protocol, but it was preoccupied with the problem of terrorism. Throughout much of the year, Guatemala had been under a state of siege: right-wing terrorists had kidnapped the archbishop of Guatemala in March, and left-wing terrorists had murdered the United States ambassador in late August. Each time the government declared a state of siege. Despite the crackdown by the military and the police, shooting and bombings occurred almost daily in the capital; and there were a number of kidnappings as the private war between left-wing and right-wing extremists dominated the political arena. Compelled by necessity to support the government, the private sector muted its criticism of the San Jose Protocol. Confronted with no forceful opposition, the Mendez government ratified the Protocol.[36]

The Honduran government ratified the San Jose Protocol in August, but it refused to deposit it--or any of the other outstanding regional agreements--until El Salvador had deposited the Protocol on Preferential Treatment which had been signed in 1966. Despite its refusal to deposit the Protocol, the Honduran government followed Nicaragua's lead and unilaterally imposed some of the consumption taxes. When the Lopez government enacted some of the provisions of the Protocol, it aroused intense opposition, especially from the north coast business sector. A number of observers blame the stiff resistance Lopez encountered on his failure to communicate the requirements of the Protocol to the poorly informed Honduran public. Ignorant of the potential effects of the Protocol, the Hondurans, says Wynia, panicked out of fear that prices on all consumer goods would rise dramatically when the Protocol was implemented.[37] However, as the discussion of Honduran politics in Chapters 4 and 6 demonstrates, the opposition to the Protocol was based on a great deal more than the Honduran public's ignorance of the Protocol's provisions.

Lopez had been under fire for months on both the economic and the political fronts. The leaders of the unions and the business community had been calling for a comprehensive development plan; they had publicly condemned the San Jose Protocol as the latest and most drastic in a series of consumer taxes which were forcing the consumers to pay for the government's corruption and inefficiency. When Lopez imposed the Protocol without warning on September 12, 1968, the entire population became very upset. North coast businessmen, workers, students, and teachers called a general strike on September 18 in San Pedro Sula. The strike was not called simply to protest the imposition of the San Jose Protocol. Rather, the San Jose Protocol was the catalyst which caused the strike. Antipathy between the government and the private sector had been growing for months over the government's lack of a coherent development policy and over other, more political, reasons.

The government declared a state of siege and managed to put down the strike and suppress its most violent critics, the banana workers and the merchants of the north coast. But tensions between the government and the private sector remained high; and when the teachers and university students struck again a few months later, they received the strong support of the merchants and workers.

El Salvador became the fourth country to ratify the San Jose Protocol on October 16, 1968; but like Honduras and Guatemala, it did not deposit the Protocol with ODECA. Opposition to the San Jose Protocol was widespread. Industrialists, merchants, unions, and the Christian Democrats all strongly opposed the imposition of new consumer taxes. The Chamber of Commerce and Industry criticized SIECA's secrecy in handling the negotiations.[38] The Salvadoran Industrial Association requested that the government establish a commission to examine the Protocol and that leaders of the business community be included as members.[39] Against the current of national opinion, the Legislative Assembly approved the Protocol by a majority of 26 to 24. The vote was split along party lines, with the 26-vote majority representing those votes belonging to the government-backed PCN. The Christian Democrats, jubilant over their gains in the March elections, had used the vote as a show of strength. Worried about the threat posed by this strong internal opposition to the Protocol, the Sanchez government announced on the day following the vote that, while the 30 percent additional import duty would be imposed on nonessentials from third countries, the 10 and 20 percent additional consumption taxes authorized but not demanded by the Protocol would not be imposed.[40]

Costa Rica was the only country in which the government was unable to obtain the legislature's ratification of the Protocol. Not coincidentally, Costa Rica was the only country in which the opposition controlled the legislature. The Partido de Liberacion Nacional (PLN) had allowed the Trejos government to impose sales taxes similar to those in the Protocol one year earlier; yet now the PLN claimed that the taxes embodied in the San Jose Protocol were actually taxes on the poor and therefore refused to ratify it. The liberal PLN deputies demanded more progressive income and other tax reforms in exchange for ratification, but the conservative Trejos was unwilling to pay such a high price.[41]

In sum, while four of the five Common Market members ratified the San Jose Protocol, only Nicaragua deposited it with ODECA. Since three countries were required to deposit the Protocol before it could be implemented legally, the San Jose Protocol lost what little credibility it had as an "emergency measure to defend the balance of payments." The Protocol had become embroiled in both domestic and regional political disputes. On the domestic level, in Honduras, El Salvador, and Costa Rica, the Protocol was manipulated by opposition parties and groups in order for them to gain political advantage at the expense of the government. On the regional level, Honduras tied its deposit of the Protocol to the Salvadoran deposit of the Preferential Treatment Protocol. Because of the growing tensions between these two countries, it was difficult for either country to change its position for fear that it would appear to have made a concession which favored its neighbor.

THE SIGNIFICANCE OF THE SAN JOSE PROTOCOL

Despite the apparent failure of the San Jose Protocol, many observers contend that it marked a turning point in the development of the integration movement. Chief among this group is Philippe Schmitter, whose interpretation of the events surrounding the adoption of the San Jose Protocol differs dramatically from the interpretation offered in the preceding pages. By the end of 1967, says Schmitter, the "latent contradictions" between free trade and declining revenues became increasingly manifest. In a pervasive atmosphere of "crisis," the Central American governments "discovered" that a number of major protocols had not been ratified and that the agreement to coordinate monetary and fiscal policies had gone unimplemented. As mutual recriminations arose, national authorities began to take unilateral "emergency" measures. To "outsiders," says Schmitter, the movement seemed on the verge of collapse.[42] However, the response of economic policy makers was to blame the excessively narrow focus of regional policy making and, "instead of retreating to some lowest common denominator of 'balanced' satisfactions, to use the crisis to redefine the scope of the integration process." While the San Jose Protocol did not directly involve adjacent policy areas, it did establish the guidelines for a common policy where none had existed before. Citing an editorial in the authoritative Mexican journal, Comercio Exterior, Schmitter states that the draft protocol represented an important "salvage operation" and appeared to prove that "the best way to get out of a curve is by accelerating."[43]

Schmitter does not claim that the Protocol was an increase in the level of regional integration--"transcendence," in the "exotic lexicon" of his theory--but that it did represent a significant increase in the scope of the integration movement.[44] Nevertheless, Schmitter strongly implies that the San Jose Protocol did make possible the "spillover," at least on the formal level of commitment, into adjacent policy areas which occurred a few weeks after the Protocol was signed. At the summit meeting of the Central American Heads of State, and in the presence of President Lyndon Johnson, the five presidents agreed to an expansive set of new goals for the integration movement: harmonization of monetary policies; agreements to facilitate the mobility of labor; agreements to strengthen the regional institutions; and recognition of the necessity of supporting regional infrastructure projects.[45] Schmitter apparently believes that the successful resolution of the crisis surrounding the signing of the San Jose Protocol gave the members the encouragement needed to take this moderate, but symbolic, next step in the integration process.

Isaac Cohen Orantes supports Schmitter's estimation of the significance of the San Jose Protocol. His analysis also appears to support Schmitter's contention that the "spill-around" process is a serious obstacle to the future progress of the integration movement:

> These measures represented important steps toward monetary and fiscal cooperation in the area. Regretfully, though, they constituted the only instance in which the participants adopted joint actions in this sector. Meanwhile, because of the lack of specificity in the terms of reference of the Central American Monetary Council, other methods of adjusting the balance of payments remained within the hands of the zealously independent central bankers.[46]

Schmitter and other theorists have misinterpreted the nature of the balance of payments problems which the San Jose Protocol was supposed to resolve. The balance of payments problems of the members were not caused primarily by the Common Market but rather by the economic and political goals and philosophies of the national political elites. Cable states flatly that the region's balance of payments troubles have been simply the result of the ideologically motivated unwillingness of the elites to generate domestic reforms, such as direct taxes.[47] Landry makes the general accusation that the integration scheme was promoted by the national elites to encourage political stability by "buying off" the middle classes with consumer goods.[48] Wynia also points to the dramatic increase in imports of luxury and other consumer goods as part of the governments' development plan designed to satisfy the demands of the privileged sectors in order to maintain political stability.[49]

The San Jose Protocol, therefore, did not necessarily represent a step forward in the integration movement. It was not an intermediate step on the path to the future harmonization of fiscal and monetary policies. Neither was it an attempt to solve a "regional" balance of payments problem. Each country had its own revenue and balance of payments problems which it had been unable or unwilling to solve domestically. Furthermore, each country manipulated and implemented the San Jose Protocol in response to its national criteria.

Viewed from Schmitter's regional perspective, the San Jose Protocol was a rational policy response by the member governments to common balance of payments problems that resulted in an increase in the level of mutual cooperation. Viewed from the domestic political perspective, however, the Protocol was manipulated by the member governments to avoid the domestic reforms which threatened to disrupt the political and economic status quo. In Schmitter's view, the signing of the San Jose Protocol and subsequent events demonstrated the growing awareness on the part of the member governments of the need to widen the focus of the integration movement. Nevertheless, on closer inspection, the events surrounding the signing and implementation of the Protocol call into serious question the commitment of the national political elites to upgrade the common interest. In sum, the San Jose Protocol represented precisely what Schmitter claims it did not: "retreating to some lowest common denominator of 'balanced' satisfaction," an apparent "spill-back" in his terminology.[50]

THE NICARAGUAN CRISIS

Pressed by the adverse effects of three years of drought on public revenue growth and agricultural production, and angered by the members' delays in ratifying and depositing the Emergency Measures, President Somoza of Nicaragua unilaterally imposed the San Jose Protocol on June 21, 1968. In addition, he imposed a 5 percent sales tax on all Central American goods not covered by the 10 and 20 percent taxes, including items produced in Nicaragua. Almost immediately, Nicaraguan border guards began demanding payment of the new duties; hundreds of trucks were turned back or delayed.

The other members reacted immediately but restrainedly to Nicaragua's unilateral actions. At the July meeting of the Executive Council, the four delegates charged that the use of differential bases and forms of collection made the tax discriminatory. The taxes, when applied *ad valorem*, were calculated on the C. I. F. value of imports;

they were computed on the basis of the factory price for nationally produced items. Taxes on imported items were paid at the customs house, but those on national production were collected at the national revenue office. Second, they charged that Nicaragua was violating Article VI of the General Treaty by imposing consumption taxes on items produced in the region but not in Nicaragua itself. Finally, they charged that Nicaragua had no authority unilaterally to impose the San Jose Protocol.[51]

The July Meeting of Presidents, attended by President Johnson, was supposed to be a showcase of regional cooperation. It turned out to be an "operacion de salvamiento" (salvage operation) during which the presidents attempted to find solutions to their financial problems and to the faltering integration program.[52] President Johnson promised additional loans for the region as a whole and for each individual country. In response, the Central American presidents pledged to press for the rapid ratification and deposit of the San Jose Protocol and the other major regional agreements which were pending. At this point, Nicaragua agreed to remove the most controversial of its taxes, especially those which focused on agricultural products imported from the other member states.

Despite the rhetoric and the spirit of cooperation evinced at the Meeting of Presidents, throughout the rest of 1968, the trade war between Nicaragua and its neighbors escalated. Nicaragua continued to block rice imports from Guatemala, despite that a SIECA investigation had shown that Guatemala had not imported the rice from outside the region and that the Executive Council had voted to reestablish free trade for the item. A similar incident occurred with Honduras. Nicaragua suspended free trade of clothing made with synthetic fibers in Honduras, charging that Honduras had illegally exempted some of the raw materials from tariffs. But when a SIECA investigation proved the charges false and the Executive Council voted to reestablish free trade, Nicaragua refused, claiming that additional investigations were necessary. Next, the Nicaraguan government blocked the entry of shirts imported from a Honduran firm, on the grounds that Honduras was exporting them at undervalued prices. Nicaragua made a request to the Executive Council that it be allowed to place a bond in an amount equivalent to the common tariff on the article, but the Council refused. Finally, Nicaragua halted the import of Costa Rican beans and maize, charging that Costa Rica had imported some of these products from Mexico.[53]

Honduras retaliated against Nicaragua's actions by closing its borders to biscuits manufactured in that country. But El Salvador charged that Honduras had illegally granted import concessions to a local firm in its purchases of raw materials for the manufacture of clothing--a charge similar to the one made by Nicaragua--and banned the import of products made by that firm. El Salvador also restricted the entry of Guatemalan cigarettes, charging that they were dumped. Costa Rica was so suspicious of the high quality of Salvadoran rice that it cut off rice imports from that country, charging that the rice was not of Central American origin. Costa Rican officials were greatly embarrassed when its Salvadoran origin was proved. But Costa Rica's real motives were revealed a short time later when that country banned rice imports from all of Central America. Costa Rica also banned the import of Guatemalan cigarettes and suspended imports of several Honduran items in retaliation for their banning of certain Costa Rican imports. El Salvador suspended imports of Costa Rican dairy products in reprisal for Costa Rica's suspension of Salvadoran rice imports.[54]

While many similar incidents had occurred in the past, they had been viewed as minor incidents which normally could be expected in the formative years of a Common Market. But this situation was entirely different. It threatened to explode into a major crisis provoked, not only by the sheer number of disruptions of free trade, but also by their underlying political motivations.

Nicaragua had created obstacles to free trade with its neighbors to protest the reluctance or inability of the member states to deposit the San Jose Protocol. Although the United States had promised additional financial assistance and the Central American presidents had pledged to fulfill their common market obligations at the July meeting, by mid-October no other government had deposited the Protocol. Consequently, according to most observers, the Somoza government acted unilaterally to alleviate Nicaragua's worsening economic position.[55] But the available evidence indicates that Somoza's primary goal was to create a crisis which would force the other countries to deposit the San Jose Protocol rapidly. Unfortunately, the other countries were not in a receptive mood. When Nicaragua imposed its sanctions, its neighbors retaliated in kind. Moreover, the Nicaraguan actions and the subsequent reprisals released a flood of "latent emotional antagonisms" which had been building up since the beginning of the Common Market. Instead of coordinating their response to Nicaragua's attempt to induce a crisis, the other four countries began to fall out among themselves, taking the same actions against each other that Nicaragua had taken against them.

In an attempt to resolve this critical situation, the Secretary General of SIECA and the Salvadoran Minister of Economy traveled to Honduras, Guatemala, and Costa Rica to try to overcome the obstacles which stood in the way of an early implementation of the San Jose Protocol. El Salvador and Guatemala deposited the agreement by the end of October; Guatemala also deposited the Protocol on Preferential Treatment for Honduras. But Honduras still refused to deposit both the San Jose Protocol and the Common Fiscal Incentives Agreement until El Salvador deposited the Preferential Treatment Protocol. And the opposition-dominated Costa Rican National Assembly still refused to ratify the San Jose Protocol. In retaliation against this apparent deadlock, the Somoza government made a second attempt to engineer a crisis which would force a resolution of the issue. The Somoza government announced that it would not attend any Common Market meetings until the other states deposited the several outstanding regional agreements, especially the San Jose Protocol.

There was a certain amount of common sense in the Nicaraguan attitude, because many important protocols ratified by the ministers of economy had not been ratified or deposited by the Central American governments. Why, asked Nicaragua, pretend that the integration movement is progressing nicely when only one country--Nicaragua--has deposited all of the protocols? Honduras had left nine protocols unratified, Guatemala and El Salvador six each, and Costa Rica one. The Common Market--and integration in general--could not progress any further until all outstanding protocols had been deposited.[56]

After a joint meeting in early December, the presidents of Nicaragua and Costa Rica issued a joint statement in which they claimed the Common Market, in its present state of "incompletion," was prejudicial to the economic welfare of Costa Rica and Nicaragua. If the Common Market were not made institutionally and operationally complete, the two countries threatened to take unilateral actions in defense of their own economic interests. To Somoza and Trejos, the "completion" of the Common Market meant that all outstanding protocols must be deposited; that countries refrain from using the deposit of one protocol as a bargaining tool for the negotiation of later protocols; that the Limon Protocol on Basic Grains be revised; that the Common Fiscal Incentives Agreement be revised after it was deposited; that a permanent court be established to deal with day-to-day problems of integration; and that the agricultural sector be "integrated" into the integration movement. If these steps toward "completion" or "perfection" of the present Common Market were not fulfilled, Costa Rica and Nicaragua threatened to refrain from cooperating under the present institutional structure and to press for a complete "restructuring" of the Common Market.[57]

In a speech broadcast over radio and television three weeks later, Somoza once again blamed the "incomplete" nature of the Common Market--a nature resulting from the bad faith of the other members--for many of Nicaragua's economic problems. Somoza used this opportunity to revive the issue of balanced growth, insisting on the need to limit free trade between Nicaragua and the more developed members, namely, El Salvador and Guatemala.[58] Then Somoza traveled to Honduras to confer with President Lopez. The two presidents issued a joint declaration which repeated the demands of the Somoza-Trejos communique: that all outstanding protocols should be deposited; that the Common Market should be perfected; and that the agricultural sector should be "integrated" into the Common Market.[59] According to one observer, this second presidential communique was less threatening and more optimistic in tone than the first.[60]

The Secretary General of SIECA appeared to support the Nicaraguan-inspired demands. To avoid a potential crisis and preserve the level of regional trade, in late January 1969 he urged the five countries to adopt the Limon Protocol on basic grains, to deposit and reform the Common Fiscal Incentives Agreement, to harmonize sales and consumption taxes already in effect, and to remove obstacles to free trade.[61]

Somoza had difficulty getting the other countries to support his idea of an integration court. At the February 1969 meeting of Foreign Ministers, Nicaragua formally proposed the establishment of the court to serve as final arbiter in integration disputes. The Honduran minister claimed that his government needed more time to consider the matter; his view apparently was shared by some of the other ministers because the meeting adjourned abruptly. No headway was made in further consultations, so the meeting of foreign ministers, planned for the end of February to consider the court, was adjourned without any discussion of the issue.[62]

By the end of February, then, it was evident that Somoza's second attempt to force the member governments to act had failed: the trade wars continued unabated; the Costa Rican Assembly had rejected the San Jose Protocol for the second time; Honduras still refused to deposit the San Jose Protocol until El Salvador deposited the Preferential Treatment Protocol. The other four countries appeared unmoved by Somoza's repeated threats. Rather than respond to the validity of many of Somoza's criticisms and suggestions, they chose to interpret Somoza's attitude as another indication of his determination to impose his will on the other Common Market members. Moreover, there appeared to be very little genuine interest in implementing the reforms demanded by Nicaragua.

Angered by the intransigence of his neighbors, Somoza made his third major attempt to engineer a crisis which would force the other member states to respond to his demands. On February 26, denouncing his "bad friends" and citing the need to defend Nicaragua's balance of payments and improve its fiscal situation, he decreed a "compensatory consumption tax" on most items originating in the other four member states for an amount equivalent to the tariffs in effect in Nicaragua on July 1, 1955. In effect, this decree reestablished a tariff barrier in Central America. To justify its actions, the Nicaraguan government reverted to the balanced growth argument. The Common Market had not developed into a customs union, as had been intended. A customs union would have weighted the distribution of import revenues in favor of the less-developed countries, in order to promote the balanced growth of the region. Instead, due to the incompletion of the Common Market, the more-developed countries were growing at the expense of the poorer countries. Thus, Nicaragua was suffering revenue losses which were endangering the country's development programs.[63]

At an emergency meeting of the Ministers of Economy, the delegates urged Nicaragua to suspend the new decree. In return, they promised to deposit the outstanding protocols. El Salvador announced that it would deposit the Preferential Treatment Protocol within two weeks; Honduras stated that as soon as El Salvador did so, it would deposit all outstanding protocols; and Costa Rica promised to make a final attempt to secure the Assembly's ratification of the San Jose Protocol.[64]

But Nicaragua appeared to be unmoved by the conciliatory gestures of the other member states. The Nicaraguan Minister of Economy stated that the new decree was intended to compensate in part for the fiscal losses Nicaragua had suffered through its participation in the Common Market. Furthermore, Nicaragua made stronger demands as its price for the normalization of Common Market relations. Not only did the Minister of Economy demand the immediate deposit of outstanding protocols and the revision of the Common Fiscal Incentives and Basic Grains Agreements, but also he called for compensatory taxes at the regional level on articles enjoying regional free trade, in order to recover part of the fiscal income lost as a result of integration while maintaining a preferential margin for Central American items as compared with those from third countries.[65]

As an indication that Nicaragua's real motives were to reform the Common Market's institutions and operations, the Minister of Economy announced that Nicaragua would no longer boycott Common Market meetings. Furthermore, he called for the Economic and Executive Councils to meet in permanent session to deal with this crisis.[66]

The four Ministers of Economy retaliated against Nicaragua. Invoking Articles XI and XIII of the General Treaty, they suspended free trade with Nicaragua by imposing a bond in the amount of the common tariff on goods originating in that country. But the tone of their communique was conciliatory. They stated that they had imposed the sanctions on Nicaragua with regret, and that they would remove the bonds as soon as Nicaragua withdrew its compensatory tax. They also agreed to maintain the Economic Council in permanent session to help reestablish Common Market relations.[67]

The five Ministers of Economy and SIECA officials were in continual contact during the next few weeks. According to one source, the five countries reached a secret agreement which would resolve the crisis.[68] On March 14, El Salvador deposited four agreements, including the Preferential Treatment Protocol. On the same day, Honduras deposited the San Jose Protocol, the Preferential Treatment Protocol, and the Common Fiscal Incentives Agreement. At an emergency meeting of the Economic Council one week later, the five Ministers of Economy reached an agreement which reestablished free trade.[69]

As Nicaragua's part of the bargain, the Nicaraguan minister announced that his government would change the nature of its compensatory tax to make it compatible with the provisions of the General Treaty. The government would not eliminate the tax altogether because it badly needed the revenue. The compensatory tax would be changed into a consumption tax on certain products regardless of origin, and any discriminatory effects of the tax or of any other consumption tax in effect in Nicaragua would be eliminated.[70] In exchange, the other ministers agreed to withdraw the sanctions they had imposed the previous month.[71]

In addition, the five Ministers of Economy agreed to work to achieve a new stage of development in the Common Market in order to prevent future crises. They established as long-range objectives the gradual establishment of a customs union; the coordination of national industrial, monetary, agricultural, and infrastructure policies; the free mobility of capital and labor; and the joint defense of their exports. However, they agreed to limit their initial efforts to an Immediate Action Plan which consisted of promoting "balanced growth," reforming the Common Fiscal Incentives Agreement, and "integrating" the agricultural sector into the integration movement by implementing the Basic Grains Protocol.[72] The ministers requested that SIECA carry out all the necessary studies and develop a working schedule for the Immediate Action Plan. SIECA was to submit a working schedule for the Plan at the next meeting of the Economic Council and its study of a possible customs union by the end of 1969. In the meantime, to avoid crises similar to the one which had just occurred, the ministers agreed to amend Article VI of the General Treaty in order to control the application of domestic consumption taxes in the five countries.[73]

Thus, Somoza's strategy appeared to be successful. On his third attempt, he had engineered a crisis which had forced the other member states--and SIECA as well--to formally and publicly commit themselves to "perfecting" the Common Market in the near future. Nicaragua had succeeded in forcing the other members to deposit all outstanding major agreements--all members, that is, except Costa

Rica, which had been unable to deposit the San Jose Protocol for domestic political reasons. This meant that cooperation on the Common Fiscal Incentives Agreement, the Preferential Treatment Protocol, the San Jose Protocol, and the Basic Grains Protocol could begin in earnest. Moreover, Nicaragua had obtained approval of an Immediate Action Plan which promised that the members would make a serious commitment to balanced growth and to the integration of the agricultural sector into the integration movement.

Somoza's strategy succeeded for two basic reasons. Most important, his suspension of free trade threatened to create a north-south split in the Common Market, isolating the more industrialized northern countries, Guatemala and El Salvador, from their lucrative trade with Nicaragua and possibly with Honduras and Costa Rica as well. Because their industrial sectors were heavily dependent on regional trade, El Salvador and Guatemala were forced to accede to Nicaragua's demands in order to reestablish free trade. The second reason that Somoza's strategy succeeded was that the cost to the member states, especially to El Salvador and Guatemala, of the resolution of the crisis did not appear high. The states had only agreed to fulfill a number of pledges and agreements which they had made several years earlier: the Common Fiscal Incentives Agreement had been signed seven years earlier and the Preferential Treatment Protocol three years earlier. On the other hand, even if only one of the major objectives of the Immediate Action Plan were fulfilled, the scope of the Common Market would be significantly expanded. Thus, to paraphrase one regional integration theorist writing at that time, the crisis appeared to be resolved in a manner which resulted in a greater consolidation of the Common Market, satisfied some of the demands of the less developed members, and involved a potential expansion of the scope of integration.[74]

However, a few days after the Economic Council meeting, Nicaragua began applying its reformed tax in a manner which still discriminated in favor of local industries. The other four countries immediately protested, charging that the "reformed" tax still violated Article VI of the General Treaty. At the May 1969 Executive Council meeting, the four countries asked SIECA to investigate the alleged discriminatory effects of the Nicaraguan tax. The Executive Council ordered SIECA to investigate all of the domestic taxes in effect in Nicaragua and in the other four countries and to report its findings to the next council meeting. Before this critical situation could be resolved, however, hostilities broke out between El Salvador and Honduras in the summer of 1969. Thus, several months after the crisis engineered by Nicaragua appeared to have been resolved, the Immediate Action Plan remained unimplemented; and Nicaragua persisted in applying a tax which was disrupting regional free trade in manufactures.[75]

CONCLUSIONS

Contrary to the generalizations made by regional integration and economic theorists about the balance of payments problems leading inexorably to regional political crises, there does not appear to be any direct relationship between economic problems at the national level and the crises engineered at the regional level. In Chapter 4, it was shown that Honduras demanded preferential treatment during a period of high growth rates, although the country was experiencing its first regional trade imbalance. Nicaragua also demanded preferential treatment, although it had the fastest growing economy in the region. When Costa Rica imposed its dual exchange rate, both its regional and third country exports had recently begun to improve dramatically; however, it had been suffering fiscal and foreign exchange shortages.

The Nicaraguan case does not easily fit the above generalization. Most observers claim that Nicaragua disrupted free trade because of its increasing regional trade imbalance, fiscal shortages, and external trade deficits. But as described above, part of Somoza's motivation was political--to force the other countries to ratify and deposit the San Jose Protocol. Moreover, the behavior of the Nicaraguan private sector during the Nicaragua-induced crisis demonstrates the exceptional nature of Somoza's behavior. Nicaraguan businessmen rose to support Nicaraguan participation in the Common Market when Somoza imposed the "compensatory" tax. They tried unsuccessfully to get Somoza to delay the decree to allow the other countries time to deposit the protocols. After Somoza ignored their requests, the major representatives of the private sector issued a joint statement in which they vigorously defended Nicaragua's continued participation in the Common Market as essential to the continued development and prosperity of the economy.[76] In addition, many representatives of the private sector traveled throughout Central America on what apparently were good will missions to urge the other governments to deposit the outstanding protocols.[77] But the Nicaraguan private sector was unable to influence Somoza's actions. This demonstrates that there was no domestic political pressure which forced Somoza to impose the compensatory tax, and moreover, that the strong domestic support for the Common Market was insufficient to persuade him to refrain from interfering with free trade. It is the peculiar double nature of the Somoza dynasty, as both the dominant political and economic elite, that enabled Somoza to prevent the other substantial economic interests outside the Somoza extended family from having much influence on policy making. Until the early 1970s, the Somozas made policy regarding the Common Market with virtually no input from the other domestic economic interests. Finally, both Luis and Anastasio Somoza, during their tenure as president, attempted to play a major regional political role, especially regarding integration issues such as the San Jose Protocol. Anastasio Somoza's apparent belligerence on this issue was a result of his desire to establish a leadership role in the integration movement. Contrary to most published accounts, his moves were not dominated by sheer economic necessity.

The rise of the issue of balanced growth, the growing demands for "perfection" of the Common Market, and the increase in the number of disruptions of free trade were due more to changing political conditions than to changing economic conditions. As this chapter has shown, and as the next chapter will show as well, domestic political changes caused a great deal of the political instability in Common Market relations and were, in fact, responsible for a number of the crises. Fagan recognizes this but attempts to deal with it solely from the perspective of regional integration theory. Accordingly, he states that changes of government interfered with "integrative learning."

> New officials in new governments who had not been participants in the negotiations of the original integration agreements and in the numerous subsequent regional meetings made the demands around which each of the conflicts centered. Officials in new govern-

ments were more likely to perceive integration as exacerbating their economic problems and to use disruptive tactics than were their predecessors. The new governments in Honduras, Costa Rica, and Nicaragua clearly demonstrated that they did not view free trade as a 'sacred cow,' as had previous governments.[78]

Fagan's "empirical generalization," however, overstates the impact of changes of government on the Common Market. There were a number of important domestic political changes, besides changes in government, which contributed to the increasing use of disruptive tactics on the part of Honduras and Costa Rica. While it is true that there had been a change of government in both countries, this is a superficial observation. There had been changes of government in Guatemala and El Salvador as well, yet both countries maintained their complete support of the Common Market. In Honduras, Lopez faced increasing domestic opposition, both because of his "illegitimate" status and because of his inability to spur the Honduran economy along the path of development. When confronted with the domestic failings of his economic policies, he attempted to disassociate his administration's policies from those of Villeda and at the same time to blame Honduras' economic problems on an external source--the Common Market. Trejos of Costa Rica made every attempt to cooperate fully with his common market partners and ratify the San Jose Protocol. It was the opposition-dominated Assembly, which blocked passage of the Protocol for political reasons, that forced Trejos to seek an alternate solution to Costa Rica's serious balance of payments and fiscal problems. As the actions of the next president of Costa Rica--Jose Figueres, the progenitor of Costa Rican participation in the integration movement--demonstrate, it was the political exigencies of the moment and not differing perceptions concerning the value of the Common Market which determined the actions of the presidents. A third type of domestic political change in Guatemala, increasing political terrorism, strengthened the government's hand and allowed it to ratify the San Jose Protocol despite significant domestic opposition.

To bolster his argument, Fagan says that there apparently were changes in national goals which paralleled the changes in government discussed above. Economic officials in Honduras and Nicaragua adopted the ECLA and SIECA-backed objective of rapid industrial development as their primary objective. At the same time, El Salvador and Guatemala maintained their commitment to the original primary goal of free trade. Consequently, both Honduras and Nicaragua provoked crises when they demanded preferential treatment and reform of the Common Market as the price the more developed countries would have to pay for the continued operation of the Common Market.[79]

However, as demonstrated in this chapter and in the previous chapter, this apparent change in economic goals was due at least as much to domestic political considerations as it was to the alleged unequal benefits which Honduras and Nicaragua were obtaining as a result of the unrestricted operation of free market forces. There was some dissatisfaction in the business sectors of both countries. But in Honduras, when Lopez attempted to take advantage of this sentiment and blame the Common Market for Honduras' economic problems, the business groups protested, pointing to the grave deficiencies in Lopez's domestic economic programs. In Nicaragua, when Somoza disrupted free trade, the business sector protested strongly and actively sought to ameliorate the impact of Somoza's actions. Thus, in some cases, there was greater support for free trade on the part of the business sector than on the part of the government. Nevertheless, not only did the government ignore the requests of the business sector, but also it was guided by what it considered to be a more crucial political imperative--political survival.

Fagan's major conclusion about the process of regional integration in Central America is that the process of "politicization" has not resulted in growth in the scope or level of integration. Although Common Market members demonstrated a "high level of mutual responsiveness" in dealing with problems involving direct obstacles to free trade, on issues concerning "equal benefits"--issues on which there had been no clear initial commitment for joint action--member countries relied primarily on avoidance and delay as methods of conflict resolution, in the belief that the "free play of market forces" would resolve the issue and that the disgruntled member would withdraw its demands. The dissatisfied member, in turn, relied on blackmail and escalation--the politics of brinkmanship--to force the other members to respond to its demands.[80]

Honduras was the first country to disrupt the

Common Market's operations in order to force its partners to accede to its demands concerning preferential treatment. When Honduras' announced refusal to deposit previously agreed-upon protocols failed to evoke the desired response, the country boycotted Common Market meetings, thus impeding the resolution of free trade problems and raising serious doubts as to whether it would continue to honor the free trade provisions of the Common Market. Even then, it was only after SIECA demonstrated that Honduras' demands involved negligible costs to the other members that they responded favorably. Honduras' use of disruptive tactics encouraged the future use of similar tactics by other dissatisfied members. They had "learned" that they could use brinkmanship tactics to force immediate consideration of their demands for "equal benefits" without seriously endangering the future of the Common Market.[81]

Fagan concludes that this rise in the level of controversy--politicization--over "equal benefits" has not resulted in an increase in the countries' responsiveness to one another's needs, a growth in integrative behavior, an upgrading of the common interests of the members, or a delegation of more authority to the regional center. When the least developed members demanded significant changes in the structure of the Common Market, the other members responded by reaffirming their original commitment to free trade and to a reliance on unregulated market forces to achieve development. Regardless of the verbiage of Economic Council resolutions and official statements by the five presidents, the Common Market members have refused consistently to expand their commitment to include policies which would regulate market forces or involve domestic structural reforms. This combination of demands for "equal benefits," the "low level of actor responsiveness," and the increasing use of brinkmanship tactics has meant that the Common Market has "bounced" from crisis to crisis since 1965, with each succeeding conflict presenting a greater threat to free trade. "At least to date, politicization in Central America has not resulted in growth in the scope or level of integration. It has not led to significant spill-overs, only to threats of spill-backs."[82] Even before the outbreak of the Soccer War, says Fagan, one could have projected a very unstable future for the Common Market, "a Common Market often on the verge of collapse and promising little or no spill-over."[83]

Schmitter is more optimistic than Fagan in his view of the status of the Common Market before the outbreak of the Soccer War.[84] Unlike Fagan, he does not see in the three crises under discussion a failure of integrative learning or a "failure" of the spill-over syndrome or of politicization. In fact, he comes to just the opposite conclusion. Fagan bases his pessimistic conclusions on the grounds that spill-over through politicization has not worked in Central America. On the other hand, Schmitter bases his relatively optimistic conclusions on his "spill-around" thesis and on what he sees as a corollary to politicization--the "crisis manipulation" of the tecnicos. Schmitter agrees with Fagan that spill-over did not work in Central America. However, Schmitter contends that there was another "expansive logic" at work, which he calls "spill-around":

> ...a proliferation of independent efforts at integration in distinct functional spheres, i.e., an expansion in the <u>scope</u> of regional tasks, without, however, a concomitant devolution of authority to a single collective body, i.e., without an increase in the <u>level</u> of regional decision-making....It is naturally expansionist, but without the element of automaticity or the degree of predictability of the spill-over syndrome.[85]

While the spill-over dynamic theoretically culminates only with complete political unification, spill-around is limited. In the Central American case, most of the spill-arounds which occurred were of the "costless" variety, involving unexploited or weakly exploited policy areas. But, according to Schmitter, the success of the spill-around dynamic in the early years of the Common Market was due to the unexpectedly favorable external environment and to the successful efforts of the tecnicos in anticipating and isolating conflicts. When the balanced growth and balance of payments controversies arose in the late 1960s, the tecnicos' strategy could not handle them. Since the initial impact of trade liberalization has worn off, a series of problems has arisen--industrial location, fiscal harmonization, coordination of agricultural policy--which cannot be postponed. Yet these problems demand the "painful, deliberate and persistent transformation of existing policies" which the tecnicos have previously avoided.[86] "Here entrenched government agencies and interest clienteles must be confronted, and there are bound to be net winners and net losers rather than the conveniently non-zero-sum game which has so far prevailed."[87]

Nevertheless, the spill-around dynamic has been successful enough in the early stages of the integration movement to have enabled the movement to cross "some minimum threshold of irreversibility," so that a spill-back is not likely to occur. But while the spill-around dynamic enabled the integration movement to cross this minimum threshold, it cannot help the integration movement achieve "transcendence."[88] In the long run, says Schmitter, transcendence, "the expansion of the authority of common institutions and the shift in the locus of loyalties and expectations," can only result from politicization.[89]

In Schmitter's analysis, the crises which plagued the Common Market in the late 1960s demonstrated that politicization was occurring. The two mainfestations of the benefits of the process of politicization in Central America were the successful crisis manipulation by the tecnicos and the broadening of the supporting coalition for regional institutions.

In order to survive, says Schmitter, regional actors--the tecnicos--had to struggle with a succession of crises. With considerable skill and imagination, they resolved these conflicts by widening the scope and level of mutual policy-making and interdependence--"accelerating through a curve". Equally important, says Schmitter, each of the three principals involved in the crises, Honduras, Costa Rica, and Nicaragua, could claim to have made important sacrifices in the interest of the emerging community. "This seemed to be an optimal pattern for regional crisis management to have taken and might have laid the foundation of 'learned experiences' which, in turn, could result in an eventual 'transcendence'--manifest redefinition of the purpose of their collective enterprise."[90]

Equally important, says Schmitter, were the secondary effects of these conflicts. Regional interests groups were forming and the political influence of national associations was growing. For example, as discussed earlier, when Nicaragua disrupted free trade in early 1969, its manufacturers' association and other business groups vigorously protested Somoza's actions, warning him of the consequences of destroying the Common Market. This was an act of unprecedented independence for them.

While Somoza believed that he could still afford to ignore the groups in 1969, by 1973 this was no longer possible.[91]

> The rise in controversiality had triggered an expansion in the clientele attentive to integration matters. Trade unions, parties, legislatures and higher executive circles found themselves able to take open public positions on the issues. Granted that many of them took a negative posture, nevertheless, the integration movement had broken important barriers of indifference. In the future, with different policies, these aroused groups could have become part of a new supportive coalition. In short, Central America seemed to be escaping from the 'inevitability' of self-encapsulation.[92]

The key variable in Schmitter's analysis is his interpretation of the role the tecnicos played in the crises which plagued the Common Market during the late 1960s. In his search for a "functional equivalent" of the spill-over experienced in Western European integration, Schmitter has assigned the Central American tecnicos a role which they were incapable of playing.[93]

Initially, says Schmitter, the tecnicos--first ECLA officials and later those of SIECA--attempted to avoid "politicizing" integration issues by concentrating on technical issues and making the Ministers of Economy the center of all decision-making. The results of the tecnicos' incremental "apolitical" strategy was the spill-around syndrome. In 1967, the "logical" long-term consequences of the spill-around pattern of institutional expansion appeared to be stagnation--"self-encapsulation." By 1969, however, the once latent contradictions between free trade and declining revenues and between import substitution policies and balance of payments problems had become manifest. The tecnicos were no longer able to confine themselves to safe, "encapsulative" strategies. Rather, in order to survive, says Schmitter, they had to struggle with a succession of crises. With considerable skill and imagination, they have resolved these conflicts by widening the scope and level of mutual policy-making and interdependence.[94] Thus, Schmitter believes that the role of the tecnicos changed substantially--from conflict avoidance to conflict resolution through crisis manipulation--

when the integration movement was confronted by a series of crises in the late 1960s.

Schmitter is essentially correct in his analysis of the early "conflict avoidance" strategy of the tecnicos, but he has misinterpreted the reason for their apparent initial success. Like most observers, Schmitter points to the success of the tecnicos in separating economic issues from the mainstream of political debate. He supports Nye's thesis that the tecnicos' early successes were based upon the attitude of the political elite toward economic change. Because the political elites were preoccupied with maintaining their own political power rather than with economic change and policy-making, the tecnicos were given virtually free rein over integration decision-making.[95]

However, Nye, Schmitter, and others have confused economic integration with economic change in general. As this study has repeatedly attempted to illustrate, economic integration was not ignored by the political elites. On the contrary, it was supported actively by political elites who saw in integration a viable alternative to other paths of development, such as agrarian reform and income redistribution, which required significant economic and political sacrifices.

As indicated in Chapter 3, since the early 1950s the Central American political leadership has strongly supported development ideologies. In an effort to encourage rapid and sustained economic growth, the post-war leaders created new public agencies, increased expenditures in infrastructure, and encouraged industrial development. The ECLA Doctrine of regional economic integration complemented the Central American development ideologies, because it promised economic growth without requiring major domestic political and economic reforms. The initial management of technical integration decision-making "quite naturally" was assigned to the tecnicos, says Wynia, because they possessed a virtual monopoly of the vital expertise needed to initiate the integrative process.[96] Irving Tragen, the former director of ROCAP, insists that the tecnicos would have had little success at all if the dominant political elites had not supported the integration program.[97] Finally, by focusing on initial policy commitments rather than on policy implementation, theorists such as Nye and Schmitter have exaggerated the importance of the tecnicos' initial successes.[98]

A close observation of the tecnicos' actions

during the late 1960s reveals that, contrary to Schmitter's thesis, they did not work toward the widening of the focus of the integration movement. For example, the tecnicos were supposed to manipulate the "balanced growth" issue by exploiting "the growing but limited convergence of the major powers and the special fears and hopes of the smaller ones."[99] This was to lead to an increase in the level of integration through an upgrading of the common interest. But the tecnicos' role during the crisis engineered by Honduras was limited to suggesting measures which would satisfy Honduras' demands. At no time did the tecnicos attempt to transform the institutional setting, because their principal concern was to preserve the existing structure. According to one tecnico, "the crisis was perceived by the technocrats as one that imperiled the existence of the program as it was." The possibility of their obtaining wide powers, he says, was never envisioned.[100] SIECA's role in the "balanced growth" crisis and in the crises that followed was limited to bringing the member states together to adopt recommendations already approved by the Ministers of Economy. The tecnicos did not want to direct the integration program or promote those activities which would cast them into a more active and less secure role. Although they occupied a strategic position in the process of change, their position was weak and dependent. The tecnicos never played the role of supranational agents devoted to upgrading the common interest by overcoming the built-in limitations in their tasks. As the crises of the late 1960s began to plague the Common Market, the goal of the tecnicos became to hold the integrative structure together, not to expand it.

> The preservation of the regional institutions, where they were entrenched, constituted the major activity of the tecnicos. The process lost its character as an instrument for building a larger entity among the participants or for their modernization; it became an end in itself. The tecnicos gave up their role as agents of change and became agents of the status quo.[101]

In sum, the tecnicos' early successes were not as significant as they have been portrayed. What success they did have was due, not to their ability to separate economic and political issues, but to the goals of the political elites. The development-oriented post-war governments used the tecnicos initially because they had the technical expertise. The tecnicos were the liaisons between the national governments and the international lending agencies, so they had a certain amount of influence due to the international support for the Central American integration effort. Moreover, the Central American presidents needed the assistance of the tecnicos in order to meet the minimum requirements of the international development agencies and the United States for development assistance for infrastructure development projects.[102] Thus, the tecnicos were permitted to form planning agencies and to secure the approval of integration treaties because they had become marginal members of the political elite. But the tecnicos never developed much influence because the governments perceived many of the tecnicos' plans as politically controversial--a threat to their traditional patterns of resource allocation. Thus, although the tecnicos occupied a key position in the integration process, they were manipulated by the political elites. As Wynia points out, the observations of Nye, Schmitter, Cochrane, and Hansen do not capture the many dimensions of national policy-making; and therefore, they tell us little about the attitudes and behavior of the national political elites.[103]

The focus on the behavior and goals of the national political elites points to the second major error of Schmitter's analysis and to the failure of the regional integration theorists' focus in general. As was indicated earlier, Fagan and Schmitter portray the series of crises which struck the Common Market in the late 1960s as having arisen inexorably from the contradictions which emerged beginning in 1966. However, as the analysis of the balanced growth and the balance of payments "crises" has demonstrated, the issues were manipulated by the national governments for domestic political reasons.

Schmitter portrays the tecnicos as rising to the occasion during these crises and resolving them by expanding the scope of the integration program. But the above analysis of the tecnicos has demonstrated that they were incapable of playing such a positive role. A more accurate focus would be on presidential decision-making during this period. As Schmitter himself acknowledges, "the threats to withdraw, the calculated delays in ratification and deposit of new protocols, the unilateral refusals to conform to regional norms and the resultant acts of recrimination have been, for the most part, tactical ploys." This brinkmanship style of forcing an issue may be regarded with alarm, he says, but it has rarely resulted in a downgrading of original commitments.[104] One may therefore share Schmitter's guarded optimism about the future of the Central American integration movement, but not for his reasons. The focus on presidential decision-making reveals that the national political leadership of the member countries was in control of the integration movement and that various governments engineered crises with no real intention of endangering the future of the integration movement. Thus, if the integration movement was <u>not</u> in danger of collapsing before the outbreak of the 1969 Soccer War, it is because of the continuing commitment of the political elites to integration.

All five governments maintained this commitment for two basic reasons. First, the Common Market had fulfilled its original commitment to free trade so well that a "spill-back" would have been very costly to all members, even to the "least developed" Honduras and Nicaragua. Regional trade had grown dramatically during the decade; and it would have been difficult, if not impossible, to find alternative markets for regionally produced manufactures in the event of a breakdown in regional trade ties. Second, each country maintained its original belief that industrialization could not be achieved on the strength of its domestic market alone; the Common Market was indispensable to the economic future of the five countries.[105]

NOTES

1. Pincus, pp. 182-183.

2. Schmitter, "Central American Integration," p. 25.

3. SIECA, <u>Carta Informativa</u>, No. 42, pp. 13-19.

4. Despite IDB, OAS, and Pan American Union recommendations for substantive tax reforms, Guatemala called for regional solutions to the balance of payments problems. "Economic Survey," U.S. State Department, U.S. Embassy, Guatemala, First Quarter, 1965, mimeographed.

5. Schmitter, "Central American Integration," pp. 19-27; Fagan, p. 39.

6. Fagan, p. 39.

7. Hansen, Central America, pp. 85-88.

8. SIECA, Carta Informativa, No. 63, pp. 5-9.

9. Fagan, p. 41.

10. Ibid.

11. SIECA, Carta Informativa, No. 74, pp. 10-19.

12. Ibid.

13. State Airgram, op. cit.

14. SIECA, Carta Informativa, No. 80, pp. 3-4.

15. Ibid., pp. 3-8.

16. Reporte Economico, June 7, 1968, p. 20.

17. Fagan, p. 48.

18. Vincent Cable, "Problems in the CACM," BOLSA Review, Vol. 3, No. 30, June 1969, pp. 345-6.

19. Economist Intelligence Unit, Quarterly Economic Review: Central America, No. 38 (June 1962) and No. 39 (September 1962).

20. Ibid., No. 35 (October 1961), No. 36 (Dec.1961)

21. Ibid., No. 42 (June 1963).

22. Pincus, op. cit.

23. El Grafico, April 19, 1968, p. 7.

24. Quoted in OEA Secretaria, "El esfuerzo interno y las necesidades de financimiento externo para el desarrollo de Guatemala" (Washington:OAS, 1969).

25. Economist Intelligence Unit, No. 2, 1968.

26. La Prensa Libre, January 9, 1968, p. 8.

27. Economist Intelligence Unit, No. 3, 1968.

28. Ibid., Nos. 1 and 3, 1967.

29. This general observation does not hold for the earlier two examples of Villeda and Ydigoras, whose political futures were in jeopardy long before the tax reform controversies arose.

30. Based on interviews with Lazar, Tragen, Barber.

31. Gary Wynia, Politics and Planners, pp. 97-98.

32. Based on interviews, op. cit.; see also Wynia, p. 98, for similar conclusions.

33. Fagan, p. 49.

34. Wynia, "Paradox," p. 333; Fagan, pp. 49-51.

35. _Reporte Economico_ (El Salvador), June 7, 1968; also reported in Fagan, p. 49.

36. _The Economist para America Latina_, Vol. 2, No. 23, November 1968, p. 37.

37. Wynia, "Paradox," p. 333.

38. _Reporte Economico_, June 21, 1968, p. 11.

39. Ibid., August 2, 1968, p. 3.

40. Economist Intelligence Unit, No. 4, 1968.

41. Ibid., p. 13.

42. However, one Central American source of unknown reliability states that the delegates who approved the Protocol believed that it was necessary to prevent the disintegration of the Common Market. _Reporte Economico_, June 7, 1968; June 14, 1968.

43. Schmitter, "Central American Integration," pp. 24-27.

44. See footnote 88, "Transcendence..."

45. Schmitter, "Central American Integration," p. 26.

46. Cohen, p. 59.

47. Cable, p. 668.

48. Landry, p. 175.

49. Wynia, _Politics and Planners_, p. 56.

50. Schmitter, "Central American Integration," p. 26.

51. Fagan, pp. 51-52.

52. _Comercio Exterior_, Vol. 19, No. 3 (March 1969).

53. _Carta Informativa_, No. 82, pp. 2-7.

54. Ibid.

55. Fagan, p. 53; Wynia, "Paradox," p. 332.

56. Economist Intelligence Unit, No. 4, 1968, p. 4.

57. _Carta Informativa_, No. 87. The alleged differences between "perfection" and "restructuring" are discussed in Chapter 8.

58. Ibid., No. 82, pp. 2-7.

59. Ibid., No. 87, pp. 2-5.

60. Fagan, p. 55.

61. Carta Informativa, No. 88, p. 1.

62. Latin American Newsletter, February 28, 1969.

63. Carta Informativa, No. 89, p.1.

64. Ibid., pp. 1-7.

65. Fagan, p. 58.

66. Ibid.

67. Ibid.

68. Ibid., p. 59.

69. Carta Informativa, No. 90, pp. 2-4.

70. This included exempting items already subject to consumption taxes, unifying into one instrument the consumption taxes already in effect in Nicaragua, refraining from discriminating against regionally produced goods, and eliminating taxes in cases where their application seriously affected trade.

71. Carta Informativa, No. 90, pp. 2-4.

72. Ibid.

73. Fagan, p. 61.

74. Ibid.

75. For details of this period, see Carta Informativa, No. 92; Latin American Newsletter, April, 1969.

76. Latin American Newsletter, March 28, 1969.

77. Fagan, p. 62.

78. Ibid., pp. 66-7.

79. Ibid., p. 66.

80. Ibid., p. 67. Fagan's use of "unequal benefits" encompasses-- incorrectly-- both balanced growth and the balance of payments issues.

81. Ibid., p. 68.

82. Ibid., p. 69.

83. Ibid.

84. Schmitter, "Central American Integration."

85. Ibid.

86. Stanley Hoffmann, "The European Processes at Atlantic Cross Purposes," Journal of Common Market Studies, Vol. 11, No. 2(February 1966), p. 88.

87. Schmitter, "Central American Integration," p. 42.

88. "Transcendence" occurs when successive redefinitions of the scope and level of the actors' commitment to regional institutions lead to increases in the level of authority "devolved" upon joint institutions until the actors ultimately agree upon a manifestly new set of common objectives. Schmitter, "A Revised Theory of Regional Integration," in Leon Lindberg and Stuart Scheingold, eds., Regional Integration: Theory and Research (Cambridge: Harvard University Press, 1971), p. 236.

89. Schmitter, "Central American Integration," p. 43.

90. Ibid., p. 44.

91. Interview with George Gowen, U.S. State Department, Washington, D.C., August 1975.

92. Schmitter, "Central American Integration," p. 44. Schmitter defines "self-encapsulation" in "Three Neo-Functional Hypotheses about International Integration," International Organization, Vol. 23, No. 1, 1969. For present purposes, it can be defined simply as stagnation.

93. See Hansen, "Reflections," p. 263, for a discussion of functional equivalents. For a more detailed presentation, see Haas and Schmitter, "The Politics of Economics of Latin American Regionalism," Monograph Series in World Affairs, III (Denver, 1965-66), p. 7.

94. Schmitter, "Central American Integration," p. 44.

95. Nye, "Central American Regional Integration," p. 27; Schmitter, op. cit., p. 41.

96. Wynia, "Paradox," p. 328.

97. Interviews, op. cit.

98. Wynia presents an excellent case study of the tecnicos in the national planning agencies in Politics and Planners.

99. Ernst Haas, "The Uniting of Europe and the Uniting of Latin America," Journal of Common Market Studies, Vol. 5, No. 4 (June 1967), p. 342.

100. Cohen, p. 79.

101. Ibid., p. 85.

102. Interviews with, Clare, Lazar, Elac, Tragen, and Lockard. The tecnicos "spoke the language" of the U.S. and other Western economic officials; they

communicated as equals, since the tecnicos had the same economic training and philosophy.

103. Wynia, "Paradox," p. 328. For example, only Wynia has studied the dimensions ofpresidential policymaking, and no one has studied the tecnicos as a domestic political elite. The tendency has been to treat the tecnicos as an external agent in the integration process; the tecnicos were supposed to create regional constituencies and manipulate the national political elites in order to widen the scope of the integration process. However, the tecnicos were also a domestic political elite, however marginal their status. The "first generation" of tecnicos who participated in the creation of the Common Market, such as Fuentes, Sol, Delgado, and Noriega, enjoyed great prestige in their countries. But the "second generation," which staffed the national and regional economic institutions in the 1960s and 1970s, enjoyed no such prestige. While the first generation had succeeded in getting the treaties and major protocols signed, the job of the second generation was to hold the integration structure together, not expand it.

From this defensive position, it was easy for the tecnicos to be coopted into the traditional socio-political structure described in Chapter 2. Just as the other potential challenges to the traditional structure, the agricultural exporters and the industrialists, had been coopted before them, the tecnicos also became part of the status quo. According to Wackerbarth (interview, op. cit.), "they simply became another part of the 'Old Boy' network which dominates the Central American political scene." Thus, an understanding of the national role of the tecnicos is a prerequisite to an understanding of the role they play in regional politics.

104. Schmitter,"Central American Integration," p. 38.

105. Fagan, p. 69, acknowledges these continuing commitments on the part of the elites, but he concludes that they were insufficient to prevent the Common Market from struggling from crisis to crisis, being often on the verge of collapse, with little promise of spill-over.

6. The Soccer War

As indicated earlier, despite the series of crises which plagued the Common Market after 1966, most observers were predicting that these problems would be resolved and that the future success of the integration movement would actually be enhanced by the satisfactory resolution of these crises. Like many observers in 1968 and early 1969, Miguel Wionczek felt that the Common Market countries had "demonstrated the ability to absorb peacefully the growing social tensions arising partly from the accelerated industrialization of the area."[1] Even the crisis which surrounded the imposition of the San Jose Protocol appeared to have been resolved by April 1969.[2]

Thus, although most observers are aware of the difficulties which the Common Market faced, they believed that it had reached "a point of no return."[3] The Central American integration experiment appeared to support the neo-functionalist theory of regional economic integration: "The Central American integration experiment is facing a new stage, confirming what is well-known from West European experiences; economic cooperation in one field within the framework of a common market creates inexorably a need for cooperation in other fields."[4] Wionczek hoped for "a gradual renunciation on the part of the member countries of freedom of action in fields which are universally considered to be the legitimate domain of a sovereign state."[5]

Most observers were completely surprised, therefore, when El Salvador launched a blitzkrieg attack on Honduras in July 1969. A series of incidents arising from two soccer matches followed by severance of relations and the outbreak of armed hostilities was culminated by the Salvadoran attack on Honduran territory. Under threat of OAS sanctions, El Salvador withdrew from Honduran territory. Since then, there have been a series of border incidents. Bilateral talks were held in 1970 under OAS auspices, again in 1973 in Mexico, and in 1978 in Peru; but these and other levels of negotiation have all failed to resolve either the border issue or the question of the status of the Salvadoran residents of Honduras. In retrospect, observers have pointed to several issues and events which were responsible for the outbreak of hostilities between the two countries.

The issue generally regarded to be the primary cause of the war is the issue of "labor mobility."[6] According to regional integration theorists, while the free movement of capital and labor is a matter which the institutions of the EEC have been able to deal with effectively, in Central America it has been a matter of "high politics."[7] Labor mobility has long been considered a political and security problem, and it has never been resolved by the regional institutions. In fact, Schmitter puts the underlying reason for the outbreak of hostilities on the failure of the regional institutions to respond to El Salvador's repeated attempts to raise the issue of labor mobility and build it into the integration process. This failure, according to Schmitter, is related to the integrationist strategy of the tecnicos, which resulted in what he calls the "spill-around syndrome." That is, collective efforts in different policy sectors were deliberately kept apart in order to keep political issues separate from the "purely economic" questions.[8]

However, while this author agrees with those who point to the issue of labor mobility as an important cause of the 1969 hostilities between Honduras and El Salvador, he does not believe that this issue was the fundamental cause of the war. Moreover, this author believes that the "spill-around syndrome" does not adequately explain the causes of the war, nor does it satisfactorily explain why the labor mobility issue was not resolved on the regional level. Due to limitations of space, this specific issue cannot be discussed at length. The labor mobility issue will be investivated below, but in the context of the other causes of the war.

The three issues which are generally determined to have set the stage for the 1969 war are, in order of importance: the migration issue, the border issue, and the question of Honduras' dissatisfaction with its participation in the Common Market. However, as the following discussion will demonstrate, these issues were insufficient in themselves to have caused war to break out between the two countries. This chapter will demonstrate that the domestic political problems of the two countries were the principal causes of the 1969 hostilities.

THE FRONTIER QUESTION

Animosity between El Salvador and Honduras is long-standing and predates the formation of the Common Market. The cycle of wars and treaties has been of considerable duration and intensity, to the point where each successive clash is seen as a forerunner to the next one. The major issue, up until the 1960s, was the determination of the border between the two countries.

Bilateral hostilities began with a war in 1839, which was quickly followed by a peace treaty. However, the treaty was rendered inoperative by a subsequent war which followed almost immediately. This war was followed by the peace treaty of 1841, which was cancelled by the war of 1845. In 1854, the two countries signed a reciprocal treaty on sovereignty and independence. In 1861-1862, there was a boundary dispute; joint inspection of the involved areas followed, and then the two countries signed a treaty of peace and friendship. Once again in 1869, a boundary dispute led to the joint inspection of certain areas; but only a partial agreement was achieved. Honduras declared war on El Salvador two more times, once in 1871 and again in 1876. In 1878, the migration issue first came into question as a security issue. Another bilateral Treaty of Peace and Friendship included provisions for preventing emigrants and discontented politicians from using the territory of the one to disturb the peace and security of the other. In 1880, both countries signed a preliminary convention to fix national boundaries, with the President of Nicaragua as mediator. However, neither side submitted the necessary documents and no award was made. In 1884, a boundary treaty drawn up after a survey and report by a Canadian civil engineer was disapproved by the Honduran Congress. In 1886, Honduras and El Salvador signed a convention for the determination of the border by commissioners. When they were sent out, however, the commissioners failed to agree. In 1895, the two countries signed another boundary convention providing for the setting up of a Mixed Boundary Commission to resolve all differences and to lay down a dividing line. But the Mixed Commission did not meet within the ten year time limitation stipulated by the treaty. So in 1906, a further convention was signed, prolonging the validity of the 1895 treaty by another ten years. In 1908, Honduran revolutionaries launched an unsuccessful attack on Honduras from El Salvador. In 1916, as a result of renewed frontier disputes, the 1895 Mixed Commission was convened; but the Commission's second ten year mandate expired during the middle of negotiations, because El Salvador had no wish to finalize the border. In 1918, a new boundary convention was signed by both countries, but El Salvador never ratified it. There is no record of any serious dispute during the "isolationist" period of the "Depression Dictators." Not until 1962 did the boundary issue arise again; another Mixed Frontier Commission was established to demarcate the land frontier, but it never met. Also, for the first time, this treaty recognized the problem of the 150,000 illegal Salvadoran immigrants in Honduras; provision was made in the 1962 treaty to legitimize their position. In 1965, a Treaty of Migration was negotiated. It provided, among other things, for the expulsion of existing undocumented immigrants. However, the treaty was not ratified until 1967; and Honduras allowed it to expire in January 1969. In 1967, there was a series of what most observers felt were "minor" frontier incidents. These incidents were investigated by a new joint commission; the frontier was submitted to mediation by a commission to be established by the foreign ministers of Guatemala, Nicaragua, and Costa Rica.

The above chronology of failures to resolve the border problem highlights two important facts. First of all, the border issue was not of sufficient gravity to cause the two countries to go to war. Second, since 1900, El Salvador had resisted Honduran initiatives to resolve the border issue, not because of potential loss of territory, which would have been minor, but primarily because the border was linked to the migration issue. Salvadoran peasants had taken up residence by the thousands on both sides of the disputed border areas. If the border issue were formally resolved, it could mean the expulsion from Honduran territory of thousands of illegal Salvadoran residents. This was a price for the border settlement which El Salvador was not willing to pay.

The frontier incidents of 1967, however, involved much more than the border issue. In May

1967, a group of Salvadoran National Guardsmen crossed into Honduran territory and captured an alleged Honduran refugee from Salvadoran justice. Antonio Martinez Argueta, connected socially with President Lopez of Honduras, was kidnapped from his hacienda and carried off to El Salvador. A short time later, there was a clash between two armed patrols which resulted in six deaths, many wounded, and two Salvadorans captured. Both countries responded by mobilizing troops along the border.

The situation was aggravated for domestic political reasons by both sides. Honduras, because of domestic discontent with the Lopez military regime, tried the age-old remedy for domestic problems--a dispute with a neighboring country. After the above incidents, the Honduran government published official maps and documents which pinpointed Salvadoran violations of Honduran territory and attacked El Salvador for refusing to agree to a final border settlement. Moreover, and an omen of things to come, Honduras began to enforce the new immigration law by expelling a number of illegal Salvadoran residents from the border area.[9] Finally, Honduras banned the export of beans to and the import of eggs from El Salvador and refused to attend the meeting of the Executive Council scheduled to meet in El Salvador in June. Thus, Honduras manipulated all three issues--the border issue, the migration issue, and the Common Market--in its dispute with El Salvador for domestic political reasons which will be discussed in detail below.

A few weeks later, forty Salvadoran soldiers were captured as they entered the Honduran city of Nueva Ocotepeque. They were apparently sent by Salvadoran President Sanchez to deliver $200,000 worth of arms to support an abortive coup--a garrison uprising--against Lopez. But armed conflict was avoided, and twelve months of negotiations resulted in an exchange of prisoners--the Salvadorans for Martinez. At the same time, Honduras returned the $200,000 worth of arms. The humiliation of the Salvadoran armed forces which resulted from the incident left a bitter residue of feeling which was a factor in the events of 1969. The domestic political reasons for the Salvadoran attack on Honduras will be discussed later in the chapter.

From the foregoing, it is evident that the frontier question has been an active issue between the two countries off and on for nearly a century and a half. However, the frontier question cannot be regarded as the primary cause of the 1969 war, because until recently neither side has been eager to pursue wholeheartedly the settlement of their common border. Undeniably though, the border was important in the events leading up to the outbreak of hostilities. By 1967, Honduras had tied the solution of the border problem to the resolution of the migration issue, just as El Salvador had avoided a settlement of the border issue because of its need for an "escape valve" for its "excess" population.

THE MIGRATION ISSUE

Most analysts believe that the migration issue was the fundamental cause of the 1969 war. For over fifty years, El Salvador had been exporting labor to Honduras. El Salvador has a population density about eight times greater than Honduras has, no unoccupied agricultural lands, a capital-intensive industrial sector, a high unemployment rate, an extremely high birth rate, and the highest degree of land concentration in Latin America. The result has been serious population congestion. With the opening up of the foreign-owned banana plantations on the Honduran north coast in the 1920s, thousands of Salvadorans began to migrate to Honduras. By 1960, 300,000 Salvadorans had taken up residence in Honduras, half of them illegally. The generally more resourceful and industrious Salvadoran immigrants readily found employment on the land or in industry, despite that there was a serious unemployment problem among Hondurans. Rising unemployment was caused by the stagnation of the banana sector and by the rapid urban population growth, 6 percent, while employment grew at only 2.6 percent. The powerful trade unions began to blame the Salvadorans for depressing the wage level and limiting opportunities for employment. At the same time, Honduran peasants, most of them landless laborers, had succeeded in getting the government to heed their demands for implementation of the 1962 Agrarian Reform Law. Both sides took out their frustrations on the Salvadorans who had settled illegally in the border areas. These settlers became particularly vulnerable in times of crisis, both internal and external. Thus, just before the outbreak of the "Soccer War" in July 1969, minor scale evictions of Salvadoran immigrants occurred in April and May. The immigrants were driven from their land under the 1962 Law and the 1965 Migration Treaty; another estimated twenty-five thousand Salvadoran settlers abandoned Honduran territory by mid-July. El Salvador supposedly became greatly alarmed over the security and well-being of its expatriate citizens. In fact, El Salvador justified its invasion of Honduras by citing reports of genocide and other atrocities which were allegedly committed against these "conacionales" during the land evictions and the "Soccer riots."[10]

THE COMMON MARKET AND THE SOCCER WAR

A few observers believe that the existence of the Common Market was itself a cause of the war.[11] On the other hand, only one analyst, Joseph Nye, appears to believe that the existence of the Common Market may have had a mitigating influence on El Salvador-Honduras relations. The war might therefore have broken out as early as 1967 if the Common Market had not existed.[12] Most analysts concede, however, that the Common Market was only a secondary issue in the Salvadoran-Honduran conflict.[13] Nevertheless, this author believes that the Common Market was a very important issue in the El Salvador-Honduras conflict, but not in the way the other observers have believed. The governments of both countries manipulated the Common Market as a domestic political issue; the significance of this fact will be discussed below. This author believes, moreover, that the Common Market became an integral part of the "postwar" settlement debate, because Honduras insisted on linking a settlement of the migration problem with El Salvador to the restructuring of the Common Market.

The fundamental causes of the war must be understood if the role of the Common Market as both one of the causes of the conflict and a part of the solution is to be understood. For this reason, the following analysis focuses on the domestic political events in the two countries and on the relation of these events to the three issues described above: the migration problem, the frontier issue, and the Common Market. This author believes that the ultimate causes of the war were domestic political problems that the two governments faced and the methods they chose to deal with these problems. Moreover, these same problems present the greatest obstacle to both a peace settlement[14] and to the restructuring of the Common Market.

THE INTERNAL POLITICAL SITUATION IN HONDURAS

Since 1963, Honduras has been confronted with two grave internal problems, one political and one agrarian. Neither problem is new, however; both have their roots in the country's past. The political problem is related to the traditional political rivalry between the National and Liberal Parties, which has been so fierce that stable government has had difficulty in operating. The major problem is that the National Party has been a power-seeking machine with little concern for the Constitution or the electoral process.

In 1948, General Carias surprised everyone when he announced his retirement from the presidency. However, through his political organization, the National Party, he chose the man who was to be his successor, Juan Manual Galvez. Galvez had held several important positions under the long rule of Honduras' "Depression Dictator"; he had also been a lawyer for the Standard Fruit Company. Carias had suppressed his political opposition, the Liberal Party, for the past fifteen years; and the Liberals were unable to field a strong candidate for the 1948 elections. Moreover, the government interfered so much in the electoral process that the Liberal Party finally refused to participate in the election. Thus, Galvez, the only candidate, was declared elected and took office on January 1, 1949.

Galvez proved to be surprisingly independent of the last caudillo. He ruled in a constitutional manner, he permitted the free organization of political parties and a free press, and he invited all political refugees to return to Honduras. Relying heavily on external assistance, Galvez made elementary moves toward developing the Honduran economy. Because Carias had done nothing about development, Galvez's reforms in road construction, industrial development, education, and social services appeared as striking departures from the past.

Galvez retired at the end of his term, departing from the Honduran tradition of "continuismo," and provided for the first free elections in Honduran history in 1954. When Galvez's term expired in that year, three candidates competed for the presidency. The National Party, which had totally dominated Honduran politics for decades, nominated its caudillo, the former dictator General Carias. But a large faction had left the National Party. Calling itself the National Reform Movement (MNR), this splinter group nominated General

Williams, the former Vice President. The Liberal Party, which had extremely limited electoral support up until that time,[15] nominated a young physician named Ramon Villeda Morales. After a free election, marred by a moderate degree of violence, Villeda Morales had won 48 percent of the total votes, or 121,213 votes. Carias had received 77,726 votes and Williams 53,041. Under the Constitution, the Congress of Deputies was to pick the President, since no candidate had received a majority. Villeda was the logical choice, since he had won by such a great margin. But the old political leadership--the National Party and the MNR faction--refused to allow Villeda to be elected, because they wanted to maintain political control. They engineered the following crisis.

Just before Congress was to vote, Galvez suddenly left the country for "medical" reasons. He handed the reins of government over to Vice President Julio Lozano. At the same time, Williams and Carias had the MNR and the National Party deputies boycott the session. Since Congress required the attendance of two-thirds of its membership for a quorum, the new president could not be elected. Then Lozano abolished the Constitution and proclaimed himself constitutional dictator, claiming that he was forced to do so because there was no Congress. Next, Lozano appointed the deputies of the MNR and the National Party as members of an advisory council charged with drafting a new constitution.

Not surprisingly, Lozano delayed elections in order to keep himself in power. The inevitable result was increased opposition. Strikes and labor disputes became common; and these, of course, were followed by increased political repression. But Lozano thought that he had control of the political situation; and he set the date for the next election for October 7, 1956. As political activity began to intensify, however, Lozano became alarmed and exiled Villeda and several other members of the opposition Liberal Party. Lozano's actions provoked a strike of university and high school students; and on August 3, 1956, an unsuccessful revolt took place. After this, Lozano cracked down on the opposition, instituting complete censorship and a state of emergency. Then the Lozano government engineered the October elections, awarding its own organization, the National Union Party, 370,318 votes and all fifty-six seats in the Constituent Assembly that was to elect the new president. The

Liberal Party was awarded 41,724 votes; and the National Party, a small group that had not defected to the Lozano organization, was awarded 2,003. Two weeks later, the Lozano-Galvez government was expelled in a bloodless coup; and a three-man military junta was set up to run the country until a fair election could be held.

The young officers replaced the military commanders of all seventeen departments, freed all political prisoners, forced the Supreme Court to resign, and appointed Villeda as Ambassador to the United States. All political parties became active as the entire country enthusiastically prepared for what was to be the first election in Honduran history not dominated by the military and the oligarchy. It appeared that Honduras had started on the road to constitutional democracy. Over 500,000 people registered to vote. This number included women and illiterates, who were enfranchised for the first time. Four times as many people voted in the September 22, 1957 election as had voted in the 1950 election. The Liberal Party won a tremendous victory, getting 62 percent of the vote, with 31 percent going to the National Party. Congress elected Villeda president; and on December 21, 1957, he was inaugurated for a six-year term. At the same time, Congress adopted a new constitution, which contained bold statements about social reform and the economic role of the state. The constitution also excluded the army from politics, or so the Congress thought. Villeda's public statements echoed those of leaders of the other "popular" political parties of Latin America, such as Haya de la Torre of Peru and Figueres of Costa Rica, where Villeda had spent his exile. Villeda called his administration "the second republic"; his speeches echoed the themes prevalent in all democratic reformist thought: "social justice," "integral development," and the "struggle without end."

But Honduras' extreme poverty prevented many of Villeda's programs from getting past the planning stages, and many more were left partially completed. Most of his efforts in the early years were focused on expanding existing programs, and this is where Villeda had the most success. During his term in office, he more than doubled the number of schools, health centers, roads, and bridges in the country. He was also moderately successful in improving housing and social security, and he strengthened the labor movement with the adoption of a modern labor code. But Villeda was not successful in achieving reforms in the two areas in which he tried the hardest. The first was the agricultural sector. The Villeda administration promulgated an Agrarian Reform Law in 1962 and established the Agrarian Reform Institute. But due to the hostile reaction of the American banana companies and the country's landowners, this program was sharply curtailed. While there is no evidence that the banana companies were involved in the overthrow of the Villeda government in 1963, their active campaign against the agrarian reform bill did encourage the landowners to participate actively in the overthrow of the government.

The second great failure of the Villeda administration was in the political realm. Villeda's goal was to institutionalize constitutional government. To this end, he set up a Civil Guard to provide a counterweight to the military and thus keep it out of politics. And he attempted to encourage bipartisan participation in the government. But he failed in both of these endeavors, and in the end they all contributed to his downfall in 1963.

The regular army resented the Civil Guard set up by Villeda, and all through Villeda's term in office there were armed clashes between the two military forces. Moreover, the influence of "Fidelismo" was another disruptive factor which helped to turn the army against Villeda. Honduran supporters of Castro disrupted Villeda's attempts at orderly reform; Fidelistas were moderately successful at penetrating the Villeda administration. Finally, however, Villeda broke off relations with Cuba when he became convinced that the Castro government was financing armed revolutionaries in Honduras. But this did not prevent the conservative elements in the society from denouncing the Villeda government as "communist infiltrated."

As for Villeda's attempts to encourage bipartisan participation in the government, the president was unable to find enough qualified people to staff his government because of Honduras' lack of trained personnel. The minority of Liberals who were capable and educated had little experience because they had been kept out of previous governments. National Party members refused to participate in Villeda's reform efforts. Villeda failed to get a civil service law passed that would have reformed the bureaucracy.

The final event which set the stage for the 1963 coup which thwarted the presidential elections planned for that year was similar to what had occurred in the 1954 elections. The National Party split into two factions in a quarrel over whom to nominate for the election. This split in the opposition guaranteed victory to the Liberal Party candidate, Rodas Alvarado. But the traditional power contenders in the National Party and the military refused to reconcile themselves to Rodas' expected electoral victory. On Octover 3, 1963, ten days before the election, the army revolted, expelled Villeda from the country, and established a dictatorship headed by Oswaldo Lopez Arellano, the commander of the armed forces.[16]

Once again, the Nationalist Party, determined to gain power at virtually any cost, had undermined the Honduran electoral process. The National Party supported the October 1963 coup, and two years later it cemented its bargain with the Honduran military. Months before the February 16, 1965 presidential and congressional elections, the National Party formally announced that if it won the majority of seats in Congress, it would elect General Lopez as president. The 1965 elections were one of the most fraudulent in the country's history. Lopez kept his part of the bargain made with National Party head Ricardo Zuniga by awarding the National Party thirty-five of the sixty-four seats in Congress.[17] This was enough to insure Lopez's election to the presidency. He gave the Liberals enough seats to keep them from open rebellion.

The Liberals had desperately attempted to get the National Party to compromise in order to elect a civilian government. But the National Party leaders--headed by Zuniga, who was rewarded by being appointed Secretary of the Ministry of the Presidency--were determined to exclude the Liberal Party from participation in the political process. In fact, the fraudulent elections of 1965 were only the second step--the 1963 coup being the first--in a masterful plot by Zuniga to lift the National Party to political hegemony at all levels of government.[18]

The National Party then began to set the stage for its takeover at the local level by preparing for the municipal elections of March 1968. Colonel Juan Melgar, head of the Northern Military Zone, was known as a "constitutionalist" and not a pro-Nationalist.[19] For this reason, Zuniga had Lopez remove Melgar from office. The local populace was very upset that such a professional and well-respected officer should be removed, but the National

Party wanted a politicized and pro-Nationalist leader in Melgar's place. Next, the Nationalists sent civilian cut-throats[20] into Florida province to threaten the president and the secretary of the local elections board, both of whom were Liberals; and the officials fled for their lives. This happened not only in Florida province; similar incidents occurred all over Honduras. After the National Party had installed its own leaders as heads of the local councils, it was guaranteed victory in the 1968 elections.[21]

During the March 31, 1968 elections, the military and civilian cut-throats hired by the Nationalists prevented thousands of Liberals from voting, through the use of violence. The workers' unions from the Tela Railroad Company and Standard Fruit published long lists of names of workers who had received terrible beatings which had prevented them from voting. Other sources reported that the military and gangs of Nationalist civilians stopped buses en route to the polling places and purged them of Liberal voters.[22]

The Liberals protested the election, but they had been so soundly beaten and they were so disorganized that they posed no threat to the minority rule of the Nationalist Party and the military. Lopez refused to investigate charges of fraud because Zuniga, his top political adviser, was behind the fraud. Then the three most powerful unions called on Lopez to restore constitutional democracy to Honduras. A short time later, the ninth Assembly of the National Workers' Unions produced a statement condemning the 1968 elections and announced its determination to fight for democracy in Honduras. In early May, there was a mass demonstration of over 10,000 workers calling for a return to constitutional rule. At the same time, leaders of the major business groups joined the union leaders in protest. They wrote a letter to Lopez which called for solutions to Honduras' grave political and economic crises.

In the face of this growing public reaction, Lopez decided to open a dialogue with the protesting groups. The Liberals refused to come to an "understanding" with Lopez. They announced that they would accept nothing less than the annulment of the March elections. Lopez attempted to maintain the dialogue in order to give the appearance that he was responding to public criticism and that a solution to the country's political crisis was at hand. Following Zuniga's advice, Lopez bypassed the

Liberal Party leadership and tried to win the confidence of several top Liberals. But the Liberals remained firm. They refused to participate on Lopez's terms. Instead, they demanded Liberal representation at all levels of government, including the government ministries. Lopez rejected their terms and broke off the dialogue in June.[23]

Paralleling the deterioration in the political situation, the Honduran economy continued to worsen. Cesar Batres, president of the National Association of Industry, added his voice to those of the leaders of the unions and the business sector who were calling for a comprehensive development plan which would include all sectors of the economy. On June 28, 1968, in the face of continued opposition to such a plan on the part of the government, the North Coast representative to the National Planning Council resigned. He condemned the San Jose Protocol as the latest in a series of palliatives offered by the government. Condemning the lack of a real development policy, he charged that the result of Lopez's presidency had been the continued impoverishment of the people and the rise of a small group of "nouveaux riches."[24]

As the Honduran balance of payments situation continued to deteriorate, the government responded by imposing more consumer taxes. To most Hondurans, the San Jose Protocol was simply the latest and the most drastic in this series of consumer taxes. Thus, when the San Jose Protocol entered into effect on September 12, 1968 without warning, the entire population became very upset, especially the population of San Pedro Sula, the north coast industrial center. The north coast businessmen, workers, and university teachers and students united in protest against the San Jose Protocol. On September 18, they called a general strike, throwing the government into a panic. Lopez hired journalists to misrepresent the events and then declared a state of siege. The military forced the store owners, at bayonet point, to reopen their stores. They carried workers forcefully from their homes to the work centers. They stopped all opposition papers and radio stations. And finally, they arrested the leaders of the strike.

The strike had been violently suppressed, but it provided the impetus for the next strike several months later. When the professors and university students struck in early 1969, they gained the support of the general population. This second general strike lasted several weeks; it ended only when the serious incidents arose with El Salvador.[25]

Lopez took advantage of the events with El Salvador in order to take the public's mind off these internal political and economic problems. All he had to do was to sit back and let passions run their course when 8,500 Hondurans were poorly treated while attending a soccer match in El Salvador. In Honduras, repercussions against Salvadorans by the the general population lasted only one day. But groups of thieves and delinquents began sacking stores, both Honduran and Salvadoran, that sold Salvadoran products. The government could easily and immediately have stopped this violence, as it did several days later, but instead permitted it to continue in order to divert public attention away from the government's crackdown on the teachers and students, who had become a serious threat to the stability of the Lopez regime. In fact, nationalistic fervor in Honduras was whipped up by official speeches and by the government-controlled press and radio stations.[26]

This intentional prolongation of animosities resulted in the growth of anti-Salvadoran feelings which had only been latent before the soccer match incidents. The land invasions and the threat that Salvadoran industrialists posed for Honduran businessmen provided fertile grounds for this anti-Salvadoran sentiment to grow. The results were boycotts of Salvadoran goods and increasing expulsion of undocumented Salvadoran campesinos.

The second major domestic problem Honduras faced in the decade of the 1960s was the agrarian problem. Before the development of the banana sector in the 1920s, Honduras had no agrarian problem. There was so much fertile land that there was plenty for everyone, big farmer and small farmer alike. For this reason, the campesinos never bothered to get title to the land. They just settled on the land without title and worked it. The land did not have any real economic value until the development of the export sector. At the same time, of course, the population continued to grow. With the beginning of the export economy, the foreign companies and the national elite took up huge sections of land for themselves. The best land quickly became concentrated in the hands of these elites. This left 35 percent of the campesinos, who composed 53 percent of the population, with no land at all.[27]

Even today, the agrarian situation remains

basically unchanged. The vast majority of the campesinos live on minifundias, which generally are on inferior land or are far away from markets and transportation facilities. In the interior, they are pushed up onto the sides of the mountains, while the fertile valleys and plains are used for grazing small herds or lie fallow--an estimated 90 percent of the arable land. Moreover, only 15 percent of the arable land in the most heavily populated sectors is used for farming. Yet these campesinos produce 70 percent of the national agricultural production, excluding bananas. Unfortunately, they consume 90 percent of it. While this is technically subsistence agriculture, the campesinos produce barely enough to stay alive.[28] Moreover, due to the small size of most of the fincas, the average campesino works 200 days or less on his finca and is unemployed the rest of the year.

The 525 largest fincas occupy as much land as the more than 120,000 minifundias, around 670,000 hectares. These big fincas are of two kinds, haciendas and plantations. A large percentage of campesinos depend on the haciendados, especially the landless laborers who serve as tenant farmers. The paternalistic hacienda tradition is so strong that the campesino is kept in line voluntarily: "He supports the system which oppresses him."[29] In sum, the hacienda system is still much the same as it was in colonial days.

The plantation system is geared toward agricultural production for export. Eighty percent of the export sector is foreign owned, and the United States banana companies control half of the exports. Moreover, these two companies control 50 percent of the north coast land, the most fertile land in the country. But only 35 percent of the banana companies' 200,000 hectares is cultivated; the rest is reserve land held for potential future use. The banana companies have such vast reserves that they do not bother to replenish the soil when they have depleted it and are ready to move on.[30]

Like the haciendas, the plantations have underutilized the land: cattle-raising employs one man per 500 hectares. While banana plantations have traditionally employed one or two men per hectare, recent advances in technology have caused a dramatic decline in employment in the banana sector. The number of workers for Standard Fruit and United Brands dropped from 35,000 in 1953 to 16,000 in 1959. Recently, one banana company fired 2,800 workers in one cut, simply by getting one helicopter to fight banana disease by aerial spraying. More recently, thousands more have lost their jobs as the companies have increased the mechanization of the packing of bananas in boxes.[31]

The campesino has continued to be pushed off his land during the last twenty years, as the big Honduran landowners have begun to cultivate land for new export crops: coffee, cotton, and cattle. At the same time, the rents that the campesinos have had to pay have more than doubled; and they do not know how to raise these higher-paying new crops. They know only about raising beans and corn. Salvadoran cotton and tobacco growers, the "co-nacionales," have aggravated the situation. They buy up good tobacco and cotton land and import an unlimited supply of peons from El Salvador; these peons displace the former campesino tenants. In a short time, these Salvadoran citizens move on to better job opportunities and land inside Honduras, while the Salvadoran cotton and tobacco growers import another group of Salvadoran peons.[32]

These Salvadoran immigrants are illiterate and have only traditional agricultural skills. They do not contribute taxes or take part in the market economy, but they do make use of the already overburdened schools and other public services. The Salvadoran peasant is used to lower salaries and poorer working conditions; and since he has no documents, he is exploited by the landowners and displaces Honduran workers.

The campesinos who have lost their land or their jobs in the ways discussed above either become squatters or flood the cities with surplus labor. Agrarian conflict begins when the landowners try to drive the campesinos off the land, by both legal and illegal means. So 35,000 campesinos have formed a union to fight for their land. Since the adoption of the 1962 agrarian reform law, there have been well over one hundred cases of agrarian conflict in areas where capitalization of agriculture, i.e., changeover to export crops, has occurred the most. There were nine very serious agrarian confrontations between unionized campesinos and armed landlords between July 1967 and July 1969, the two-year period during which political opposition to the Lopez government began to increase dramatically.[33]

The Villeda Morales administration had passed the agrarian reform law in 1962 and had established the National Agrarian Institute (INA) to apply the law. But it was not until the agrarian issue reached crisis proportions early in 1969 that the Lopez administration began to enforce the provisions of the law. The Lopez government resisted the pressures from the campesinos to enforce the law for years, because the terms of the law were prejudicial to the interests of the banana companies and the big landowners, the backbone of the civilian support of the Lopez government. When the Lopez regime was forced to accede to the campesinos' demands, it also had to protect the interests of the major landholders, both foreign and domestic.[34]

Thus, in early 1969, the Lopez administration seized upon certain provisions of the 1962 law in an attempt to find a solution to the agrarian reform problem --a solution which would minimize political conflict among all parties involved in the dispute. In particular, the INA seized upon Article 68 of the Agrarian Reform Law, which restricted ownership of the land to Hondurans by birth. The corollary was that only those campesinos who were Hondurans by birth could participate in the agrarian reform program. This provision was eminently rational. There were already over 150,000 undocumented Salvadoran squatters, fully 50 percent of the Salvadoran population residing in Honduras; and an indiscriminate land-giveaway program would have encouraged further massive immigration from El Salvador to the "host" country. Therefore, it was reasonable that, under the political and economic circumstances, participation in the agrarian reform program be limited to Honduran citizens.[35] However, this provision began to take on political connotations very quickly, because of the refusal of the Salvadoran government to agree to a final resolution of either the border or the migration issues. Moreover, by the time the Lopez regime got around to implementing the Agrarian Reform Law, not only had friction between Honduras and El Salvador grown concerning the above two issues, but also and more importantly, Lopez needed some way to contain the growing domestic opposition to his administration.

The INA began to evict Salvadoran squatters and to parcel out the land to Honduran citizens, in strict accordance with the provisions of the 1962 Agrarian Reform Law. It appears that, initially, all that was intended was to find the most immediate solution to the agrarian reform issue. The government was unwilling to expropriate land from big landowners, and its colonization projects had failed.[36] The path of least resistance was, quite logically, to expel illegal Salvadoran squatters from government-owned lands. Unfortunately, the Lopez regime also saw in this issue a chance to exploit the migration and border issues in order to bolster its sagging political support. Thus, the Lopez regime manipulated the agrarian reform issue in an attempt to foment an anti-Salvadoran spirit among Hondurans in an effort to place the blame for Honduran political and economic troubles on El Salvador.

The migration issue was made more serious by Honduras' agrarian problems. Honduras and El Salvalor had signed what was to have been the definitive migration treaty on September 21, 1965. It stipulated that documented Salvadorans could not be expelled from Honduras. But Article II stipulated that the 150,000 Salvadorans without documents would have to establish legal residency in Honduras. New immigrants would not be accepted without documents, proof of nationality, and health shots. Moreover, El Salvador had agreed to enforce these laws and prevent illegal emigration. Furthermore, El Salvador agreed that illegal Salvadoran immigrants in Honduras should be deported at the discretion of the Honduran government.

But El Salvador never attempted to fulfill its obligations, and few illegal Salvadoran residents made any attempt to legalize their status. In Honduras, the disorganization, growing political instability, and corruption among civilian and military authorities made the terms of the treaty inoperable. When the treaty came up for renewal in 1969, Honduras refused to renew it because of El Salvador's refusal to work toward a settlement of both the border issue and the migration issue.[37]

In the meantime, the number of land invasions by campesinos in Honduras began to escalate. A large number of the invading campesinos were illegal Salvadoran immigrants; in many cases a majority were Salvadoran. Because they did not qualify for land under the Agrarian Reform Law, they were expelled. But only illegal Salvadorans were affected. When campesinos invaded land owned by Salvadorans, the campesinos were expelled. Moreover, many Salvadorans were Hondurans by birth and were therefore eligible for land under the terms of the Agrarian Reform Law.

As tensions grew between Honduras and El Salvador, the Lopez administration took advantage of the situation to dramatize the Honduran trade imbalance with El Salvador. This anti-Salvadoran campaign on the Common Market issue paralleled the growth of domestic opposition to the Lopez regime. Although the Honduran campaign for "balanced growth" and preferential treatment was aimed at all four of its common market partners, resentment was channeled against the "colonial" nature of trade relations between Honduras and El Salvador. By the time hostilities had broken out between the two countries in July 1969, even the more knowledgeable and sophisticated Hondurans were denouncing "the expansionist desires of Salvadoran industrialists to consolidate Salvadoran-Honduran economic complementarity; that is, Honduras should abandon industrial development and continue to supply El Salvador with raw materials."[38]

THE INTERNAL POLITICAL SITUATION IN EL SALVADOR

Like Honduras, El Salvador has both a political problem and an agrarian problem. These problems became very serious shortly before the outbreak of hostilities between El Salvador and Honduras. As in Honduras, El Salvador's political and economic problems are closely related.

El Salvador has had an "agrarian problem" for over a century. On four separate occasions, in 1872, 1875, 1885, and 1932, the Salvadoran peasants have revolted in protest against the abject misery in which they live.[39] El Salvador has the highest degree of land concentration in Latin America. While 1.9 percent of the population controls 57.5 percent of the land, those who live on small plots of land--81.4 percent of the proprietors--control 21.9 percent of the land.[40] When one adds the large number of landless laborers, the picture becomes even bleaker. The result of this tremendous concentration of land in such a tiny country is that the agricultural sector has 484,400 man-years of labor but needs only 280,000; thus, there is a labor surplus of 276,300 man-years in the agricultural sector. As a result, the average campesino works only 122 out of 280 working days each year.[41]

To make matters even worse, between 1950 and 1966, the agricultural sector grew at an annual rate of 2.4 percent; and from 1957 to 1966, it grew only 0.3 percent per year. This occurred because, despite that thousands of campesinos faced near starvation in the countryside, the oligarchy maintained its policy of taking latifundia lands traditionally used for basic grains production and changing it over into production of export crops: coffee, cotton, and sisal hemp. This "expropriation" was still occurring for cotton growers in the early 1960s.[42] In the face of the near-starving masses--93 percent of the rural population--[43] this increasing scarcity of basic grains drove grain prices up; and as a result, the latifundistas increased the rents considerably. The rise in grain prices was insufficient to cover the rise in rent, and many campesinos were expelled because they could not afford the higher rents. This made way for the capitalist renter who had access to tractors and fertilizer. This, says Abel Cuenca, was in keeping with the Salvadoran government's "agrarian reform" program, which stressed higher yields and increased production at the expense of the former tenants.[44]

Thus, the historical concentration of land into the hands of a tiny minority, the development of the export sector, and the attempt by the Salvadoran government to capitalize the agricultural sector created a tremendous overpopulation of the land available to the campesinos. In the face of nearly certain starvation, the campesinos migrated to Guatemala, Nicaragua, and especially Honduras. They came to Honduras to work on the banana plantations on the north coast and to squat on lands on the Honduran side of the common border with El Salvador. By the late 1950s, there were over 300,000 Salvadorans in Honduras, over 12 percent of the Honduran population.

When the Honduran government hardened its position on the border and frontier issues, the government of El Salvador became very apprehensive. For years, the Salvadoran oligarchy had used Honduras as a pressure valve in order to maintain domestic stability and thus its own hegemony. Although the Salvadoran government negotiated settlements with Honduras on both the border and the frontier issues, El Salvador could not afford to allow the status quo to be altered. If Honduras stopped the influx of Salvadoran peasants or forced tens of thousands of illegal Salvadoran residents to return to El Salvador, the Salvadoran government would face a grave internal political and economic crisis. When Honduras began expelling illegal Salvadoran residents in April and May of 1969, therefore, the Salvadoran government became greatly alarmed. In view of the political unacceptability to El Salvador of the return of any significant number of its former citizens, it is ironic that an immediate result of the Salvadoran attack on Honduras was the flood of an estimated 100,000 refugees into El Salvador.[45]

El Salvador justified its invasion of Honduran territory as necessary to protect the lives of its citizens residing in Honduras, after the Honduran government allegedly began to discriminate against Salvadoran citizens in its enforcement of the 1962 Agrarian Reform Law and the 1965 Treaty of Migration. However, the reasons for the Salvadoran invasion of Honduras are much more complex. As indicated earlier, migration problems alone were insufficient in themselves to have led to armed hostilities.

The key to understanding why El Salvador invaded Honduras lies in the domestic political situation of El Salvador. The migration issue, the border problem, and the changing Honduran attitudes toward the Common Market all played a role in inciting El Salvador to attack Honduras. However, it was the underlying instability of the domestic political system and the increasing opposition to the Sanchez government that caused the government to exploit El Salvador's conflicts with Honduras in the hope of creating "national unity."

The underlying instability of the domestic political system is the result of the determination of the traditional coffee planters' aristocracy, the cafetalera oligarchy, to prevent even modest changes in the political status quo. For the first seventy-five years, the coffee sector was a force for change. Because the coffee growers needed thousands of cheap rural laborers, they challenged the ancient latifundia structure and "freed" thousands of young campesinos--"mozos colonos." The new production force, represented by coffee, caused great political upheavals during the last decades of the nineteenth century: coups d'etat, assassinations, and wars between the feudalistic traditional sector and the new coffee sector.[46] But these conflicts did not explode into civil war, because the latifundia produced basic grains at the lower elevations, while the high, dryer elevations were needed for coffee growing. These higher elevations had no previous value. It was not until many years later that the "cafetaleras" came down into the valleys in search of more land. By then, the cafetaleras had developed into an economic and political elite powerful enough to force the latifundistas to recognize them as legitimate power contenders and to share the reins of government.

In protest against the "liberation" of their land and mistreatment by the coffee growers, the campesinos rose up in armed rebellion in 1833, 1872, 1875, 1885, and 1898. The response of the oligarchy every time was violent suppression. With this end in mind, by the end of the nineteenth century, El Salvador had developed a professional military; and by the beginning of the twentieth century, it had created a National Guard whose express purpose was to keep peasants, workers, and students from challenging the status quo. As the oligarchy became more and more dependent on the military as its guarantor of political stability, the military assumed more importance as a legitimate power contender. The unquestioned dominance of the coffee aristocracy came to an end in 1932, when the civilian president Araujo was unable to put down a large-scale popular uprising.[47] The coffee aristocracy became alarmed and asked the vice president, General Hernandez Martinez, to engineer a coup and take over. He immediately established a repressive regime composed of the army, the National Guard, and the police. He declared a state of seige and brutally put down the insurrection. Thousands of innocent peasants were murdered in 1932, and thousands more fled to Honduras in fear for their lives. Between 1932 and the end of his reign in 1944, Hernandez executed a large number of peasants for alleged involvement in "communist plots."

The coffee oligarchy had turned to the military in an attempt to maintain its political and economic hegemony, but in doing so it had paved the way for the increasing militarization of the government. After 1932, the military not only became an equal partner in the governing elite, but also it usually elected one of its own officers to the presidency. From then until 1944, under the Hernandez dictatorship, the economic and political life of the country stagnated. The commercial interests and the young industrial bourgeoisie became increasingly discontented, and politically subversive feelings and movements began to take shape. Taking advantage of the international fight against fascism, the discontented groups rose up in 1944 and overthrew Hernandez. The workers, students, and middle class united with the young industrial bourgeoisie in opposition to the coffee oligarchy. But this was a natural and spontaneous reaction to the crimes of the dictatorship and the oligarchy; it was therefore not an organized, politically conscious act. The coffee oligarchy remained intact; and within months, with the aid of the military, it had engineered another controlled election and installed Castaneda Castro as the new dictator. But in 1948, when the oligarchy attempted to prolong Castaneda's term, the more moderate elements of the armed forces, with the full support of the industrial bourgeoisie, replaced him with a military junta.

From that moment, the industrial bourgeoisie became very influential. This was the period of a rapid increase in the pace of industrial development, the promotion of industrial protection laws, social security and public health legislation, and investment in physical infrastructure. But the industrial elite did not clash with the traditional oligarchy in the beginning. Industrialists had not yet seen the benefits of improving the distribution of income in the rural sector or of raising export taxes on coffee. Moreover, coffee sales and prices were very high during the 1950s. Therefore, the oligarchy was fairly complacent and did not see the dangers of the new but modest reforms being implemented. The industrial elite had not supplanted the traditional elites. It had simply forced them, with the aid of the young military officers, to accept the industrial bourgeoisie as a legitimate power contender, just as the coffee oligarchy had done to the latifundistas many years earlier.

Major Oscar Osorio emerged as the leader of the junta and as the next president. His administration was a government of compromise. He was committed to reform, but he had no desire to undermine the strength of the military or the coffee oligarchy. But underneath the façade of cooperation within the framework of PRUD,[48] the government party, there was a constant struggle between the oligarchy and the industrial bourgeoisie. The oligarchy, with the support of reactionary army officers, failed in a coup attempt in 1952. Thus, observers both inside and outside El Salvador saw no difference between the military regime of Castaneda and those that followed. They interpreted changes as merely the result of internal bickerings of the armed forces and palace coups.[49]

But the "Revolution of 1948" did mark a turning point in the economic and political development of El Salvador. Allied with the young industrialists, the military reformers, first in the Osorio administration and then during the Lemus administration, rapidly expanded infrastructure and industrial development and introduced the first meaningful social welfare legislation. At the same time, however, neither regime made any attempt at agrarian reform or any other measure which would challenge the economic position of the traditional oligarchy. They had no intention of disturbing the mid-twentieth century Salvadoran society, which differed little from that of the nineteenth century.[50] Nevertheless, the military's decision to accelerate the pace of industrial development unavoidably brought about changes in the economic structure which were bound to have a strong impact on the socio-political structure. Acting in the interest of the industrial elite, for example, the Lemus regime (1955-60) seems to have gone a step further than the Osorio regime. While Lemus concentrated on carrying out and expanding the projects implemented and envisioned by Osorio, his regime also claimed responsibility for the "improvement of the living conditions of the workers in the countryside,"[51] in an attempt to widen the internal market for domestically produced consumer goods. In fact, Abel Cuenca, writing in 1957, claimed that an essential policy of the Lemus regime was the development of the internal market for the "national industry of transformation" through the elevation of agricultural workers' salaries.[52]

This was the point at which the interests of the traditional oligarchy and those of the industrialists came into direct conflict. The oligarchy was opposed to the domestic reforms necessary to develop internal markets, and it was still powerful enough to prevent even modest changes in these areas. Even though the oligarchy was small and discredited politically, it had a uniformity of interests and was politically experienced. On the other hand, the supporters of development were disorganized, had conflicting goals, and were politically inexperienced. The industrial bourgeoisie was unwilling to challenge the oligarchy on these issues, because conflict would be very costly. The only way the supporters of development could have developed El Salvador's internal market would have been to overcome the resistance of the oligarchy. Moreover, because of the weight of the institutional structure inherited from the dictatorial past and the "oligarchic mentality" of all the elites, the industrial elite was not prepared to attempt to secure popular support for its development goals.[53]

Thus, the fear of mobilizing the public, the uncertain outcome of direct conflict with the oligarchy, and the fear of losing what political influence they did have caused the industrial bourgeoisie to back down on its attempts to develop the internal market. As an alternative, they began to seek peaceful penetration of the markets of their neighbors, first through bilateral schemes and then through the Common Market.

The Common Market path to development was supported by the traditional oligarchy after 1958, because it was an alternative to domestic reform. From 1948 to 1958, the oligarchy had dramatically increased capital flight; between 1950 and 1956, the amount invested abroad had doubled.[54] But by 1960, with the establishment of the Common Market, a number of landowners changed their attitude and responded favorably to the idea of investing in industries geared toward serving the regional market. The result was the fusion of economic interests into one broad elite, "la gran burguesia."[55] The Common Market encouraged this fusion of agrarian and industrial capital; but while the Common Market made "la gran burguesia" economically stronger, at the same time it did not eliminate their political differences. Moreover, the Common Market could not solve El Salvador's domestic problems; it merely served to postpone them. The "contradictions" within the "gran burguesia" would rise to the surface in the future.[56]

The emerging conflict with Honduras brought the contradictions within "la gran burguesia" into the open. The industrialists, the moderate groups within the army, and the professional and middle sectors had elected Colonel Sanchez to the presidency in 1967, because he promised to implement the reforms necessary to promote the development of the small and medium-sized enterprises, which depended on the widening of the internal market. But the majority of the traditional oligarchy, aligned with the conservative military officers and the National Guard, totally opposed Sanchez's reform program. The conflict with Honduras separated the two groups even further. The main concern of the industrialists was to prevent anything from disturbing the operation of the Common Market, because their livelihood depended on it. They especially wanted to maintain Salvadoran trade with Honduras, because Honduras was El Salvador's major trading partner. On the other hand, the traditional oligarchy was primarily concerned with preventing the mass return of immigrants from Honduras. If these campesinos returned to El Salvador, the pressures for domestic reform would be even greater. In the end, the concerns of the traditional oligarchy, supported by the conservative sector of the military, superseded those of the industrialists and the moderate officers. While there are several reasons why El Salvador invaded Honduras, a major reason is that the traditional elites still held the preponderance of power when they chose to exercise it.[57]

The other point to be made about the inability of the industrialists to defend their interests in the Common Market by avoiding armed conflict with Honduras, is that the Common Market proved to be incapable of preventing the outbreak of hostilities, either through the benefits it had imparted to El Salvador or through the mediation of its institutions. Thus, those observers who believe that the Common Market may have had a mitigating effect on Honduran-Salvadoran relations are not familiar enough with the internal political situations of the two countries.

The ideological split within the Salvadoran economic elite was not the only cause of growing political instability in El Salvador. The other destabilizing factor, and the one that encouraged the military to reinforce the traditional oligarchy's anti-Honduran position, was the growing political opposition to the Sanchez regime. This opposition was of two kinds: the fragmentation of the government party (the PCN) caused by the growing disaffection of the conservative oligarchy and military for the reasons discussed above; and the growth of formal opposition to the PCN in the form of the Christian Democratic Party and the left-wing Revolutionary Action Party (PAR).

For the last forty-five years, the military has totally dominated Salvadoran politics. Since 1931, every chief executive has been a military officer. Franklin Parker made a most accurate assessment of Salvadoran politics in 1964:

> Nothing is plainer about the politics of the country since 1948 than that the army retains control, regardless of the means through which manipulation takes place, and that whatever obedience it has rendered has been to the interests of El Salvador's aristocratic society rather than to the country at large.[58]

Osorio created the Partido Revolucionario de Unificacion Democratica (PRUD) as a vehicle for his election to the presidency in 1950. He had patterned PRUD after the Mexican PRI, apparently with the goal of unifying his country behind the reformist goals of the "Revolution of 1948." But Osorio and those that followed him used the government party as an instrument of control and dominance. By 1956, the ideals of democratic government, symbolized by the "Revolution of 1948," had been forgotten. To Osorio, politics were "inappropriate" in a country whose first priority was economic development.[59] PRUD did everything necessary to keep politics from raising its ugly head. One month before the 1956 presidential elections, the Osorio government banned three of the five presidential candidates who were challenging the PRUD candidacy of Lt. Colonel Jose Maria Lemus. One of those banned was the major challenger, a civilian named Roberto Canessa, who was very popular, but who had no military support.[60] The other two candidates withdrew from the campaign in disgust, since the outcome of the election was a foregone conclusion. All six candidates had been in substantial ideological agreement. They all supported a continuation of Osorio's social welfare programs, and they all believed in preserving the basic structure of Salvadoran society. Thus, the only reason for the Osorio regime to eliminate political competition was to preserve the hegemony of the military in politics.

After engineering the 1956 presidential elections, PRUD engineered the elections for the Legislative Assembly in 1956, 1958, and 1960, to provide President Lemus with unanimous support. PRUD also swept all local elections in 1956 and 1958. But by 1958, PRUD's heavy-handed control of the elections had aroused wide-spread vocal opposition, which Lemus found impossible to ignore. The opposition parties called for a new electoral law which would insure an honest count of votes and guarantee minority representation in the Legislative Assembly.[61] Lemos ignored their demands; and when, in November 1959, the all-PRUD Assembly passed a watered-down electoral law, it satisfied none. Protest against the Lemus regime mounted; and when the government once again awarded PRUD all seats in the April 1960 Assembly elections, the volume and violence of street demonstrations increased sharply. Lemus used the army to crush the demonstrations and riots, and opposition to his regime became even more intense. On September 5, the government declared a state of siege; and many students and other protesters were killed or wounded in the mounting confusion. Finally, on October 26, the army deposed Lemus in a bloodless coup and installed a junta to run the country.

Lemus was ousted by his military peers because he could not deal effectively with the growing civic unrest. Thus, the 1960 coup was essentially the result of a revision of power alignments within the military and not a revolution of any sort. However, the three civilian members of the junta had very close ties with the University; and their participation did cause a shift to the left in national politics. But this shift was in the spirit of the "Revolution of 1948"; it was a "controlled revolution" through which the military would enact necessary reforms while maintaining domestic tranquility. The reforms called for by the junta were basically the same as those called for but quickly forgotten by the "Osoristas" in 1948: a labor law, an agrarian reform law, new tax reforms, and a minimum wage law. But the most significant promise the junta made was to provide for free elections as soon as possible. In keeping with its goal of giving El Salvador its first real chance at democracy, the junta permitted the formation of new political parties. The Supreme Court even recognized a party with a "Fidelista" orientation, the Revolutionary Party of April and May (PRAM). By January 23, 1961, El Salvador had nine legal political parties. On that day, they were scheduled to meet to draw up a new electoral reform law under which they would later compete for office.[62]

Two days later, however, a new junta composed of more conservative elements took over the country in a violent coup. The new junta exiled two members of the old junta, arrested the other four, and dissolved the pre-electoral congress. The oligarchy and the conservative army officers had become alarmed over the threat to the political status quo posed by the previous junta's attempt to promulgate a fair electoral law and to allow the full play of democratic forces (i.e., the participation of "communistas" and "Fidelistas" in the electoral process), according to a spokesman for the new junta.[63] Leftist street demonstrations and the formation of new political parties sympathetic to "communista" and "Fidelista" ideologies created the fear among the traditional power holders that the broadening of the political process to include all elements of society would cause the political structure of the past to collapse. The conservatives therefore felt that they had to act before the new electoral law could be promulgated. After deposing the previous junta, the new junta eliminated the four political parties which it labeled as subversive: it arrested the leaders of PRAM, exiled Osorio of PSD, and prevented PRD and PAD from participating in the creation of a new electoral law. These were the same four parties which had joined together to protest the PRUD-dominated 1960 elections and to demand a new electoral law. The five remaining parties all accepted the established order and therefore were no threat to the continued dominance of the military.

However, the new junta actually implemented more social and economic reforms than envisioned by the previous junta. Opposed by both the extreme left and the die-hard reactionaries, the junta issued 335 decrees in a short time, including decrees for a higher minimum wage, a reduction of rents, a social security system, an increase in income taxes, exchange controls to prevent capital flight, and reforms of the civil service system.[64] Thus, the new junta was as committed to moderate social and economic reform as the previous governments; but it stood in fundamental opposition to the widening of the political process.

Because PRUD was too closely associated with Lemus, the new government organized the National Conciliation Party (PCN) as the mechanism through which it would control the country. Like PRUD in previous elections, the government-backed PCN was awarded all fifty-four seats in the Constituent Assembly that ruled until 1964. In the April 1962 presidential elections, Colonel Julio Rivera, the PCN's candidate, was the only candidate on the ballot. The other parties boycotted the election just as they had done in the past, because the results of the election were preordained.

But the time had passed when the military could manipulate the electoral process at will and at the same time fulfill its mandate, the maintenance of political and economic stability. In each succeeding election since 1948, the government had faced increasing demands for free elections and electoral reforms, accompanied by increasing political instability. The 1962 elections were no different. Following the junta's emasculation of the leftist political parties and the elimination of all opposition to Rivera, various left-wing groups staged a series of minor bombings and demonstrations which caused the new Rivera regime to clamp down immediately on left-wing political activity. In September 1962, the government passed a law which provided for a prison term for anyone who "praises, diffuses, indoctrinates, or propagates" any doctrine contrary to "democracy." The law also banned strikes, work stoppages, and other activities "inimical to public order."[65]

Rivera had campaigned vigorously on a platform of Alliance for Progress reforms with the hope of securing majority support and thus of becoming the first Salvadoran president to be truly legitimate. But not only had Rivera failed to secure widespread support for his regime on the part of moderates and leftists, but also his support for the Alliance for Progress was vehemently denounced by the conservative oligarchy, which launched an extensive media campaign branding the reforms as "communist inspired." Faced with mounting opposition from both the right and the left, the Rivera regime had to find some way of securing the support of the responsible opposition groups and parties. Otherwise, the new government would be confronted with the same paralyzing political instability which had caused Lemus' downfall. Rivera's solution was a law passed in August 1963 which created a system of proportional representation for filling the seats in the National Assembly. The government-backed PCN would still dominate, but the opposition parties would be allowed to participate in the Assembly for the first time in many years. This new law, coupled with the new period of economic prosperity engendered by participation in the Common Market, helped to create a new atmosphere in El Salvador. Just before the 1964 elections, moreover, the Rivera administration passed a new electoral reform law which promised that the government would not tamper with electoral procedures or results.

The government retained 60 percent of the Assembly seats for the PCN in the 1964 and 1966 elections, parcelling out the remaining twenty of the fifty-two seats to the major opposition parties. The Christian Democratic Party quickly emerged as the second largest party in El Salvador: the government awarded the Christian Democrats fourteen seats in 1964 and fifteen seats in 1966. At the same time, the Christian Democrats began to develop a strong power base in the urban areas. Christian Democratic candidate Napolean Duarte was elected mayor of San Salvador in 1964 and again in 1966 by a landslide.[66]

Rivera's strategy was initially successful in winning a general consensus for the political dominance of the "oficialista" PCN. This appears to have been borne out by the results of the 1967 presidential election, the first election in the country's history in which several candidates actively campaigned for office, the government refrained from tampering with electoral procedures, and the overwhelming majority of the population peacefully accepted the outcome.

But the limits to the government-sponsored "evolution in liberty" were made manifest in the elections of March 10, 1968. Support for the Christian Democratic Party had increased dramatically; and after the 1968 election, the party had won control of the urban areas by a wide margin, winning mayoralties in all the principal towns. The Christian Democrats gained four seats in the Legislative Assembly, reducing PCN control in the Assembly to one vote over absolute majority.[67]

The government would not have accepted an opposition majority in the Assembly, especially in view of the Christian Democrats' full support of the teachers' strike which went on throughout the election period. But the government managed to prevent the elections from developing into a "crisis," i.e., becoming an all-out test of strength between the PCN and the Christian Democrats, because the government party had complete control of the electoral machinery in the rural areas. The 1964 electoral reform law was observed by the government in the urban areas, where the dramatic increase in political activity and political awareness made fraud increasingly difficult. But fraud was still easy to perpetrate in the rural areas, where illiterate peasants were coerced into voting for the PCN.[68] As the Christian Democratic Party increased its dominance in the urban areas, this rural-urban dichotomy threatened to lead to trouble in the near future.[69]

The attempt of the moderate military officers to insure political stability and increase the legitimacy of their rule had failed. On the one hand, Rivera and Sanchez aggravated the ideological divisions within the military with their policies of liberalization and reform; but, on the other hand, the conservative elements were still powerful enough to frustrate most of the reformists' programs. Moreover, Sanchez proved to be unwilling to allow the democratic reforms initiated by Rivera to be carried to what appeared to be their rational conclusion, the beginning of a working constitutional government with meaningful party competition at the highest level.

Sanchez had come to power in 1967, supported by the moderate officers and the middle class. Besides stability, he promised to promote economic development and social tranquility. But the oligarchy, the National Guard, and the "gorilas" in the military opposed his modest reforms, just as they had opposed those of Lemus, Rivera, and Osorio; and they continually threatened him with coups (indeed, they attempted several). They forced him to give up the projects proposed by Minister of Economy Valdivieso and also to get rid of Valdivieso.

The failure of Sanchez to fulfill his campaign promises led to a wave of student, teacher, and worker strikes, which began in late 1967 and rose to crisis proportions by mid-1968. This series of strikes became the catalyst which caused the Sanchez government to seize upon the border, migration, and Common Market problems with Honduras in an attempt to rally public opinion behind it.

The internal divisions of the military and the weakened position of the Sanchez regime allowed a new figure of power to appear on the scene by mid-1968, National Guard Chief Jose Alberto Medrano, a close ally of the oligarchy.[70] As the student, teacher, and worker strikes continued, Medrano increased his power and influence by putting the strikes down until finally, in May 1968, the government closed the University.[71]

Medrano played an important role in the invasion of Honduras. In 1968, he organized 60,000 campesinos into 15,000 "cells" and gave them military training in what was officially termed an escalation in El Salvador's fight against communism.[72] But the only time this group (called ORDEN) was used was in July 1969, when it spearheaded the invasion of Honduras. According to several Honduran sources, the military invasion of Honduras was preceded by two waves of campesinos, armed with machetes and ancient firearms, who were affiliated with ORDEN.[73]

The generally accepted view is that El Salvador prepared rapidly for war in the emotionally charged climate following the Soccer Riots of 1969, without thinking of the economic and political repercussions.[74] However, there is other evidence, like the formation of ORDEN, which suggests that El Salvador was gearing up for a possible, if not anticipated, armed conflict with Honduras. In fact, one outside source states plainly that El Salvador had been planning such an invasion for over a year.[75]

While the available evidence is not strong enough to support a conspiratorial theory, it does demonstrate that, at the very least, El Salvador was preparing for a possible offensive attack.[76] In the year preceding the war, El Salvador received two deliveries of weapons from the United States. Every soldier who participated in the invasion was equipped with a new M-3 rifle.[77] Moreover, the Salvadoran army had set up supply bases along the border where they planned to attack, long before the outbreak of hostilities.

In January 1969, Honduras signed a migratory treaty with El Salvador; but El Salvador continued to build up its military forces along the border. Honduras had wanted the border issue to be settled at the same time, but El Salvador insisted on limiting the treaty to the migration question. Then, as described earlier, Honduras began to evict a small number of Salvadorans under the agrarian reform law during April and May of 1969. The Salvadoran press reacted bitterly, claiming wholesale discrimination was being committed.

As tensions rose on both sides, a final series of events occurred just before hostilities broke out. The World Cup Soccer qualifying matches between El Salvador and Honduras began on June 8. On that day, Honduras defeated El Salvador at home. The Salvadoran government claimed that there were anti-Salvadoran incidents following the game (which the Hondurans have since denied) and waged a hot anti-Honduras campaign in the press and on radio. They also increased their attacks on the "unjust" Honduran expulsion of Salvadorans from their land. The press incited Salvadorans to "give the Hondurans back what they gave" in the second soccer game, to be played in El Salvador. From the time of the Honduran team's arrival in El Salvador, angry mobs were stationed in the front of their hotel. A military escort was necessary to get the team to the stadium safely. Moreover, many Honduran fans were molested upon their arrival in El Salvador. Although the Salvadoran team won the second game, Salvadoran crowds attacked Hondurans the entire length of the 196 kilometer drive back to the frontier. Almost immediately, Salvadoran residents in Honduras came under attack. The INA intensified its expulsions of Salvadorans; and great crowds of Hondurans went around threatening Salvadorans, causing many to flee to El Salvador. An estimated 25,000 fled to the border, but El Salvador closed that avenue of escape to them on June 24. On June 27, El Salvador broke diplomatic relations with Honduras and closed the border to Honduran commerce and vehicles. After rejecting all attempts at conciliation and mediation, El Salvador launched a surprise attack against Honduras on July 14, a full month after the soccer incidents and following a continuous propaganda war designed to justify its eventual military action.[78]

With its superior army, El Salvador planned to move quickly into Honduras and occupy the provinces along the common border. The "gorilas" wanted to use the occupied land for resettlement purposes (their model was the 1967 Arab-Israeli War), while the moderate military officers wanted to use the occupied territory as a powerful bargaining tool for future migration and border treaties. However, just after the Salvadoran army crossed the border, it was halted by unexpectedly stiff Honduran resistance. The army's plans for a quick and easy victory shattered, El Salvador allowed itself to be persuaded by the OAS to withdraw under the threat of economic sanctions and a Honduran guarantee that its Salvadoran minority would not be the target of any further violence.

THE AFTERMATH OF THE SOCCER WAR

The Soccer War did nothing to resolve the internal political instability of either regime. In fact, the domestic political problems of both regimes were compounded by the war. The "gorilas" in El Salvador felt they had been cheated of the fruits of victory and refused to allow a settlement of outstanding problems with Honduras; many, in fact, wanted to finish what they had started. Moreover, rather than quiet the opposition, the war and its immediate after-effects increased dissatisfaction with the Sanchez regime. The right was afraid of what it saw as a revolutionary situation created by the rapid influx of refugees and the resulting increase in demands for agrarian reform. The industrialists and the middle sectors objected to the breaking of economic ties with Honduras and the disruption of all Common Market trade. Meanwhile, the Sanchez regime intensified its propaganda campaign against alleged Honduran atrocities committed against the "conacionales" in an attempt to unify the Salvadoran population. Honduras reciprocated by decrying the many atrocities committed during the Salvadoran advance.

Since the Soccer War, El Salvador and Honduras have both attempted to make political capital, especially during election years, by exploiting the nationalistic sentiments of the people. This will be discussed in the next chapter.

The immediate effect of the war on the Common Market was a disruption of trade. But third party trade ties were restored within a year, and intraregional trade continued to increase after 1969. The most significant impact of the war was to paralyze the common market institutions. Except for SIECA, these institutions have continued to be inoperable to the present day. The process of restructuring the market and the relationship of restructuring to the after-effects of the Soccer War will be discussed in the next chapter.

SUMMARY

The three bilateral issues--the border, migration, and Common Market problems--certainly increased the chances for and the magnitude of armed hostilities between El Salvador and Honduras. Moreover, the war would not have occurred if these problems had not existed. But the three problems, although they increased the tensions between the two countries, were not sufficient to cause El Salvador to launch an invasion of Honduras.

The border issue alone, even including the incidents of the 1967-1969 period, would not have led to armed conflict. Rather, it would simply have continued to be a secondary issue which eventually would have been resolved. Linked to the border issue was the migration issue. By 1967, Honduras had tied a solution of the migration issue to the resolution of the border problem. As discussed earlier, between 1962 and 1969, the two countries had signed a series of agreements specifically designed to defuse the issue. The Common Market did not really become an issue until Honduras began to exploit it for political purposes. Honduran disaffection with its Common Market status did lead it to aggravate relations with El Salvador. El Salvador certainly had every reason to try to maintain good relations with Honduras, because Honduras was El Salvador's biggest trading partner, and Salvadoran industry was totally geared to the Common Market. But the importance of the Common Market to the Salvadoran economy did not prevent El Salvador from invading Honduras and jeopardizing the future of the Common Market. As Nye points out, however, the prestige of the Common Market, along with the visit of President Johnson to the region in 1968, may have helped to delay an intended Salvadoran invasion.

Honduras certainly had no desire to provoke an armed conflict with El Salvador. The Lopez regime was hoping to precipitate a Common Market crisis similar to the ones engineered earlier by Nicaragua and Costa Rica. In this way, Honduras hoped to force El Salvador to agree to preferential treatment for Honduras in the Common Market. At the same time, however, the Lopez regime's manipulation of the migration and border issues got out of control, causing great alarm in El Salvador.

El Salvador's motives for attacking Honduras are questionable. The Sanchez regime claimed it invaded Honduras only to protect the rights of the Salvadorans residing in Honduras. Certainly, the danger of a mass return of Salvadoran refugees from Honduras threatened to aggravate El Salvador's worsening political and economic situation. But it was the internal political weakness of the Sanchez regime that incited it to invade Honduras.

Until the late 1960s, both sides had every reason to prevent the build-up of bilateral tensions. The factor that caused these bilateral issues to escalate into armed conflict was the domestic political situation in each country. Both countries were--and still are--military governments which lacked genuine popularity. Each country faced a crisis of legitimacy which caused it to manipulate the bilateral problems with its neighbor in an attempt to forge internal unity by rallying the population around the banner of patriotic nationalism.

The ease with which the national elites of both countries were able to arouse the nationalistic sentiments of most sectors of the population calls into serious question one of the most commonly held assumptions concerning Central American political culture. In his pioneering work on Central American integration, Joseph Nye states that the lack of strong nationalistic ideologies in Central America made possible the regional integration movement. Nye does not deny that the countries of Central America possess a degree of national consciousness. He cites the ability of the Guatemalan government to rally public support over the recurrent issue with Great Britain concerning British Honduras, the troubles between El Salvador and its Central American neighbors over illegal Salvadoran migration, and the Honduran-Nicaraguan border dispute that was settled by a decision of the International Court of Justice in 1960, as proof that there is a modest level of national consciousness in the countries of Central America. But, he says, the sense of national consciousness has not been intensified by ideology to the point of excluding the secondary but important sense of "Central Americanism."[79]

In his later work, Peace in Parts, Nye concludes that, not only did the lack of strong nationalistic sentiments encourage the growth of regional integration, but also the growth of the regional integration movement apparently caused a decline in the confrontations of the type mentioned above. The sole exception was the Soccer War, and Nye contends that a single case does not prove his thesis wrong.[80]

Nevertheless, Nye's analysis fails to account for the inarticulate, emotional type of nationalism which erupted during the El Salvador-Honduras conflict. At no time does Nye recognize the depth of nationalistic sentiments among the Honduran and Salvadoran people. Neither does he discuss the manipulation of this nationalistic sentiment by the national political leadership. In other words, this "inarticulate" nationalism may have been increasing in scope and magnitude ever since the end of World War II as the result of the process of political "modernization" or "development." It would be misleading to portray the Central American leadership as a group of "modernizing elites" attempting to utilize nationalistic sentiments to create a nation-state and sustain a development effort. However, this chapter's discussion of the development of the Salvadoran and Honduran political systems since 1948 demonstrates that there has been a continually growing political consciousness among the urban population of both countries and among a large segment of the rural population. This growing political awareness caused many citizens to feel that their government was not legitimate. Perceiving this, the national political leadership, losing ground to its political opposition, attempted to increase its legitimacy, or at least to strengthen its position, by evoking nationalistic sentiments against an external opponent. This escalation of nationalistic sentiments culminated in the Salvadoran attack on Honduras.

The second source of friction which may have

triggered an increase in nationalistic sentiments was the Common Market. Reviewing the frictions caused by distribution issues, Nye rejects the idea that they had any direct connection with the war.[81] But Gary Wynia supports the thesis of those observers mentioned at the beginning of the chapter who believe that one of the causes of the war and of the resultant undoing of the Common Market was the unleashing of the "once latent emotional antagonisms" among the Central American countries--antagonisms attributable to the "agonizing pressures of development."[82]

The basis for Nye's conclusions rests on the fact that it was the state which gained from its participation in the Common Market, and not the state which lost, that launched the attack.[83] This chapter has shown, however, that the Honduran government was dissatisfied with its status in the Common Market, and that this dissatisfaction encouraged Honduras to become more aggressive in its bilateral relations with El Salvador. Honduran disaffection with its "colonial" economic relationship with El Salvador and the growth of anti-Salvadoran sentiment led to discrimination against the illegal Salvadoran residents in Honduras. This discrimination, in turn, led to the Salvadoran reprisal, an armed attack on Honduras. In short, this chapter has shown that there is a more direct link between the frictions created by participation in the Common Market and the outbreak of the Soccer War than Nye's analysis suggests.

NOTES

1. Miguel Wionczek, "The Central American Common Market," Intereconomics No. 8, 1968, pp. 237-40; see also Schmitter, op. cit., p. 7, 21-4, 27.

2. Schmitter, pp. 26-7.

3. Wionczek, "The C.A.C.M."

4. Ibid. See also Schmitter, p. 44.

5. Ibid.

6. Schmitter, p. 45; Fagan, p. 69-72; Wionczek, "The Rise and Decline of Latin American Economic Integration," Journal of Common Market Studies Summer 1970, pp. 56-8.

7. For a good discussion of the distinction between high and low politics, see Hansen, "Reflections..."

8. Schmitter, p. 85.

9. _El Dia_, May 6, 1967 (Honduras).

10. Interview data. See also Arturo Zeledon Castillo, "Anatomia de un genocidio," _Estudios Centroamericanos_ No. 254-255, November 1969, San Salvador.

11. However, among those few are some important names: Wionczek, "The CACM" and "Rise and Decline"; Aaron Segal, "Mini-War in Central America," _Ventures_ October 1969; Carias, op. cit.; Monteforte, op. cit.; and Antonio Camillo Flores, Mexican Foreign Minister, in a speech to the U.N. General Assembly, September 24, 1969.

12. Joseph Nye, _Peace in Parts_ (Boston: Little, Brown, 1971), pp. 119-123. However, Nye criticizes the integration program for failing to achieve the coordination of social policies necessary to secure a regional solution to the basic problems involved--migration, and labor mobility in general.

13. However, this does not include Honduras, which charges that the Common Market issue was of eminent concern to Honduras and El Salvador.

14. Another issue which complicates the negotiation of a peace settlement is that El Salvador never formally declared war on Honduras; thus, it is virtually impossible to get El Salvador to sign a "peace treaty."

15. In the 1950 municipal elections, the Liberals had 8,104 votes, compared with the National Party's 77, 593 votes. Harry Kantor, _Patterns of Politics and Political Systems of Latin America_ (Rand McNally: Chicago, 1969), p. 139.

16. For a general treatment of Villeda's failure to institutionalize democracy in Honduras, see Charles Anderson, "Honduras: Problems of an Apprentice Democracy," in Martin Needler, _Political Systems of Latin America_ (Princeton: Van Nostrand, 1964). For a detailed account of the failure of the Lopez regime to achieve legitimacy, see Rafael Leiva Vivas, _Un Pais en Honduras_ (Tegucigalpa: Offset Calderon, 1969).

17. Refer to Chapter 4 for further details.

18. Based on interviews with Central American government officials. According to one source, "Lopez es solamente el fonografo al que Zuniga le da cuerda de cuando en vez." (Lopez is only the phonograph which Zuniga turns on from time to time).

19. Melgar became head of the government following Lopez's removal.

20. One source called them "dos gallos con el gatillo."

21. See Leiva, Chapter 2.

22. Derived from newspaper accounts of the period.

23. Leiva, op. cit.

24. El Cronista (Honduras), June 29, 1968.

25. Marco Virgilio Carias, Analisis sobre el conflicto entre Honduras y El Salvador, pp. 51-2.

26. Based on interview data.

27. See State Airgram, op. cit., for data on land concentration.

28. According to the latest U.N. study, in both El Salvador and Honduras the daily per capita caloric intake is well below minimum nutritional levels.

29. Carias, op. cit.

30. Ibid., pp. 27-30.

31. Interview with Mario Martin, Honduran Embassy, Washington, D.C., November 1975. He can be considered a "tecnico."

32. For a case study of the politically destabilizing effects of the development of an export-oriented agricultural economy, see Mitchell Seligson, "The Peasant and Agrarian Capitalism in Costa Rica," unpublished Ph.D. dissertation, University of Pittsburgh, 1974.

33. See the accounts of the period in El Dia and El Cronista.

34. Monteforte, op. cit., Vol. 1, p. 269, states, however, that the Honduran oligarchy is the weakest in Central America. This does not mean that the government did not feel pressure to protect the oligarchy's interests. Villeda was overthrown partly because of what landowners saw as a "communist threat" in the form of an agrarian reform law that was mild, even by Alliance for Progress standards. Later on, the weakness of the oligarchy enabled the agrarian reform law to be implemented. But local military commanders consistently intervened in agrarian conflicts on the side of the landowners.

35. Interviews, op. cit.

36. Interview with Stern, op. cit.

37. See Carias, pp. 47, 56-7; El Dia, January 20,

March 13, 1969. Fagan, p. 71, blames Honduras for its failure to renew because of pressure to implement the agrarian reform law.

38. Carias, pp. 5-7.

39. Ibid., pp. 12-17.

40. Monteforte, p. 196.

41. Carias, p. 9-15.

42. Abel Cuenca, _El Salvador: Una democracia cafetalera_ (Mexico: ARR-Centro Editorial, 1962), p. 137.

43. Almost three-fourths of Salvadoran children under the age of five are nutritionally deficient.

44. Cuenca, pp. 51-2.

45. Interview, with Wackerbarth, op. cit. See also Economist Intelligence Unit, "Central America: Review," No. 3, 1969.

46. For an account of the traditional Liberal-Conservative confrontation in Latin America, see Ronald McDonald, _Party Systems and Elections in Latin America_ (Chicago: Markham Publishers, 1971).

47. The uprising had been provoked by the government when it refused to acknowledge the workers' victories in some local municipal elections.

48. The Revolutionary Party of Democratic Unification.

49. See Cuenca, p. 114; Franklin Parker, _The Central American Republics_ (London: Oxford Press, 1964), p. 153.

50. Parker, Chapter 6.

51. _Prensa Grafica_ (El Salvador), June 30, 1957.

52. Cuenca, p. 152.

53. Information in this section based on interview data.

54. Derived from unpublished AID statistics.

55. Cuenca, p. 152.

56. While many observers recognize that the Salvadoran elite has recently developed a "broad economic base," they apparently do not comprehend the fragility of the bonds that unite the various groups. See, for example, Vincent Cable, "The Football War and the CACM," _International Affairs_ 43, (October 1969), p. 660. One incident which demonstrates the essential incompatibility of the long-range inter-

ests of the traditional oligarchy and the new, progressive members of the Salvadoran elite is the reaction of the traditional oligarchy to the Alliance for Progress reforms attempted in El Salvador in the early 1960s. While the reforms were generally accepted by the moderates, the traditional oligarchy launched a rabid media campaign against the Alliance for Progress, branding it as communist-inspired and revolutionary. The traditional elites easily stopped the modest reforms, despite support of these reforms by the moderates.

57. Jorge Arieh Gerstein,"El conflicto entre Honduras y El Salvador," *Foro Internacional* (Mexico City) 11:4 (April-June, 1971), p. 556; Dr. Gonzalez Camacho, Salvadoran Vice-Minister of Economy, in *Diario de Hoy* (San Salvador), September 1, 1971.

58. Parker, p. 153.

59. Interview with Tragen.

60. Canessa was killed by government agents in 1960.

61. The seriousness of the problem of tabulating the votes was demonstrated in the 1956 election; while the Election Council's official count was 750,000 votes cast, most observers believed that this was a fraudulent total. Some estimates placed the actual number of votes at 150,000. See Anderson, in Needler, pp. 64-5.

62. Ibid.

63. *Diario de Hoy* (El Salvador), January 26, 1961.

64. Kantor, p. 115.

65. Ibid., p. 116.

66. McDonald, p. 269.

67. "Evolution in Liberty" is the PCN slogan.

68. Economist Intelligence Unit, *Quarterly Economic Review*: "Central America," No. 2, 1968, pp. 9-10.

69. The continued threat that the Christian Democrats pose for the military is discussed in Ch. 7.

70. Widespread but unsubstantiated rumors circulating in 1969 had it that Medrano was the most important Central American on the CIA payroll.

71. *El Dia* (Honduras), February 24,28; March 9, 11; May 11, 1968.

72. *El Cronista* (Honduras), November 8, 1968.

73. Carias, p. 66.

74. Cable. p. 661.

75. Economist Intelligence Unit, "Central American Review," March 1969.

76. It is not likely that El Salvador was arming its military with sophisticated weapons for defensive purposes. The Salvadoran government knew quite well that the Honduran government had no intention of launching an attack on El Salvador and that, furthermore, the Honduran military could not have launched a successful attack. While the Salvadoran military is the most professional in Central America, the Honduran military is trained only for counterinsurgency and only up to the sergeant level. The chief function of the officer corps has been to keep the government in power; and there is a great deal of corruption in Honduras. From 1962-69 the military had been budgeted $50 million, but the troops still had worn-out equipment; some rounds of ammunition were so old they would not fire. The Honduran military hierarchy had pocketed the money; they had never expected a war to break out with any of their neighbors. See Carias, Chapter 2.

77. *El Cronista* (Honduras), December 21, 1967, reported the purchase of fighter planes, and Carias, p. 56, reports their delivery. But Cable, p. 661, disputes this charge; he states that El Salvador's air force before the war consisted of eight World War II Mustangs. It is possible the El Salvador ordered them but did not receive them in time to utilize them in the war.

78. See *Prensa Grafica* and *Diario de Hoy* (El Salvador), April through July, 1969.

79. Nye, "Central America," pp. 30-31.

80. *Peace in Parts*, p. 119.

81. Ibid., p. 121.

82. Wynia, "Paradox," p. 329.

83. Nye, *Peace in Parts*, p. 121.

7. Reconstruction: 1969-1978

Despite the insistence of each side in the El Salvador-Honduras dispute that it has consistently sought a rapid and definitive solution to outstanding problems, the two countries are apparently no closer now to resolving their differences than they were in 1970. At the same time, most observers agree that there can be little progress on the integration front until the Honduras-El Salvador dispute is resolved.

In view of the apparent lack of progress, both in the normalization of relations between El Salvador and Honduras and in the restructuring of the Common Market, this chapter seeks to answer the following questions. First, what has delayed for so long the settlement of the El Salvador-Honduras dispute? Second, how has this impasse affected the Common Market negotiations? Third, what issues other than this bilateral dispute have contributed to the continued stagnation of the Common Market and its institutions? Finally, what are the future prospects of regional integration in Central America?

THE *MODUS OPERANDI*

While nationalistic passions remained at a fever pitch for months following the July 1969 Soccer War, by November the situation had stabilized to the point that the foreign ministers of all five Common Market countries were able to meet together. By early December, they had developed a plan designed to break the deadlock between the two adversaries and repair the damage to the integration movement. The foreign ministers adopted a three-pronged approach. A working group composed of three Salvadorans, three Hondurans, and a moderator, was created to resolve the bilateral problems. The Economic Council, composed of the five Ministers of Economy, was to meet to formulate the interim procedures which would allow the market to function. A third group, an ad hoc commission of economists and jurists, was instructed to make a more detailed study of how the Common Market might be restructured. Although the plan was logically conceived, it failed to live up to expectations. Cease fire violations and general instability along the border did not form a backdrop conducive to bilateral talks; and it was nearly a year after the fighting--June 1970--before agreement was reached on creation of a six kilometer demilitarized zone along the border, to be policed by OAS military observers. Symptomatic of the problem, this accord was reached at a meeting of the five foreign ministers and not at a meeting of the bilateral working group.[1]

The major difficulty in pursuing bilateral talks was that neither belligerant was willing to address itself to the topic most important to the other. Honduras insisted on negotiations on the border dispute before it would discuss any other issue. El Salvador was prepared to talk about anything except the border dispute and saw particular merit in discussing the principle of unimpeded Salvadoran migration, the protection of Salvadoran residents in Honduras, and above all, the restoration of trade relations.

Despite the Salvadoran success in battle, the government could show few concrete gains. El Salvador, which previously had been able to use Honduras as an escape valve for its landless and its poor, now had no such outlet. Not only was further migration of Salvadorans to Honduras out of the question, but also some 65,000 refugees had to be fed, clothed, housed, and employed. One of the alleged war aims had been to gain equal treatment and full protection for Salvadorans residing in Honduras; but more than ever, they were regarded as a fifth column and found themselves objects of hatred and scorn.

The economic picture was equally glum. Honduras had been El Salvador's second largest trading partner, taking more than 10 percent of total Salvadoran exports and more than 25 percent of its intraregional exports. And Salvadoran exports to Honduras were nearly double its imports from Honduras. Now, trade between the two countries was at a standstill; and Honduras, by blocking its section of the Pan American Highway, was also impeding Salvadoran trade with Nicaragua and Costa Rica.

El Salvador, therefore, was eager to return to the status quo *ante bellum*; but it was unwilling to discuss the border problem. Honduras could document its current border; and in addition, it could forcefully stake a claim to substantial portions of Salvadoran territory. El Salvador, unhappy with its limited area, was reluctant to raise the question. Moreover, the government could afford no major concessions before the congressional elections of March 1970.

Meanwhile, the Hondurans needed concessions badly. Honduras had been the victim of aggression; yet it had received no assistance and little sympathy. Having followed the advice of the United States before the war and put its meager resources into economic development rather than into weapons procurement, Honduras felt deceived when the United States refused even to sell ammunition when Honduras' existing stocks were depleted during the war. Honduras also felt betrayed when the OAS refused to brand El Salvador an aggressor. Humiliated by its military and diplomatic performance during the war, Honduras was in no mood to lose the peace.

Honduras had few high cards to play, however. Inconveniencing El Salvador by keeping the Pan American Highway closed to Salvadoran traffic was, indeed, Honduras' major bargaining lever and one that could not be relinquished without winning something important in return. Political considerations, moreover, precluded Honduran action on readmitting Salvadorans or on guaranteeing equal treatment of Salvadoran residents as long as the prevailing national mood was anti-Salvadoran and anti-Common Market. On the other hand, persistent border tensions and fear of another Salvadoran invasion lent urgency to settlement of the border dispute.[2]

Lack of progress on bilateral issues was paralleled by lack of progress on Common Market problems. When the economic ministers first met in January 1970, all of the member states except Honduras were prepared to allow the Market's executive organs to resume formal operations immediately. Honduras, however, maintained that the conflict had terminated the Common Market's legal framework and insisted that a *modus operandi* be worked out to govern the Common Market, until a more complete restructuring could be negotiated.

Throughout 1970, negotiations on a *modus operandi* continued. Honduras, finding its deficit with its Common Market partners increasing and its foreign exchange reserves dropping, renewed many of the arguments advanced by Nicaragua before the war. As its price for continued participation in the Common Market, Honduras insisted that its industrial development receive special assistance and demanded that means be found to liquidate its chronic regional trade deficit. In a manner reminiscent of the March 1969 crisis, the Hondurans spoke of the need to reduce the cost that integration had forced on the consumers. Honduras furthermore spoke of the need for expanding industrial production on a rational basis by adopting a regional policy which would govern the establishment of new industries and the expansion of existing industries. It also called for weeding out "fictitious" industries that did not contribute to industrialization. Finally, Honduras spoke of the need for member states with positive regional trade balances to make specific commitments to increase their purchases from countries running a negative balance of trade.[3]

By September 1970, the economic ministers had reached agreement, in principle, on a _modus operandi_. Bowing to Honduran demands, the other four countries agreed to establish a permanent agricultural and industrial development fund that would have the long-term goal of helping countries correct persistent trade deficits. Each country would contribute to this fund in proportion to the relative benefits it received from the Common Market. The ministers also agreed to work out coordinated agricultural and industrial policies to correct imbalances in the rates of development of the member countries, to promote new basic industries and decide where new industrial plants should be located, and to grant fiscal and tariff benefits through joint agreements reached on a regional level. Finally, the ministers agreed to take the necessary steps to see that the protocol providing for the free trade of basic grains was applied throughout the region and that no country would purchase these grains elsewhere, as long as they were available within the Market area. From September 8 to the end of November, details of the agreement were fleshed out. Then, in December, as the economic ministers were preparing to give their final approval to the _modus operandi_, El Salvador suddenly refused to sign.[4]

El Salvador's eleventh-hour reversal of direction, like its decision to attack Honduras, was largely the result of military pressure on the government to take a firm stand. But it was also based on a reevaluation of the economic situation. The Salvadorans had realized all along that Honduras would be the major beneficiary of the *modus operandi*; and they had been particularly unhappy about the development fund, an innovation that appeared to subsidize Honduran growth partly with Salvadoran funds. Having balanced its interest in keeping the Common Market alive against its disinclination to assist the Honduran economy, El Salvador had initially concluded that its own gains from a functioning Common Market would outweigh any marginal advantage for Honduras.

A number of things had changed, however, between the end of the war and December 1970. At first, the Salvadoran economy seemed to be in a precarious position. It needed Honduran staple food products, such as beans and corn, and Honduran markets for manufactured items and petroleum products. But alternative sources of supply gradually developed, and more intensive and imaginative exploitation of markets at home and abroad compensated for the loss of the Honduran market. As these economic adjustments were made, El Salvador's interest in compromise waned; and the government began to consider a tougher bargaining position, even at the risk of Honduran withdrawal from the Common Market. Moreover, the Salvadorans were reasonably certain that the other members once again would play the role of conciliator and, in order to prevent the collapse of the Common Market, would force Honduras to be more accommodating. Salvadoran President Sanchez was eventually persuaded that it made little sense to make concessions in order to revive the Common Market unless El Salvador, in turn, could achieve some of its own political objectives.[5]

The *modus operandi*, as it finally developed, was far from the short-term transitory document that had been envisioned originally. A compensatory development fund to help the economic laggards at the expense of the Market's main bnenficiaries, a transfer of decisions on industrial development from individual governments to Common Market institutions, and a coordination of agricultural policy came close to representing a basic restructuring of the integration movement. The Salvadorans became justifiably concerned that they were bargaining away some very real economic advantages without carefully considering the long-term effects that such measures might have on their development.[6]

By December 1970, Honduras' balance of payments difficulties had become critical. Unable to obtain the economic concessions contained in the _modus operandi_, and angered by the sudden Salvadoran refusal to sign the agreement, Honduras moved to reduce its steadily increasing trade deficit by suspending the Common Market's internal trade provisions. On December 30, the Honduran Congress passed Decree 97, which applied the Common Market's common external tariff to imports from within the Market and gave the Minister of Economy authority to negotiate bilateral trade agreements granting tariff concessions based on reciprocity. Tariffs for certain goods were lowered sufficiently to permit imports from outside the region at lower prices than had been paid previously for regional imports. It was hoped that the savings from the purchase of extraregional goods would more than compensate for any loss in regional exports due to retaliation by the other four members. In addition, Honduras hoped to find extraregional markets for at least some of the goods customarily sold within the Common Market. In a very real sense, however, Honduras was resorting to the same kind of grandstand play that El Salvador had used when it refused to sign the _modus operandi_. By boldly ending preferential treatment for Common Market products and, in effect, by unilaterally withdrawing from the Market, Honduras hoped to shock the other members into action. Honduras counted on the neutral three to force El Salvador to make some compromises.[7]

The other Common Market states were indeed stirred into action. They immediately required a deposit on imports of Honduran products equal to the tariff being imposed by Honduras, and they pledged not to conclude bilateral agreements with Honduras outside the Common Market framework. Meeting on January 12, 1971, the foreign ministers of Costa Rica, Nicaragua, and Guatemala issued the Declaration of El Alcazar, committing themselves to continue the Common Market. El Salvador chose to interpret the Declaration as setting up a four-member Market and proposed formalizing such an arrangement. Costa Rica, experiencing increasing trade deficits itself and concerned that, in a four-member market, it might move into the position vacated by Honduras, blocked such a move. The Costa Rican government refused to participate in any Common Market meeting at which Honduras was not present and declared, for essentially tactical reasons, that a Common Market without all of the original members would not be viable.[8]

COSTA RICA ENGINEERS A CRISIS

In June 1971, six months after the Honduran de facto withdrawal from the Common Market, Costa Rica surprised its neighbors by imposing without warning a dual exchange system which authorized importation of "essential" goods at the official rate of 6.65 colones to the United States dollar, while all other goods were to be imported at the free rate of 8.60 colones. Moreover, Minister of Economy Carlos Castillo, the former Secretary General of SIECA, announced that Costa Rica was going to require customs bonds for certain products manufactured in El Salvador, Guatemala, and Nicaragua.

Castillo justified these actions on two separate grounds. Costa Rica was forced to impose the dual exchange rate because its balance of payments situation once again had begun to deteriorate. The selective customs bonds were necessary because, since El Salvador, Nicaragua, and Guatemala had suffered a dramatic decline in their trade with Honduras, certain industries within these countries had been "dumping"--selling below cost--their merchandise in Costa Rica. In order to protect its own industries and to prevent any further illegal dumping, Costa Rica immediately had to impose the customs bonds on shoes, textiles, clothing, soap, and edible oils.[9]

A number of observers had become convinced earlier of the seriousness of the Costa Rican charges of dumping and of the need to take remedial action. In a June 9 press conference, which followed a meeting in San Jose to discuss Costa Rica's problems, Guatemalan Minister of Economy Miron Porras stated that the Costa Rican market was being inundated with low-priced Common Market goods as a result of the closing of the Honduran market, and that local Costa Rican industry was being gravely affected.[10] In a private interview, Jonas Vasquez, Manager of the Guatemalan Chamber of Commerce and formerly a member of the Guatemalan delegation to the San Jose meeting, stated that Guatemala, El Salvador, and Nicaragua had to accommodate Costa Rica in order to avoid further deterioration of the integration movement. While he would not admit that Guatemalan industry was dumping excess goods in Costa Rica, he did admit that a few industries had cut prices substantially. Furthermore, Vasquez said that he and the other delegates appreciated the immense competitive pressure such tactics imposed on Costa Rican producers. Although price cutting was limited to the few industries mentioned above, the political impact apparently was substantial. This was particularly true for the shoe industry, where the large number of small-scale Costa Rican producers were threatened by two large shoe manufacturers, ADOC of El Salvador and INCATECU of Guatemala. Finally, it appeared that El Salvador and Guatemala were going to respond favorably to Costa Rica's request that they limit exports to Costa Rica in certain industries to 1970 levels. Castillo had promised that El Salvador and Guatemala would be provided with a detailed statistical analysis of the problems Costa Rica faced, and this analysis would enable them to fulfill Costa Rica's request.[11]

It is for the above reason that Costa Rica's neighbors were surprised by Castillo's sudden imposition of a dual exchange rate and the customs bonds. They had apparently informally agreed to accommodate Castillo's requests at the San Jose meeting. El Salvador and Guatemala immediately reciprocated by detaining all Costa Rican merchandise at the border. In addition, Salvadoran Minister of Economy Interiano sent a cable to Castillo reminding Castillo of his promise on June 9 that he would not adopt any trade measures until he had visited the other Common Market countries to explore solutions to Costa Rica's problems. In a press interview, Interiano refuted Castillo's charges of dumping--at least on the part of El Salvador--by citing trade data which indicated that Salvadoran exports to Costa Rica were below 1970 levels and by citing the high freight charges paid to the Somoza ferry--charges which made dumping difficult, if not impossible. Finally, Interiano questioned whether there was any substance to Costa Rica's alleged economic troubles, because Castillo, a well-trained economist, was unable to describe precisely the nature of Costa Rica's problems.[12]

Guatemala, El Salvador, and Nicaragua held a meeting in Managua to try to adopt a common policy toward Costa Rica. El Salvador and Guatemala had already detained Costa Rican goods at the border; but the Nicaraguans made clear that they could not risk a boycott of Costa Rican trade, since they shipped half of their exports to Costa Rica. Because the three countries could not agree on a unified position, they decided to request that Castillo attend so that they could further probe his intentions.

Castillo readily agreed to appear at the Managua meeting. Because the three countries had failed to agree on a common policy, he felt that he would be able to control the terms of the negotiations. Castillo began his presentation by insisting on the need to "restructure" the Common Market. Specifically, he demanded that the other countries accept the modus operandi that had been rejected six months earlier. Castillo declared that until the other countries agreed to sign the modus operandi, Costa Rica would apply its new free exchange rate to Central American imports. Effectively, it would impose a 30 percent tax on those products.

In response to Castillo's demands, Interiano reportedly said that "two can play at that game." He warned Castillo that, if Costa Rica persisted, the government of El Salvador would retaliate with similar measures. The Guatemalan minister of economy backed up this threat. Castillo then reportedly declared, "You know this means the end of the Common Market." Interiano replied, "So be it." This rejoinder produced the climax of the meeting: Castillo held out a Kleenex in his hand, lit it, and said, "There goes the Common Market." At this point, the meeting adjourned.

When the meeting resumed, Castillo offered a compromise proposal that became the final agreement. The agreement appeared to resolve the current crisis and to promise several long-term benefits as well. The Ministers of Economy agreed that Costa Rica, El Salvador, and Guatemala would lift their recently imposed trade restrictions on June 22 and that the ministers and the Monetary Council would study Costa Rica's exchange controls. It was understood that, within one week, Costa Rica would begin to apply the official exchange rate to intraregional imports. In addition, the Ministers of Economy agreed to establish, by July 2, a Normalization Commission which would regulate trade among the four countries by enforcing all of the provisions of the General Treaty. At the same time, the proposal did not appear to present further obstacles to the eventual return of Honduras to the Common Market. It was understood that the Normalizing Commission was a temporary substitute for the Economic Council. When Honduras signalled its desire to return to the Common Market, the Normalizing Commission would be dissolved and the Economic Council reestablished.[13]

Both observers and participants had high praise for the compromise agreement. One United States embassy official labeled it "a workable, possibly even brilliant" compromise and stated, "This arrangement has all the classic simplicity of which successful solutions are made." However, one Nicaraguan official, while praising the proposal, wondered whether Castillo had "purposely led the Common Market to so dangerous a brink" in order to win acceptance of this plan. If so, the official said, Castillo's statesmanship was exceeded by his recklessness.[14]

Several Central American officials supported the Nicaraguan's suspicions by pointing to the domestic economic situation in Costa Rica. The manager of the Salvadoran Industrial Association pointed out that the president of the Costa Rican Chamber of Commerce was involved in the shoe trade and suffered greatly from the loss of the Honduran market and from the subsequent dumping practices of the Salvadoran and Guatemalan shoe industries. He was able, according to this source, to use his influential position to exert greater private sector pressure on the Costa Rican government to protect domestic industry. As a result, despite that the majority of Costa Rican businessmen supported their country's continued participation in the Common Market, Castillo allegedly responded to the political pressure exerted by a minority of influential businessmen and engineered the crisis to gain some trading concessions from Costa Rica's trading partners. These concessions would prevent Costa Rica from occupying the position in the Market vacated by Honduras.[15]

Another argument circulating throughout Central America at the time was that Figueres had inherited a relatively sound monetary and fiscal situation in 1970 and had proceeded quickly to dissipate that inheritance. With the sour fruits of maladministration about to be harvested, Costa Rica sought to place the blame on regional economic development, according to this argument.[16]

However, Salvadoran Subsecretary for Integration Gonzales offered a very different analysis of the Costa Rican crisis. According to Gonzales, Castillo did not "abandon the Common Market" under pressure from Costa Rican businessmen. Castillo had already been assured by El Salvador and Guatemala that he could obtain the concessions he needed to satisfy the minority of Costa Rican businessmen who had been hurt by the loss of the

Honduran market. He engineered the crisis after he had obtained these promised concessions. Therefore, Gonzales and other Salvadoran and Guatemalan officials began to realize that Castillo had a deeper motive than simply demanding minor trade concessions for Costa Rica.[17]

At a meeting in Antigua in January, it was Castillo who had suggested June 30 as a deadline for the government of Honduras to announce its willingness to return to the Common Market. As this deadline approached, it became clear to Castillo that Honduras was uninterested in returning to the Common Market except on its own terms and that the other three members were willing to proceed without Honduras. Castillo had either to provoke a crisis or to live up to his commitment to go to a four-country market after June 30. Since Costa Rica initially would be the most disadvantaged member of the four-country market, Castillo opted for the crisis in a final attempt to win approval of a return to the five-country market.

Several facts support Gonzales' observations. First, Castillo, as Secretary General of SIECA in 1970, had created the _modus operandi_ for Honduras. He still supported the guided-economy aspects of the _modus operandi_; ideologically, he still considered himself an ECLA man and could not abandon his years of hard work in the integration movement. Second, the Costa Rican government feared the consequences of participating in a Common Market without Honduras, its major trading partner.[18]

Thus, when Castillo made his presentation at the Managua meeting, the Salvadoran delegates realized that he was not simply demanding trade concessions; he was also seeking to "restructure" the Common Market along the "dirigista" lines of the _modus operandi_. Moreover, according to one confidential source, Castillo did not have a compromise proposal prepared when he went to the Managua meeting. According to this source, when El Salvador and Guatemala "called Castillo's bluff," Castillo surrendered. Then, the Guatemalans permitted Castillo to save face by allowing him to propose a plan they had devised; it was this plan which became the Managua agreement.[19] Although Castillo formally proposed the final agreement, it was not the vehicle for restructuring the Common Market that Castillo had demanded initially. Rather, it closely resembled the Salvadoran proposals for "normalization" that Castillo had rejected after Honduras had imposed Decree 97 on January 1. In fact, the agreement appeared to provide a mechanism for smoothing the period of transition from a five- to a four-country market. Although the door was left open for Honduran participation, in practice the agreement excluded Honduras from the Market for a minimum of six months, because it did not directly address itself to Honduras' demands. As trade patterns adjusted to the loss of the Honduran market and pressure from business interests for remedial action decreased, it would become increasingly difficult for any government to insist upon far-reaching "restructuring."

In conclusion, Castillo had engineered a crisis in an attempt to force El Salvador, Guatemala, and Nicaragua to accept the *modus operandi* as the price for Costa Rica's suspension of its discriminatory treatment of Central American commerce. Adoption of the *modus operandi* would have allowed Honduras to return immediately to the Common Market. Unfortunately, Castillo overplayed his hand. All he obtained were some minor trade advantages which allowed him to assure Costa Rican industrialists that they would be protected from extreme competition. He failed to resurrect the *modus operandi* or to pave the way for Honduras to return to the Common Market.

The establishment of the Normalizing Commission signified that the control of the future of the Common Market passed from those demanding "restructuring"--namely, Honduras, Costa Rica, and Nicaragua--to those basically satisfied with the status quo but willing to make some concessions to "perfect" the market. The Salvadoran-Guatemalan "victory" did not signify that these two countries had decided to eliminate Honduras from the Common Market. Rather, while they were prepared to make certain concessions in order to encourage Honduras to return, they wanted to control the negotiations.

A final series of events demonstrates the complete failure of Castillo's efforts. A short time after the creation of the Normalizing Commission and the de facto creation of a four-country market which excluded Honduras, the three neutral countries signed an agreement with Honduras in Tegucigalpa. This agreement established a second four-country market. The Agreement of Tegucigalpa was applauded by participants and observers, because it signified the determination of the three neutrals to maintain common trade policies with Honduras. The neutrals had agreed to avoid quantitative export controls and other instruments which violated the terms of the General Treaty. In March 1973, Costa Rica,

Guatemala, and Nicaragua renewed their commitment to proceed simultaneously on the basis of mutually agreeable trade lists. But in August 1972, Nicaragua had negotiated a bilateral treaty with Honduras. Afraid of allowing Nicaragua to gain a competitive trade advantage, Guatemala and Costa Rica rapidly negotiated bilateral treaties with Honduras. By May 1973, the attempt to form a second four-member market had been superseded by three sets of bilateral treaties, which effectively restored conditions to what they had been before Honduras implemented Decree 97 in December 1970.[20]

Integrationists like Castillo had struggled to avoid the proliferation of bilateral treaties. Because they violated both the spirit and the letter of the General Treaty, these bilateral agreements marked a dramatic setback for integration forces.

THE CENTRAL AMERICAN ECONOMIC AND SOCIAL COMMUNITY

The *modus operandi* had represented an attempt to solve the Common Market's problems by "perfecting" the current institutional and operational structure--that is, by trying to accommodate the dissatisfied "least developed" members, within the framework of a common market which maintained a focus on free trade and industrialization. Because the attempts to secure the approval of the *modus operandi* had failed, integrationists became convinced that the only way to salvage the five-member Common Market was to "politicize" it--to push the integration movement to a higher level of cooperation.[21]

SIECA's concern with the Common Market's problems led the Secretariat, in close collaboration with ECLA, to prepare a comprehensive study which it submitted to the Ministers of Economy in October 1972.[22] This report, popularly known as the "Decade Study,"[23] surveyed the causes of the current crisis and suggested the outlines of a regional, integrated, development strategy. It stressed the need to make national growth policies conform to the integration objectives. The study made the following basic recommendations: (1)the role of the public sector as a promoter of growth should be strengthened; and a closer association of interests between the public and private sectors must be fostered, in order to achieve a common development orientation; (2)policies should be developed that will insure reasonable participation by all the countries in the costs and benefits of integration; (3)agricultural development must be accelerated, since it is the main source of employment, production, savings, and purchasing power; (4)a continued stimulus for industrial expansion must be provided in order to rationalize existing production and reorient future output, so as to enhance the net benefits that accrue from industrialization to the regional economy; (5)a uniform social development policy should be adopted, and the participation of all sectors of the population in an integrated growth process must be increased; (6)a common policy on trade and export promotion is desirable, in order to project Central America as an economic bloc in its economic relations with the rest of the world.[24]

David Nott reports that most Common Market professionals believed that, without the scheme, the Common Market would flounder.[25] "It is important," say Lizano and Wilmore, "because for the first time since the late 1950s, technocrats have had the courage to act as agents of change in presenting a coherent set of controversial proposals for reform."[26]

Nevertheless, the Decade Study was not received with unanimous approval. E. L. Barber, a senior AID economist, points out that the Decade Study does not contain much that is new. The only new approach is the commitment to "balanced development," which combines a balance among countries with an improved balance of sectors and social strata within each country. The other objectives, Barber says, are not new. "They have served as the declared principles of economic integration for many years and have been espoused on more than one occasion by all of the Central American governments." The Decade Study involves "little departure from the original charter of the Common Market as set forth in the General Treaty of 1960."[27] Even a number of tecnicos did not support the Study. The president of CABEI, in fact, had the harshest criticism of the plan. He called it "a set of platitudinous generalities."[28]

In range of subject matter, the Decade Study paralleled the _modus operandi_ reports prepared in late 1970. In fact, the Study incorporated most of the recommendations of the earlier reports. The essence of the Decade Study was a five-country free trade area, with strong emphasis upon full trade freedom, coupled with controls on future industrial investment to insure that the less developed countries received a more adequate share. Thus, it was a compromise approach that attempted to balance the interests of those satisfied with the past performance of the Market and those unhappy with existing arrangements. On the one hand, in terms of preserving a free market economy in the region, the Decade Study sturdily resisted controls on trade. On the other hand, with the intention of guaranteeing the less developed members a relatively larger share of the industrial base at some time in the future, the Decade Study introduced substantial governmental control on the allocation of new investment.[29]

The proposal to establish controls on the location of new investment--the backbone of the "balanced growth" proposals introduced in the early 1960s--was still very controversial. As shown in Chapter 3, since the beginning of the Common Market, there had been widespread resistance _in principle_ to intercountry investment controls throughout the region, but especially in El Salvador and Guatemala. Both the Integrated Industries scheme of the 1960s and the _modus operandi_ in 1970 and 1971 had failed because El Salvador and Guatemala--indeed, most of the private sector in Central America--were ideologically opposed to the extent of economic planning embodied in the integration industries and investment controls proposals.[30]

In conclusion, when SIECA presented the Decade Study to the Ministers of Economy in October 1972, it did not receive an enthusiastic welcome. It is true that, if implemented, the Decade Study would have gone a long way toward resolving the problems which have caused repeated crises in recent years. However, most of the proposals had been presented many times before; the SIECA proposal was not the fundamental reassessment of the Common Market that it was supposed to be. The Decade Study did not contain anything that would make it any less controversial or any more successful than the previous attempts at "perfecting" the Common Market.

Efforts made in 1972 to "perfect and restructure" the Common Market culminated in a meeting sponsored by SIECA in Guatemala in early December. This meeting created the new forum for discussing future negotiations, the Tripartite Conference of Ministers of Economy and Finance and the Presidents of the Central Banks. This Tripartite Committee had been formed in response to the earlier crises which had plagued the Common Market. The meeting also established a technical working group known as the High Level Committee. Composed of one representative from each country with SIECA as its technical secretariat, the High Level Committee began operating in May 1973. Its purpose was to develop a work plan and priorities for restructuring, using the Decade Study as a guideline. The High Level Committee met several times during the latter part of 1973 but announced no significant progress.

Some of the countries had delayed in appointing a representative to the High Level Committee in an apparent attempt to forestall the restructuring process. When Guatemala finally did appoint a representative, he was Alfonso Alonso Lima. Robert Allen of ROCAR characterized Alonso's appointment as "Guatemala's 'slow man on the job' approach to the High Level Committee."[31] According to Alonso himself, with the breakdown of the Common Market structure after 1969, Guatemala justifiably began to feel that its interests were better served by more vigorous efforts at the national level than in a Central American framework. Alonso said that President Arana was much more concerned with "pacification" and "internal social development" than with Central American integration, about which he knew little. Alonso took pains to explain that he had no line responsibility to Economic Minister Molina and that his instructions came from Foreign Minister Arenales.[32] This is an important point. It signifies that, because the Guatemalan leadership was disaffected with the way the Common Market negotiations appeared to be moving rapidly along the path of resturcturing and away from the original commitment to free trade, the Guatemalan leadership wanted to keep the negotiations out of the total control of the tecnicos. In the Guatemalan case, at least, the "politicos" were to maintain control of their representative to the High Level Committee.

Isaac Cohen, the co-author of the Decade Study and later the chief assistant to the Guatemalan who replaced Alonso on the High Level Committee in July 1974, says that the other reason that Guatemala had appointed Alonso was because it had been running a very strong balance of trade with its Common Market neighbors. Guatemala, Cohen said, was basically satisfied with the present situation and was, therefore, providing no leadership for change.[33]

The other problem the High Level Committee faced in late 1973 and early 1974 was the attempts of El Salvador and Honduras to use the High Level Committee as a forum to air their grievances against each other. Salvadoran High Level Committee member

Luis Buitrago charged that the Committee tended to favor Honduran positions and to discriminate against Salvadoran positions on a number of issues.[34] But SIECA Secretary General Roberto Mayorga denied these charges. He said that SIECA tried to be impartial and that it was the Salvadoran and Honduran attempts to use the High Level Committee for political confrontations that threatened to destroy it.[35]

In a move that demonstrated that the Common Market members were at least interested in preventing any further deterioration of regional economic relations, the Ministers of Economy agreed in 1973 to extend the San Jose Protocol for another five years and postponed for two years the expiration of fiscal incentives, which were given to new industrial firms in the region. The ministers affirmed their commitment to use this two-year extension to revise the common customs schedule and to establish a new common industrial development policy.[36]

According to pro-integration forces, 1974 was a year of positive results for the Common Market. The seven meetings of the High Level Committee held during the year were devoted to analyzing the SIECA proposals outlined in the Decade Study. On the basis of these proposals, the High Level Committee reached an agreement to clarify and accelerate the process of Common Market reorganization in a new treaty. The agreements essentially repeated those of the Decade Study: balanced development; integrated industrial development; the eventual formation of a customs union; cooperation on agricultural, scientific, technical, and social matters; control of foreign investment; common social and agricultural policies; and the need for tax harmonization.[37]

The last meeting of the High Level Committee in 1974 was held on December 9 in Guatemala. At that meeting, SIECA submitted a preliminary draft of the "Treaty Creating the Central American Economic and Social Community." The Draft Treaty was based on the Decade Study but covered areas not previously envisaged by that study; it sought to achieve the total economic and social union of Central America.

One official called the positive achievements of 1974--achievements culminating in the new Draft Treaty--the last attempt of the tecnicos to act as the agents of change in the integration process--"Rosenthal's swan song," according to Robert Stern.[38] Rosenthal and the other leading tecnicos had become very discouraged over the apparent apathy of the member governments toward the reconstruction effort. Rosenthal made a final attempt to convince the member governments that they really did need the Common Market to insure the future economic well-being of their economies. As David Lazar, the Director for Central American Affairs for the United States Department of State put it, "Rosenthal really opened their eyes when he presented the new Draft Treaty." Guatemala, in particular, appeared to have made a dramatic change and to have adopted a very positive attitude.[39]

However, the available evidence does not support this optimistic assessment of the tecnicos' influence on the member governments. The Guatemalan change of heart is a good example. The real reason for the Guatemalan about-face stems from domestic political changes which occurred in mid-1974. Kjell Laugerud "won" the presidential election in March and took office in July. That same month, he appointed a new representative to the High Level Committee, Carlos Enrique Peralta. Peralta had been an integration activist during his tenure as Minister of Economy during the Mendez administration a decade earlier, and he immediately began to play a positive and active role in the High Level Committee meetings. In fact, Secretary General Mayorga of SIECA said that Peralta was perhaps a bit too eager to push through a new integration treaty.[40]

What brought about this sudden change of policy? Was it simply because Laugerud was more of an integrationist than Arana? The evidence does not support this contention, although many observers, including a number of Guatemalans, believed this to be true.[41] The underlying motivate behind Laugerud's positive and public support of the restructuring process appeared to stem from his illegitimate victory in the presidential elections. Laugerud apparently attempted to use the Common Market issue in an effort to gain popularity among the masses. Besides the appointment of Peralta to the High Level Committee, Laugerud and his running mate, Mario Sandoval, made a series of speeches in which they pledged their strong support to the integration movement. Sandoval had angered the private sector by proposing that the government raise duties on exports. While the effort to use the integration issue in this manner appeared to be politically futile, at least one key Guatemalan economic official believes that these political considerations underlay Laugerud's decision to play a fairly active role in the integration movement.[42]

In October 1975, the High Level Committee presented to the governments the final document on the reorganization of the Common Market and the establishment of a Central American Economic and Social Community. The Treaty was to be the central topic of discussion at the Meeting of Presidents of Central America and Panama, which took place on October 31 and November 1. However, despite the great enthusiasm which preceded the meeting, the governments did not even discuss the new Treaty. Treaty discussions hinged on the successful outcome of bilateral negotiations between El Salvador and Honduras--negotiations which preceded the meeting. But the ninety-minute talk between Honduran President Melgar and Salvadoran President Molina failed to produce an agreement on the demarcation of the border. This, in turn, prevented the opening of negotiations on the new treaty.[43]

The presidents agreed to meet again in February 1976 to make another attempt to resolve the Honduras-El Salvador dispute and to open negotiations on the new treaty. But the meeting was cancelled because of the tremendous earthquake which struck Guatemala that month. The meeting was rescheduled for March; but President Molina of El Salvador requested that the meeting be postponed once again, because he was preoccupied with congressional and municipal elections scheduled for that month.[44] Since then, all attempts, both bilateral and multilateral, to resolve the dispute between El Salvador and Honduras and begin negotiations on the new treaty have failed.

In sum, the attempt by the tecnicos to move the integration process forward by securing the member governments' approval of a new, more comprehensive integration treaty--by "accelerating through another curve"--has so far been unsuccessful. Between October 1972, when Rosenthal introduced the Decade Study, and October 1975, when the High Level Committee presented the final version of the Draft Treaty, the tecnicos had attempted to regain the leadership role they had played in the 1950s. However, conditions had changed greatly by the early 1970s. During the 1950s, integration was not very controversial; and much progress could be achieved at the technical and ministerial levels. Nevertheless, given the domestic and regional political situations in the 1970s, it became apparent that only negotiations at the highest political level, the Meeting of Presidents, could be expected to yield any meaningful results at the fromal level of commitment. Although the presidents have met many times since the "restructuring" negotiations began, they have failed to make a public and formal commitment to move the integration program forward.

OBSTACLES TO RESTRUCTURING

According to most observers, the primary obstacle to progress on the integration front, at least in the short run, is the dispute between Honduras and El Salvador. As indicated earlier, it is generally believed that the reconstruction process can begin only when the Salvadoran-Honduran dispute is formally resolved.

As this chapter has demonstrated, this dispute has played a major role in frustrating the various attempts to move the integration process forward. El Salvador sabotaged the modus operandi in December 1970 and again in 1971, because the modus operandi appeared to favor Honduras. Honduras withdrew from the Common Market in January 1971 because of Salvadoran intransigence. Both El Salvador and Honduras used the High Level Committee for political confrontations between July 1973 and July 1974. Discussions on the new Draft Treaty since October 1975 have been hamstrung by the inability of the two countries to reach an agreement on the demarcation of the border.

Little progress was made in resolving the dispute in 1971 and 1972 because the new president of Honduras, Ramon Cruz, was a "legalist"--a hardliner who refused to compromise on Honduras' initial demands that the border problem be formally resolved before there could be progress on any other issue. Moreover, El Salvador was unable to compromise its bargaining position because of the presidential elections of 1972. When Lopez ousted Cruz in a coup in December 1972, most observers believed that negotiations could begin in earnest. It was widely thought that he would stop all of the "nationalistic nonsense" inspired by Cruz and quickly come to terms with El Salvador.[45] Thus, Central Americans were greatly disappointed when Lopez appeared to adopt Cruz's "legalistic" approach. In May 1973, a new round of negotiations began in Mexico City. On August 22, 1973, the OAS announced that both nations had agreed to negotiate a general treaty which would be signed in the months ahead.

However, the Mexico talks were broken off in December 1973. Honduran Foreign Minister Batres said the talks never got beyond the reiteration of initial bargaining positions. El Salvador refused to accept international arbitration of the border dispute, but Salvadoran Foreign Minister Borgonovo denied that El Salvador had any territorial ambitions. Lopez reiterated the Honduran position that Honduras would not return to the Common Market until the border issue was resolved.[46]

1974 was a year of little progress, although Lopez and Molina apparently had managed to establish a dialogue. Special talks were held in Miami in July 1974, and Lopez and Molina met several times. Despite the optimistic pronouncements which followed every meeting, nothing concrete was achieved. At the beginning of 1975, both Lopez and Molina announced that a major goal of their administrations was to resolve the dispute. Negotiations began at the regional level as well, as the five presidents met in January, February, and March. At the February meeting, the presidents declared that the resolution of the Honduras-El Salvador conflict was absolutely indispensable to the strengthening of the Central American community; and they announced their intention to meet every month until the issue was resolved. In a declaration issued after the February meeting, El Salvador and Honduras agreed to explore the "possible resumption of diplomatic relations in the near future."[47] A few days after the February meeting, President Lopez announced that peace between the two countries was close at hand and that he and Molina had agreed to continue their direct contacts in order to facilitate the implementation of a peace agreement. However, Lopez cautioned, peace with El Salvador would be based on a delimitation of the border.[48]

But the negotiations between Lopez and Melgar did not continue. On March 21, 1975, in a national address on television, President Molina stated that the results of his talks with Lopez made him optimistic that a solution to their differences would be found by the end of 1975.[49] Ten days later, Lopez was removed by the Armed Forces Superior Council as Commander of the Armed Forces; and Colonel Juan Melgar was installed. The armed forces shakeup continued throughout April, as those officers loyal to Lopez were "reassigned" to diplomatic posts, a form of exile in Central America. Then, on April 22, the Armed Forces removed Lopez as Chief of State; and Melgar was appointed to replace him.[50]

On April 24, the new Honduran Foreign Minister Galvez stated that Honduras remained open to a speedy solution of the Honduran-Salvadoran conflict. But, he said, there had been no serious progress since the special talks in May 1973. He then called for a meeting of the Central American presidents, which was the best medium for resolving the dispute.[51] On May 3, Melgar met with Molina in El Salvador. They spoke of the possibility of promptly negotiating a definitive solution to the dispute, a solution which would include the opening of the Pan American Highway and the resumption of diplomatic relations.[52] Negotiations at the foreign minister level began in June; and Melgar and Molina met again on July 8, reaffirming their desire to reach a rapid settlement. However, on July 11, Melgar announced that the negotiations would be left to the general staffs of the armed forces for the foreseeable future. Later on, he said, a second phase of negotiations at the foreign minister level might be possible.[53] This apparent "cooling off" was due mainly to Melgar's increasing preoccupation with the increasing political instability in Honduras. However, Foreign Minister Galvez blamed Salvadoran intransigence for preventing any positive achievements since May. The two presidential meetings, he said, resolved nothing. Galvez said that he had presented El Salvador with another proposal which would resolve the dispute, but the Salvadorans had not even responded. Thus, he said, the dialogue established by Lopez had been brought to a standstill.[54] Galvez's view was reinforced by the outcome of the ninety-minute meeting between Melgar and Molina on October 31, 1975, when the two presidents were unable to agree on the demarcation of the border. A new round of negotiations was sparked by the new OAS Secretary General Orfila in January 1976. The Honduran foreign minister and the Chief of Staff of the Armed Forces met with the Salvadoran foreign minister in Miami on February 2, 1976. Molina and Melgar met at the border on February 23. Nothing was accomplished at either meeting.

A series of border incidents in May and June of 1976 increased tensions to the point where another outbreak of violence seemed likely. Armed conflict was avoided when the two countries agreed to allow an OAS "observer team" to patrol the common border. This team of Latin American observers was still patrolling the border as of mid-1978.

Border incidents continued to embitter relations between the two countries throughout 1977. Melgar and Molina met for the last time in January 1977, but they made no progress. El Salvador's newly "elected" president, Carlos Humberto Romero, and Honduran president Juan Melgar met in Washington in October 1977; but they resolved nothing. Then in December 1977, the two countries selected former Peruvian president Jose Luis Bustamonte as mediator for another round of negotiations, which began in Peru in April 1978.

The major factor that has prevented El Salvador and Honduras from resolving their dispute is the same factor that proved to be the catalyst which ignited the Soccer War--domestic political problems. Both the Salvadoran and Honduran political leadership want to normalize relations, but neither government is strong enough internally to compromise its widely publicized bargaining position. As one Central American government official puts it, "To do so would be political suicide."[55]

As indicated in the previous chapter, before the outbreak of the Soccer War, each country had been exploiting its bilateral problems with the other in an attempt to curtail domestic political opposition to--and perhaps to increase support for--the increasingly unpopular military regime. The war compounded the domestic political problems of both regimes. In El Salvador, the "gorilas" in the military felt that they had been cheated of the fruits of victory and refused to allow a settlement of outstanding problems with Honduras; the right was alarmed by the influx of refugees and the resulting increase in demands for agrarian reform; the industrialists and the middle sectors objected to the breaking of economic ties with Honduras and the disruption of regional trade. The Salvadoran government responded by intensifying its anti-Honduran propaganda campaign in an attempt to unify the Salvadoran population. In Honduras, finding the population temporarily united in its opposition to El Salvador, Lopez intensified his anti-Salvadoran campaign in an attempt to maintain this unity in the face of increasing economic difficulties.

Most observers had predicted that the dispute would be resolved as soon as the nationalistic passions inflamed by the conflict had cooled off. But this did not occur. Instead, both countries have attempted to make political capital by exploiting the nationalistic sentiments of their constituents, especially during election years.

During the March 1972 presidential elections and the February 1974 parliamentary elections, the Salvadoran government assiduously exploited anti-Honduran feelings in order to beat back the challenge by the Christian Democrats.[56] Unwittingly, Molina robbed himself of the flexibility necessary to achieve a compromise solution to the border, migration, and Common Market issues. According to one key observer, the government of El Salvador had created a monster in whipping up super-patriotism at the grass roots level. Unlike the case in Honduras, Salvadoran business interests had nothing to gain from the conflict. It was the intellectual super-patriots, the middle class, and the popular masses who, having been aroused to xenophobia by government propaganda, were prepared to destroy the government if it showed the least bit of "softness" toward Honduras. Thus, the observer said, it would be "political suicide" for Molina to give up one square kilometer of territory.[57]

To make matters worse, Molina's attempt to exploit the nationalistic sentiments of the masses did not have its anticipated effect of bolstering support for the military regime. The ruling PCN never recovered from its massive electoral defeat of 1972. The military wanted to declare a dictatorship, but it was prevented from doing so by two forces which opposed this move. The United States pressured Molina to maintain at least a semblance of parliamentary government. Equally important, the oligarchy was--and still is--powerful enough to insist that certain of its members occupy key positions in the government.

Opposition continued to mount against Molina from both the right and the left. Molina's attempt in late 1972 to begin Alliance for Progress-type reforms greatly alarmed the oligarchy. Because Molina believed that certain moderate reforms were necessary and inevitable, he faced increasing opposition from the oligarchy and those members of the military who were allied with the oligarchy in certain business ventures. On the other hand, Molina increasingly resorted to fierce repression to prevent peasant and student demonstrations protesting the slow, almost nonexistent pace of reform. In November 1974, the National Guard killed fifty peasants and wounded two hundred, invoking bitter memories of the 1932 peasant massacre.[58] Another "peasant massacre" occurred in Frbruary 1975. Then, in July 1975, twelve students were killed, forty were wounded, and twenty "disappeared" in what many observers described as another "massacre."[59] One source reported in late 1975 that, despite the growing political opposition and increasing resort to violence on both left and right, Molina was "safe for the moment" because his opposition was factionalized.[60] Foreign diplomats in El Salvador state that Molina was fortunate to stay in office until the February 1977 presidential elections.[61]

In sum, no politician in a domestic political situation such as the one Molina faced could have made the controversial political decisions necessary to achieve a compromise with Honduras. Molina's successor, Carlos Humberto Romero, has even less domestic support. Romero, who took office on July 1, 1977, won the March 4 presidential election only through massive electoral fraud, perpetrated by the ruling PCN. Fraud and violence also seriously marred the municipal elections of March 1978.

It was widely believed that when Lopez ousted Cruz in December 1972, he would bring an end to the extreme nationalism inspired in Cruz's attempt to bolster the sagging support for his regime. Although Lopez was more flexible than Cruz on the border issue, domestic political problems prevented him from seeking a compromise solution. First, the military was divided over which course the negotiations with El Salvador should take. Both governments were military regimes, and many officers saw the problem as essentially military rather than political. Second, the Honduran industrialists felt that they were benefitting greatly from their virtual monopoly of the closed Honduran market and did not look favorably upon the normalization of trade ties with El Salvador. Third, peasant organizations had begun a campaign to force the government to enforce the agrarian reform laws; and Lopez faced increasing opposition from both right and left in his attempts to satisfy the demands of the peasants without destroying the ruling coalition of military and right-wing elements.

Lopez's position as president was further weakened by the "administrative restructuring" begun in December 1972 by the armed forces. This "restructuring" ostensibly represented the move on the part of the younger colonels, average age thirty-six, to accelerate the implementation of social reforms and the economic development policies instituted by the Lopez government. Then, on April 1, 1975, the Superior Council of the Armed Forces removed Lopez as Commander-in-Chief and installed

Melgar. While Lopez retained the presidency, the tradition in Honduras is that "an officer who does not command troops does not have power." This was confirmed on April 22, when Lopez was also replaced as president by Melgar.[62] The military shakeup continued on May 2, when Melgar, who had close ties to the conservative San Pedro Sula business sector, was forced to give up his post as Commander-in-Chief. A younger officer, more receptive to reform, replaced him.[63] In sum, Melgar, a compromise choice for president with little room for independent political action, has been unable to provide the strong leadership necessary to resolve Honduras' dispute with El Salvador.

Finally, it is important to point to a factor present in both military regimes which almost guarantees that the outstanding problems between Honduras and El Salvador will not be resolved in the near future. Both military establishments are factionalized, although the Honduran case is more extreme. In El Salvador, a committee of ten full colonels, split into two factions, makes the key political decisions; and the president is apparently one of these ten, although "first among equals." In Honduras, the Superior Council of the Armed Forces, composed of twenty-two colonels split into three factions, makes all of the major decisions. In both cases, the president is the leader of one of these factions; and in both cases, his faction is in the minority. As indicated earlier, the military in both countries is deeply divided over the proper course the negotiations with the other country should take. Coupled with the committee nature of the decision-making process, this split means that neither president can exercise the political leadership necessary to achieve a political compromise.

In sum, because of the increasing political instability and the major political changes taking place in both countries, there is no likelihood of any significant change in the formal relations between El Salvador and Honduras in the near future. Moreover, as long as the two countries maintain their respective bargaining positions, there can be no progress toward the restructuring of the Common Market.

The second reason for the failure of the attempts at reconstruction is the partially successful attempts at "normalization." That is, after the 1969 war and the resulting El Salvador-Honduras impasse, the member governments moved rapidly to find alternate markets for the goods formerly exported to Honduras. Then, in late 1972 and early 1973, the three neutrals negotiated bilateral trade treaties with Honduras. A direct violation of the General Treaty, the bilateral treaties seriously jeopardized the restructuring program. The event was dramatic proof that all five countries valued increased trade levels--a return to the status quo ante bellum--over reconstruction.

It is important to note the similarities between the two periods in which bilateral treaties assumed importance (the late 1950s and the mid-1970s). In the late 1950s, as detailed in Chapter 3, the member governments were so satisfied with the benefits of the bilateral treaties that initially they were reluctant to abandon them in favor of the Common Market, or rather, a "free trade area" followed by a "customs union." In the current period, most of the member governments are so satisfied with the benefits of the bilateral treaties that they are reluctant to support actively the restructuring process, which they feel entails more sacrifices than benefits.[64] In both cases, the member governments have demonstrated that their consistent and primary concern has been the maintenance and expansion of regional trade, and that all other integration issues are secondary. In the earlier period, an external catalyst, financial assistance from the United States, was necessary to spark an interest in the integration movement. No such catalyst has provided a similar service in the 1970s. There is no issue large enough, says Cohen, to move Central America to rally around the cause of integration.[65]

There is another obstacle to the restructuring movement, directly related to the "normalization" movement, which calls into serious question Hogan's optimistic conclusion that changing economic conditions will force the member governments to revitalize the integration process. This obstacle is the widespread ideological opposition, especially in El Salvador and Guatemala, to many of the proposals in the restructuring program. David Lazar repeatedly has stressed the low esteem in which government is held in Central America. Thus, in general, Central American businessmen do not want much interference on the part of national governments or regional institutions in their business dealings. Of course, they want preferential treatment and high profits, but they strongly oppose what they interpret as the negative aspects of government interference: investment controls, restrictions on the location of plants, limits on profits, price controls, labor reforms, and higher taxes--in short, the very prerequisites for any successful attempt to restructure the integration movement.[68]

Daniel Clare points out that Guatemala's development goals and philosophy have remained unchanged since the early 1950s.[69] As described in Chapter 3, Guatemala consistently has supported the "free trade brand" of integration. Just as consistently, Guatemala has resisted SIECA's attempts at planning on the regional level. According to Carlos Rivera, Secretary General of the Central American Chambers of Industry and a Guatemalan national, both the private sectors and the governments of Guatemala and El Salvador deeply mistrust SIECA, charging that it is too "CEPAListа" and that its inclinations are too "dirigista." SIECA still adheres to the ECLA doctrines of regional economic planning and balanced growth. The businessmen and the governments have "seen the handwriting on the wall" and are aware that certain social and economic changes are going to have to take place, on both the national and regional levels. However, they want these changes, which include a functioning, restructured Common Market, to occur within the context of a free market economy.[70]

Those governments which have supported SIECA's calls for regional planning and balanced growth--Costa Rica, Nicaragua, and Honduras--have not done so consistently, and they have been unable to ignore the demands of their private sectors for "normalization" of trade ties at the expense of restructuring. Thus, even Costa Rica, with Carlos Castillo as Minister of Economy, hurriedly negotiated a bilateral treaty with Honduras in order to assure Costa Rican businessmen of access to the Honduran market.

In summary, there are three fundamental obstacles to restructuring: the impasse between El Salvador and Honduras and the domestic political problems which have made its resolution difficult; the ideological opposition to much of the restructuring program; and the ability of the member governments to satisfy their basic desire to maintain and expand regional trade outside the legal framework of the Common Market. The bilateral dispute between El Salvador and Honduras has been the greatest short-term obstacle to restructuring. However, in the long run, the other two closely related factors will prove to be the greatest obstacles to the creation of a Central American Economic and Social Community.

"INTEGRACION DE HECHO SI NO DE DERECHO"

Does the failure to move the integration program forward at the formal level mean that the integration movement has stagnated since 1969? Absolutely not, reply those who strongly support the cause of integration in Central America. The integration process is irreversible, says Irving Tragen: "There is no way that it can be stopped."[71] This sentiment is widespread among the supporters of integration, both participants and observers.

David Lazar says that there are two levels of negotiations on both the Honduran-Salvadoran dispute and the restructuring issue. Despite the failure to cooperate at the formal level, there has been an increasing amount of informal cooperation, Lazar and other integrationists contend. This informal cooperation dates from 1974, when Rudolfo Solano, the highly respected Costa Rican representative to the High Level Committee, began calling for "integracion de hecho si no de derecho"--integration by fact if not by law. According to Solano, the idealistic Decade Study and the Draft Treaty which followed were not practical documents. In addition, the formal "legalistic" efforts at restructuring faced several major bottlenecks. Therefore, Solano argued for a "micro" approach to integration in which individual pragmatic goals could be pursued--informally, if necessary--in the hope that, by strengthening economic links in a variety of ways, the Common Market countries would find themselves more disposed to resolving the political issues involved in concluding the new Treaty.[72]

As evidence to support their contention that this second, more pragmatic effort at cooperation is working, integrationists point to sectoral developments of the last few years. The Ministers and Vice Ministers of Economy have attempted to find common policies to deal with the energy crisis, and they have made decisions on the administrative aspects of the integration treaties. The Vice Ministers of Economy have made recommendations concerning integration industries. They are especially concerned about the need to strengthen the textile and footwear industries and emphasize the need for more agro-industries. In addition, the Vice Ministers of Economy have attempted to find incentives for industrial development; and they have approved amendments making the provisions of the fiscal incentives agreement more flexible. The meetings of the Central American Monetary Council have continued, and the directors of the national planning councils have met to reaffirm the desirability of coordinated planning of development within the context of Central American integration. The Chiefs of State have held many meetings at which they have publicly affirmed their desire to continue the integration process as an instrument of socio-economic development. The presidents have issued declarations stating that the integration process is irreversible, and that Honduras should be given preferential treatment.

In the export sector, the establishment of the Union of Banana Exporting Countries at the beginning of 1974 marked the initiation of a joint decision to obtain higher price levels for agricultural products. Later efforts were geared toward obtaining special treatment with respect to coffee prices.

In the industrial field, considerable progress has been made in preparing the studies of the Central American Institute of Reasearch and Industrial Technology. The studies stress the need for local industries to develop the capacity to export outside the region, and a new proposal has been made to embark on regional projects in the near future. The IDB has extended technical cooperation to help Honduras in its preparation to develop a pulp and paper plant geared to the world market. CABEI has granted several loans for the expansion of regional industries.

CABEI has also made many loans for the expansion and extension of the Central American telecommunications network and for integration highways. Several regional and international agencies--SIECA, CABEI, ECLA, IDB, and IBRD--have coordinated their efforts to carry out various studies on integrated electrical development.

According to integrationists, the most significant accomplishment has taken place in the agricultural sector. In October 1974, the Ministers of Agriculture met for only the second time in ten years. They made SIECA their permanent secretariat and established a special working group composed of the directors of price stabilization agencies, SIECA, and appropriate regional and international organizations. This group was formally assigned the task of drawing up an action plan for the integration of the agricultural sector, with a view to raising food protection and consumption levels. Special emphasis was placed on basic grains and agricultural self-sufficiency in the region.

What is most significant about this meeting is what was not publicized about it. According to Lazar, all five countries have committed themselves to the establishment of a regional storage system, a regional price and incentives system, agreements on which country plants what and how much, and a regional export policy. Lazar believes that this is the most dramatic indication to date that all five countries are interested in solving their development problems through regional cooperation. The agreement had to be informal; and thus there was no formal document, because neither El Salvador nor Honduras would have been able to sign such a document publicly. This is one of a number of indications, according to Lazar, that El Salvador and Honduras have made a pact to keep their bilateral disagreement isolated and not allow it to interfere with their mutual interest in restructuring the Common Market. In this regard, says Lazar, Honduras' and El Salvador's publicly announced "non-negotiable" stands with respect to the border and migration issues are not to be taken at full face value.[73]

Irving Tragen offers evidence in support of Lazar's contentions. He has seen, first hand, evidence that El Salvador and Honduras are already trading in cement and a few other items; of course, this trade is on an equitable basis only. The Honduran trucks change to Guatemalan license plates at the border, and the commodities do not carry any identifying labels. Tragen says that the countries have made an "agreement to disagree" on the border issue while quietly cooperating on economic issues. In fact, says Tragen, Honduras quietly made it known in late 1975 that it was willing to sign the Draft Treaty without having made final arrangements with El Salvador. This was a direct contradiction of its public statements both before and since. If true, Honduras' new attitude could lead to further progress in the Common Market negotiations. This does not mean that Honduras can agree to the immediate establishment of a five member market. On the contrary, while Honduras may agree to the provisions of the new treaty as desirable, for years to come, all that can be expected is progress at a more informal level. At best, says Tragen, two four-country markets will be established, replacing the bilaterals now in existence.[74]

There are other indications that Honduras may be softening its hardline bargaining positions with regard to both El Salvador and the Common Market negotiations. Up until 1974, Honduran businessmen profitted enormously from the captive Honduran market, but the Honduran economy did not benefit from its isolation from the regional market. In fact, the gap between Honduras and its neighbors widened. The Honduran government had issued Decree 97, says Tragen, because it really believed that the removal of Honduras from the Common Market would stimulate increased taxation and industrial production for the domestic market. But the reverse happened; the economy stagnated because of the same domestic problems discussed in detail in earlier chapters. While other countries found new markets to absorb their regional exports, Honduras did not. Honduras now realizes, says former Minister of Economy San Martin, that it must rejoin the Common Market if it wants to avoid severe economic hardships.[75] In recent years the IDB repeatedly has warned Honduras that the future infrastructure and other development investments that the IDB will make relate to the region as a whole. The IDB, says one top IDB official, is very reluctant to invest in Honduras if it stays outside the Common Market.[76] In addition, Honduras desperately needs financial assistance from CABEI because of the devastating impact of floods, drought, and Hurricane Fifi in 1974. As a signal that Honduras may be ready to negotiate on a more pragmatic and less "dirigista" or "legalistic" level, Honduras rejoined the Regional Federation of Industries in 1975. Furthermore, Tragen feels that Honduras needs the benefits of a rejuvenated Common Market so badly that it appears to be willing to modify its legalistic stance with regard to its dispute with El Salvador and its stand on "balanced growth."[77]

There is a final factor which has emerged during the past few years which appears to have altered the disposition of El Salvador and Guatemala toward the restructuring movement: the emergence of a Christian Democratic movement in Honduras. According to Tragen, one of the major reasons that Guatemala and El Salvador have agreed to concede to Honduran demands for preferential treatment is that they are very much afraid of the potential for the emergence of a strong Christian Democratic movement in Honduras.[78]

As indicated earlier, the Christian Democratic

Party is the chief opposition in both El Salvador and Guatemala. Earlier chapters have described the rapid growth in political strength of the Christian Democrats in El Salvador to the point where they would be virtually the inevitable winners of any honest election. The Christian Democrats were actually robbed of the 1972 presidential elections in El Salvador. Napolean Duarte, the popular mayor of San Salvador, won the election; but Molina "won the recount" through massive electoral fraud. Molina was able to take office only after former President Sanchez had put down an uprising of army officers who objected to the ballot rigging. Molina then "exiled" these officers by making them ambassadors, and he exiled Duarte to Guatemala. However, opposition to Molina and to the ruling PCN grew to the point that the National Opposition Front (UNO), of which the Christian Democrats are the leaders, appeared destined to win the March 1976 congressional and municipal elections and the 1977 presidential election. However, just as before the 1972 presidential election, the government engineered a series of electoral "reforms," which guaranteed PCN victories in every election. First, the PCN obtained control of the entire local administrative machinery which oversaw the 1977 and 1978 elections. Second, the PCN-dominated government moved the rural polling places from the towns to the villages, where the PCN had greater control. Finally, the government moved the 400 voting booths for the 175,000 working class voters of San Salvador all the way across town, making it very difficult for these pro-UNO voters to get to the polls.

After the election of PCN candidate Romero in the 1977 presidential election, large-scale rioting broke out when the UNO charged the government-backed PCN with stuffing the ballot boxes. The government responded by declaring a state of siege and by exiling Claramount, the losing candidate, to Costa Rica.

Similar events surrounded the March 1978 local elections. The government invented a new set of election laws that virtually prevented the opposition from campaigning. As in the March 1976 local elections, all opposition parties boycotted the elections, guaranteeing a PCN victory. Violent protests erupted following the elections, and the government declared another state of siege.[79]

The Guatemalan military has faced a similar Christian Democratic challenge in the last few years. In the March 1974 presidential elections,

General Rios Montt, the Christian Democrat who headed the National Opposition Front, obtained 78,000 votes against 38,000 for Laugerud in the capital city. Before the other ballots could be counted, the government took control of the radio stations and halted ballot counting for twenty-four hours. Daniel Varilla reported that the government voided 180,000 ballots to prevent Rios Montt from emerging with an overall majority. This allowed the election to be decided by the Congress, which naturally chose Laugerud, Arana's hand-picked successor.[80] Despite this "defeat," the Christian Democrats made strong gains in the Congress between 1974 and 1978. Like their Salvadoran counterparts, they will be a strong threat in any honest election.

The events which followed the presidential election of 1978 demonstrated the growing influence of the Christian Democrats. In a close three-way race, where no candidate received a majority, the president was to be elected by Congress. Since the candidate of the government-backed party, General Romero Lucas Garcia, could not obtain enough votes in Congress to assure victory, the government made a deal with the Christian Democrats. In return for voting for Lucas Garcia, the Christian Democrats were "awarded," through a "recount," additional congressional seats. They were also given a number of mid-level government posts.

The Christian Democratic movement in Honduras is led by Ferdinand Galvez (a relative of the ambassador to the United States, Roberto Galvez). The Christian Democrats are strongly supported by university students and young adults in their twenties and thirties. They are children of the Liberal and National Party members, and they believe in the "democratic reformist" ideals of Villeda Morales. In the opinion of the young, as well as in that of the peasants' and workers' unions, the traditional political parties have lost their legitimacy. According to Tragen, the Christian Democratic Party will be a potent political force in the future, and the Honduran military had better accommodate it. The choice, he says, is between democracy and repression.[81]

Because both Guatemala and El Salvador have robbed their Christian Democratic Parties of the presidency, these two countries are afraid of the emergence of a strong Christian Democratic Party in Honduras. Serious domestic political troubles in their countries could result from a Christian Democratic victory at the polls in Honduras. In a real sense, says Tragen, Guatemala and El Salvador are conceding much to Honduras on the issue of preferential treatment, because they hope that this will strengthen the hand of the military regime and maintain its conservative, non-nationalistic, non-Peruvianistic orientation. Thus, internal Honduran political stability is a vital concern to El Salvador and Guatemala. The Guatemalan and Salvadoran strategy, apparently, is to prevent the rift between the military regime and the traditional Liberal and National Parties from growing to the point where the Christian Democrats, by supporting the military's development plans and calls for unity, could emerge the victor in the presidential elections scheduled for 1979.[82]

There are several factors, however, which have tempered the optimism of a number of observers concerning the informal progress made in the restructuring effort. Several officials have warned this author about taking Tragen's, Castillo's, Lazar's--in fact, all integrationists'--optimism at face value, because integrationists have a stake in economic integration. They want to see it work and have been working toward that end for almost two decades.[83]

For example, the October 1974 Grain Protocol will be a significant achievement, if its provisions are ever fulfilled. However, there have been a number of events which contradict this effort to attain regional self-sufficiency in basic grains production by 1980. For domestic political reasons, in 1975, President Oduber of Costa Rica announced that a major goal of his administration was to enable Costa Rica to achieve national self-sufficiency in basic grains production by 1980.[84] National self-sufficiency in basic grains is a major goal of every government in Central America. The best example is El Salvador, where the government launched a strong self-sufficiency drive after the conflict began with Honduras, the country's major supplier. With financial and technical backing from AID, El Salvador's yields in basic grains production improved so much that its yields are now among the highest in the hemisphere. By 1972, the Salvadoran farmer could market corn, rice, and sorghum at prices below those prevailing in the other Central American countries. During this same year, El Salvador was one of only three Latin American nations which could boast of net grain exports.[85]

El Salvador initiated this move for short-term political reasons: the desire to become independent of Honduran exports, and the need to avoid the political instability threatened by the growing food shortages of the 1960s. However, the long-range implications are clearly not favorable to the future success of the Common Market. El Salvador has transformed itself into a grain exporting country, and Costa Rica and the other Central American countries are eager to follow El Salvador's example. Furthermore, AID has established bilateral programs in each country--programs designed to help the Central American countries achieve agricultural self-sufficiency. This means that, in a reinvigorated Common Market, Honduras and Nicaragua will no longer have a comparative advantage in agricultural products with respect to their Common Market partners. While the future of the Common Market rests on specialization (this was recognized in the Draft Treaty, and specialization was the goal of the October 1974 Grain Protocol), El Salvador now has a relative advantage in both the agricultural and the industrial sectors. This advantage means that there may be very little that Honduras will be able to export to its neighbors.

A similar problem exists in the industrial sector, where there are a growing number of industries with a level of excess capacity so high that the regional market will not be able to absorb it. Because the "easy" import substitution phase has nearly run its course in Central America, there is little that Honduras can do to gain a relative advantage in the industrial sector. Thus, most economists believe that Honduras' future lies, not in developing goods for the regional market, but in developing industries which can compete on the world market.

The second issue is the dispute between El Salvador and Honduras. While it is true that the two countries have been cooperating quietly in a number of areas, Honduras has refused to compromise its bargaining position. In November 1975, Foreign Minister Galvez reiterated his position that, while Honduras was willing to establish a dialogue with El Salvador at any level, it would not change its bargaining terms. Galvez has consistently opposed the attempts of other government officials, such as Minister of Economy San Martin's attempt, to find compromise solutions.[86] On February 10, 1976, a pro-government newspaper stated that most Hondurans demand a total solution and would reject a partial settlement of the dispute. The newspaper assured the public that a hardline approach would be maintained.[87] On February 18, 1976, President Melgar, responding to public criticism, reiterated his position that the government would not negotiate with El Salvador "behind the people's backs."[88] Moreover, as pointed out earlier, it would be political suicide for the Salvadoran leadership to give up one square kilometer of territory to Honduras. Thus, due to internal public opposition to a negotiated settlement on both sides, it will be years before any real progress can be made.

The third issue, which relates to the Guatemalan and Salvadoran fear of the emerging Christian Democratic movement in Honduras, is the growing political instability in the region. At this moment, it does appear that El Salvador and Guatemala may be willing to concede to some of Honduras' demands for preferential treatment. However, there are also other trends which indicate that neither government may be willing nor forced to do so in the future. In Guatemala, ever since the beginning of the Arana administration, there appears to have been a deliberate attempt to eliminate the organized political opposition. Laugerud has continued the campaign inaugurated by Arana. Although it was reported earlier that the Christian Democrats had made some substantial gains in Congress since the 1974 presidential elections, very recently a move was launched which, if successful, would rob the Christian Democrats of much of their electoral power. Under the leadership of the government, all of the other political parties have joined together in opposition to the Christian Democrats in order to change the municipal election law. In Guatemala, the local mayor controls the voting machinery that operates during the presidential elections. Consequently, the municipal elections held every two years assume disproportionate importance. The government-backed move has resulted in a new law which states that municipal elections will be held every four years, to coincide with presidential elections. In Guatemala, the party in power tends to win municipal elections during presidential election years; the Christian Democrats won large victories in the "off-year" elections. The new law will enable the government-backed parties to gain at the expense of the Christian Democrats in the next election. With pro-government politicians controlling the electoral machinery, the Christian Democrats are not likely to win an election even if they win a plurality of votes.[89]

A more flagrant attack on the political party

system is occurring in El Salvador, where the growth of widespread opposition has greatly alarmed the army and the oligarchy. Because the National Opposition Union headed by the Christian Democrats appeared likely to win the March 1976 elections, the government attempted to put every obstacle, both legal and illegal, in the opposition's path. Throughout the month of November 1975, the government refused to give legal status to the National Opposition Union. When the government finally gave the Union legal status in December, it refused to accept the Union's slate of candidates. The government charged that one of the candidates was not legally qualified to run for office. Finally, on March 5, 1976, the opposition withdrew its candidates from the election in disgust, leaving the PCN unchallenged at the polls.[90] As discussed earlier, during the 1977 and 1978 elections, the government so manipulated the electoral machinery and instituted such restrictive campaign laws that the opposition candidates did not have a chance. These attempts to destroy the political opposition seem destined to push El Salvador along the road pioneered by Guatemala, where, as one source says, active participation in conventional opposition politics is often the quickest way to the cemetery.[91] In sum, if the Guatemalan and Salvadoran military regimes are able to eliminate their organized political opposition, there will no longer be any need for them to fear the "demonstration effect" of a vigorous Honduran Christian Democratic movement.

NOTES

1. Interview with Wackerbarth.

2. Ibid.

3. Interviews with Barber and Tragen. See also U.S. Department of State, ARA/LA, "Current Situation of the CACM," April 15, 1974, unpublished.

4. Ibid.

5. Interviews with Wackerbarth and Lazar.

6. Interviews with Stern and Barber.

7. Interview with Wackerbarth. See also Congreso Nacional de Honduras, "Medida para impulsar la produccion nacional y normar el comercio exterior," Decreto No. 97, December 31, 1970.

8. Interview with Cohen.

9. State Department Airgram, ROCAP/Guatemala, Office of Planning and Finance, "Preliminary Analysis of Costa Rica's Balance of Payments Problem," September 29, 1972, unclassified.

10. El Imparcial (Guatemala City), June 10, 1971.

11. Interview with Daniel Clare, U. S. State Department, Washington, D.C., August 5, 1975.

12. La Prensa Grafica, June 18, 1971.

13. Interviews with Cohen, Wackerbarth, and Barber.

14. Ibid.

15. Interviews with Costa Rican economic officials, July 1974; interview with Michelle Bova, U.S. Department of State, August 12, 1975.

16. Interviews with Guatemalan and Salvadoran economic officials, July 1974.

17. Ibid. Also, interview with Wackerbarth.

18. Based on interview data.

19. Based on a confidential interview between a Salvadoran economic official and a U.S. State Department official. Author interviewed the State Department official in August 1975.

20. La Nacion (San Jose), June 8, 1973, p. 47.

21. Interviews with Lazar, Wackerbarth, Tragen, and Barber.

22. SIECA, "El desarrollo integrada de Centroamerica en la presente decada," October 1972. It was principally the work of two authors, Gert Rosenthal of ECLA and Isaac Cohen Orantes of SIECA. Both are tecnicos from Guatemala.

23. It is also known as the Rosenthal Report.

24. Ibid.

25. Nott, p. 373.

26. Lizano and Wilmore, "Second Thoughts on Central America," p. 306.

27. E.L. Barber, "Analysis of the SIECA/UN Report: Integrated Development of Central America in the Present Decade," December 14, 1972, unpublished State Department Memorandum, p. 2.

28. Latin America, Vol. VI, No. 42 (October 20, 1972). See Lizano and Wilmore, op. cit., for a

detailed economic analysis.

29. Barber, "Analysis," pp. 11-15.

30. Interviews with Tragen, Lockard, Stern, and Cohen.

31. Interview with Robert Allen, ROCAP/Guatemala, July 30, 1974.

32. Ibid. Allen interviewed Alonso on June 10, 1974.

33. Interview with Cohen.

34. Interview with Allen, who talked to Mayorga on July 26, 1974.

35. Interview with Luis Buitrago, formerly Salvadoran representative to the High Level Committee, and currently an IDB official, in Washington, D.C., March 1976.

36. U.S. State Department, "Latin American Economic Integration," p. 36.

37. IDB, Annual Report, 1974, pp. 125-6.

38. Interview with Stern.

39. Interview with Lazar.

40. Interview with Allen.

41. Ibid.

42. Interview with Cohen.

43. Latin America Vol. IX, No. 44 (November 1975).

44. Ibid. Vol. X, No. 10 (March 5, 1976).

45. Ibid. Vol. 8, No. 3 (January 18, 1974).

46. Ibid. Vol. 7, No. 52 (December 6, 1973).

47. FBIS, Vol. 6, February 14, 1975, Paris AFP.

48. Ibid., February 18, 1975, Voz de Honduras, Tegucigalpa; and February 21, 1975, Madrid EFE.

49. La Prensa Grafica (San Salvador), March 21, 1975, pp. 56, 60.

50. Melgar, a conservative officer, was chosen by the young colonels who had been planning to oust Lopez for months in order to accelerate the pace of social and economic development. Melgar was chosen as a compromise candidate to keep the right-wing military officers from revolting. At the same time that this "restructuring" was occurring, however, a great scandal emerged over the lowering of the

banana tax. It was discovered that Lopez had accepted a bribe from the banana companies in excess of one million dollars, and in return he had agreed to lower the banana tax. The Liberal and National Parties had demanded that the armed forces remove Lopez because of the scandal, and on April 20, Honduras' National Investigation Commission reported that it had uncovered evidence that Lopez had accepted the bribe. Lopez was removed by the armed forces two days later. A short time later, Minister of Economy Bennaton was arrested and jailed for being the intermediary in the bribe scandal. A member of the "Old Boy" network of tecnicos, Bennaton was visited in jail by the other Central American Ministers of Economy and Carlos Castillo.

51. FBIS, April 25, 1975, Madrid EFE.

52. Ibid., May 5, 1975, Buenos Aires Latin.

53. Ibid., July 15, 1975, Voz de Honduras.

54. Ibid., September 9, 1975, San Pedro Sula Radio SWAN (Honduras).

55. Interview with Cohen.

56. As discussed below, the Christian Democrats actually won the election, but Molina "won the recount" through massive fraud.

57. Interview with Cohen.

58. Latin America Vol. IX, No. 9 (February 1975).

59. Ibid. Vol. IX, No. 31, 32 (August 1975).

60. Ibid.

61. Vision Letter Vol. 25, No. 20 (October 1975).

62. FBIS, April 2, 1975, Tegucigalpa Domestic Service; April 4, 1975, Madrid EFE; April 22, 1975, Tegucigalpa Domestic Service.

63. Latin America Vol. IX, No. 7 (May 2, 1975).

64. Interview with Tragen.

65. Interview with Cohen.

66. J.L. Hogan, Economic Officer, U.S. Embassy in Guatemala, Department of State Airgram, April 10, 1974, unclassified. IDB's Annual Report 1974, p. 127, states that regional trade as a percentage of total trade declined from 25 percent in 1968 to 20 percent in 1974.

67. Ibid.

68. Interview with Lazar.

69. Interview with Clare.

70. Interviewed by Lazar in Guatemala City on March 21, 1974; interview with Lazar.

71. Interview with Tragen.

72. Ibid.; Tragen talked with Solano in April 1974.

73. Interview with Lazar.

74. Interview with Tragen.

75. Interview in Washington, August 5, 1975.

76. Interview with Elac.

77. Interview with Tragen.

78. Ibid.

79. Latin America Vol. VI, No. 41 (October 1972); Vol. IX, No. 40 (Oct. 1975); Vol. XI, No. 7 (Feb. 1977); Vol. XI, No. 9 (March 1977); Vol. XII, No. 1 (March 1978).

80. Ibid. Vol. VIII, Nos. 10-12 (March 1974).

81. Interview with Tragen.

82. In August 1975, the Christian Democrats attempted to take advantage of this growing rift by helping the military force the Liberal and Conservative Parties to cancel a demonstration intended to demand a return to constitutional rule. Recently, however, the military regime has swung back to the right: most of the younger, more reformist officers have been demoted or assigned dead-end jobs. It is difficult to predict what impact this change will have on the military's promise to restore civilian rule through a free election in 1979.

83. Interviews with Stern, Clare and Wackerbarth.

84. Interview with Bova.

85. L. Harlan Davis, "Foreign Aid to the Small Farmer: The Salvadoran Experience," Inter-American Economic Affairs Vol 29, No. 1 (Summer 1976), p.88.

86. FBIS, November 22, 1975, Voz de Honduras.

87. El Cronista (Tegucigalpa), February 10, 1976.

88. FBIS, February 19, 1976, Panama City ACAN.

89. Latin America Vol. X, No. 2 (January 9, 1976).

90. Ibid., No. 10 (March 5, 1976). The government did finally accept the UNO slate, but harassment on UNO candidates continued.

91. Interview with Clare.

8. Conclusions

This study has attempted to analyze the major events and processes which compose the history of the integration movement in Central America and to examine the goals and roles of the major actors. The thesis of this study has been that the two perspectives from which the integration movement generally has been analyzed, the perspectives of economic and regional integration theory, have provided valuable insights and information. Taken together, however, they fail to answer adequately all of the important questions concerning the nature of the Central American integration process and the reasons for its apparent failure. A third focus has been introduced: domestic politics and the role of the political leadership in the integration movement. The object has been to clarify a number of misconceptions about the nature and the process of the Central American regional economic integration movement.

Recent "orthodox" economic analyses of the benefits of the Common Market have demonstrated the utility of competition and the market mechanism in Central America. In conjunction with several other factors, the Common Market's impact as the "engine of growth" between 1960 and 1966 was primarily the result of the expansion of free trade and increased competition. By traditional standards, all five countries, even Honduras, gained substantial economic benefits by participating in the Common Market.

At the same time, orthodox theorists have shown the disutility of industrial planning to the extent envisioned by ECLA. ECLA's strategy of concentrating on the modern sector was the biggest failing of the integration program, because the member governments failed to exploit their comparative advantage in agriculture and agro-industries.

Nonetheless, orthodox economic theory has no explanation for the apparent failure of the Common Market after 1969. It acknowledges the rise of the "balanced growth" and "balance of payments" issues, but it does not support the thesis that these problems were a direct consequence of the "least" developed members' participation in the integration program. If any economic factors can explain the demise of the Common Market, from the perspective of orthodox theory, one would have to say that, because the Common Market concentrated on the modern sector, it ceased to be an engine of growth after 1966. The implication is that the problems which arose after 1966 were the result of the Common Market's failure to provide sufficient tangible economic benefits. Finally, orthodox theory assumes economic goals are primary; political questions are outside the framework of the economic analysis.

Neo-orthodox economic thought of the type fostered by ECLA does not acknowledge many of the achievements claimed by more orthodox supporters of the integration movement. While orthodox economists claim that, in general, competition forced greater industrial efficiency and kept price levels constant, ECLA and SIECA economists prefer to point to the areas where lack of cooperation produced industrial duplication and to discreet instances where import substitution caused a rise in consumer prices. Thus, from the neo-orthodox view, the greatest failing of the Common Market program of the 1960s was that it relied too heavily on the market mechanism. The "inevitable" result was the rise after 1966 of the "balanced growth" and "balance of payments" issues. Thus, the "improper" focus of the integration program was a direct cause of the crises which led to the collapse of the Common Market after 1969.

Because of the vociferousness of the ECLA and SIECA economists and the receptivity to this doctrine of the members who were dissatisfied with their share of the benefits, the neo-orthodox view became wide-spread among observers of the Central American Common Market. Political scientists in general and regional integration theorists in particular began to adopt ECLA's analysis as the starting point for their own observations. They inherited ECLA's mistrust of the United States, the free market mechanism, and competition.

But regional integration theorists have only used the ECLA analysis as a starting point. While they agree with ECLA that the balanced growth and balance of payments crises arose almost inexorably as a result of the focus of the Common Market, integration theorists point to the tecnicos' strategy of avoiding politically controversial issues as the major reason that the integration movement failed to progress to a higher level after 1966. Somehow, the integration theorists believe, "politicization" would have worked out and led to an increase in the level of integration, if only the tecnicos had pursued a different strategy.

First of all, states this group of observers, the tecnicos depended too heavily on external financial and technical assistance, principally from the United States. Thus, the member governments did not have to sacrifice any financial resources to obtain the majority of the benefits they received from the integration institutions and from most of the integration programs. As the cost and controversiality of the integration programs rose, the commitment of the member governments remained at a very low level, because they were not obligated to increase their support of the integration program. The United States was always there to pick up the slack. Thus, Haas and Schmitter concluded that only if the members were compelled to fall back on their collective resources would the behavior patterns be triggered which would make the "expansive hypothesis" of integration theory prevail.[1]

Second, integration theorists point to the failure of the tecnicos to increase the authority and influence of the regional institutions and to develop a regional constituency. Therefore, when the crises of the late 1960s arose, the regional institutions were incapable of effectively resolving them. Moreover, because the tecnicos had not developed a regional constituency, they were not able to protect regional interests against the increasing unilateral actions in defense of national interests.

The third analytical perspective and the one introduced by this study is the role of the politicos in the integration movement. This study has attempted to analyze the role played by the Central American political leadership by examining both the impact of domestic political events on regional politics and the impact of the regional integration program on domestic politics. The conclusions drawn from this framework of analysis challenge a number of the observations based on the other two perspectives. This author's framework challenges the economists' conclusion that the balanced growth and balance of payments crises arose after the Common Market stopped being the "engine of growth." These two crises were not the result of the members' participation in the Common Market; rather, they were based on domestic political considerations. This third perspective also questions the conclusion drawn by the regional integration theorists, that the key variable in the decline of the integration movement was the role played by the tecnicos. By examining the role played by the tecnicos and the politicos in both regional and domestic politics, this study has concluded that the major variable which determined the course which the integration movement pursued and its subsequent deterioration was the role played by the politicos. During the 1960s, the politicos manipulated the integration issues to further their domestic political interests. They supported the Common Market in order to maintain the domestic economic and political status quo; thus, they prevented the internal changes upon which the future of the integration movement depended.

This study has demonstrated that an appreciation of domestic politics is necessary to understand fully the forces which shaped the integration program and those forces which later caused it to collapse. In every facet of the discussion--the roles and goals of the major actors, the major events or "crises" which occurred during the late 1960s and early 1970s, and the underlying processes (neo-functionalism, spill-over, etc.) allegedly at work--the focus on domestic politics has proven to be an indispensable analytical tool.

THE GOALS OF THE POLITICOS

The fundamental assumption of every integration theorist has been that the political elites of Central America were not interested in economic change. According to Nye, Cochrane, and others, this fact was crucial to the early success of the integration movement, because it provided the degree of separability of economic and political matters that functionalist theory says was necessary to allow the tecnicos to operate.[2] Thus, most observers assumed the politicos were indifferent to economic questions and therefore to the integration movement, because their indifference was essential to enable the functionalist process to begin. However, as Chapters 2 and 3 have shown, while the political elites may have been indifferent to the integration movement in its earliest stages, as soon as it demonstrated a potential for significant economic payoffs--between 1958 and 1960--the politicos became greatly interested.

Far from being indifferent to questions of economic development, the politicos had specific development goals and philosophies. As Chapter 2 has demonstrated, the politicos traditionally had sought external assistance in promoting the economic development of their countries. This enabled them to secure the resources necessary for economic development without upsetting the political and economic status quo. The politicos interpreted the potential benefits of the Common Market in light of this historical tradition of "reaching out." Thus, the politicos saw in the Common Market a chance to increase the pace of economic growth and industrialization and simultaneously to avoid the domestic political and economic upheavals which economic change normally entailed. In other words, the politicos had specific goals which they hoped the Common Market would enable them to achieve. They wanted to finance infrastructure development through external public assistance and to industrialize their economies by peacefully penetrating their neighbors' markets.

The dramatic change in the pace of the integration movement after 1958 is understandable only if the goals of the politicos are taken into account. Similarly, the crises which led to the deterioration of the integration movement had their roots in the change of heart of some of the member governments. While El Salvador and Guatemala remained committed to their original goals, in the late 1960s, Honduras and Nicaragua evolved a different set of goals which conflicted with their original objectives. At the beginning of the Common Market period, the political elites had shared a commitment to free trade and to the market mechanism. But in the late 1960s, Honduras, Nicaragua, and Costa Rica demanded that the focus of the Common Market shift from trade expansion and the market mechanism to industrial planning and redistribution of the benefits received from participating in the integration program.

This study has also demonstrated that the tecnicos' goals were much more complicated than the integration theorists had earlier suggested. Most of these observers portray the tecnicos as essentially allies of ECLA and, as such, more of an external force for change than marginal members of domestic political elites. While Nye, Cochrane, Schmitter and others acknowledge that these men were marginal members of a domestic political elite, they ignore the fact that the tecnicos had goals designed to improve their precarious domestic political status. Thus, while the tecnicos did seek ECLA's assistance to enable them to begin the process of economic development, they were also using ECLA as a base of power and influence with which they could improve their domestic political and economic status.

Secondly, the goals of the tecnicos did not coincide with those of ECLA. The tecnicos were more committed to rapid growth through free trade expansion than they were to ECLA's "go slow" policy which concentrated on industrial planning. This commitment is evidenced in the 1958-1960 period discussed in Chapters 2 and 3, a period in which the tecnicos failed to play the role ascribed to them--"integration mafia"--and instead allied themselves with the politicos in order to accelerate the process of integration. The two groups of actors did not share the same objectives, but they agreed on the means necessary to achieve their objectives.

THE ROLE OF THE POLITICOS

As indicated earlier, regional integration theorists assumed that the politicos did not play a major role in the integration movement, because the neo-functionalist dynamic could not operate without their indifference. The tecnicos, say Cochrane and Nye, could bring about regional economic integration only because of the politicians' disinterest in integration.[3]

But the attempts of the tecnicos to foster a strong integration program proved to be relatively unsuccessful until the politicos began to take an active role in the integration movement. The history of the early years of the integration movement, through the signing of the Multilateral Treaty of 1958, shows that the integration movement was doomed to years of frustration and stagnation, unless the politicos saw some real advantages to be had in undertaking such a task.

The active interest of the politicos in the

integration program began when the United States promised to increase its financial assistance to the area, if the member governments would support the integration program. The politicos seized the opportunity to increase the foreign public and private investment in their economies. Observers have attributed this dramatic acceleration in the pace of integration which occurred between 1958 and 1960 to the United States' offer to subsidize the integration effort. While this study has confirmed the importance of U. S. assistance as an external catalyst, it has also demonstrated that the direction the integration program took after 1958, if not the speed with which it progressed, was principally a function of the goals of the tecnicos and politicos, who did share at least two important economic objectives--the rapid expansion of free trade and the increase in public and private investment. Most observers stress the external influence of the United States; they claim that the sudden shift in the focus of the integration movement from industrial planning to free trade expansion was the price the Central American elites had to pay for United States financial assistance. However, Chapters 2 and 3 have demonstrated that the Central American elites shared the belief in free trade and the market mechanism. But the tecnicos had been unable to break with ECLA and change the focus and the pace of the integration movement until the political leadership became actively involved. Thus, the key variable which determined the direction which the integration process took in the early 1960s was the role of the politicos.

This study has demonstrated that the actions of the politicos were also a key factor in the deterioration of the Common Market in the late 1960s. The politicos' role is seldom acknowledged by other observers, who generally believe that it was the failure of the tecnicos' integration strategy which caused the crises to arise in the late 1960s. This demonstrates the integration theorists' lack of concern for the complex nature of the tecnicos' dual role as both domestic and regional actor.

Integration theorists treat the tecnicos as an external agent in the integration process: the tecnicos were supposed to create regional constituencies and manipulate the national political elites in order to secure their own goals. However, the politicos initially used the tecnicos because they had the technical expertise. The tecnicos were the liaison between the politicos and the international lending agencies; the Central American presidents needed the assistance of the tecnicos in order to meet the minimum requirements of the international agencies and the United States for financial assistance and for infrastructure development projects. Thus, the tecnicos were permitted to form planning agencies and to secure the approval of integration treaties because of their key role in the integration process and in regional politics in general. But the politicos never allowed the tecnicos to develop much influence, because the governments perceived many of the tecnicos' plans as threats to the traditional patterns of resource allocation. Thus, despite their important role in the integration program, the tecnicos were manipulated by the politicos.

As indicated in Chapter 5, no other study has examined the role of the tecnicos as a domestic political elite.[4] The "first generation" of tecnicos who were "present at the creation" of the Common Market enjoyed great prestige in their countries and throughout the region. But the "second generation," those who staffed the regional and national economic institutions during the 1960s, enjoyed no such prestige. While the first generation of tecnicos had succeeded in getting the treaties and major protocols signed, the second generation had the job of holding the integration structure together, not expanding it.

From this defensive position, it was easy for the tecnicos to be coopted into the traditional socio-political structure described in Chapter 2--which is what they had wanted all along. Just as the other potential challengers to the traditional structure--first the agriculture exporters and then the industrialists--had been coopted before them, the tecnicos also became part of the status quo. As one official explains it, "They simply became another one of the 'Old Boy' networks which dominate the Central American political scene."[5] In sum, without understanding the role and the goals of the tecnicos with respect to the domestic political process, it is difficult to describe accurately their role in regional politics.

CRISES: THE POLITICS OF BRINKMANSHIP

According to most observers, the series of crises which struck the Common Market in the late

1960s arose inexorably from the contradictions which began to emerge in 1966. However, as demonstrated in Chapters 4, 5, and 6, the balanced growth, balance of payments, and Soccer War issues did not arise automatically as a result of the member governments' participation in the Common Market. Rather, these issues were raised and then manipulated by the national governments for domestic, as well as regional, political reasons.

Most observers believe that, not only did the balanced growth issue arise automatically as a result of unregulated market forces, but also it is the greatest obstacle to the restructuring of the Common Market. However, the discussion in Chapter 4 has demonstrated that Honduras benefitted greatly from its participation in the Common Market and that the causes of its development problems were domestic political bottlenecks. The balanced growth issue did not arise inexorably, as Honduras perceived that it was not benefitting equitably from participation in the integration program. Rather, the issue emerged in Honduras after an abrupt political change and during the early stages of the Common Market. Lopez faced increasing domestic opposition, both because of his illegitimate status and because of his inability to spur the Honduran economy along the path of development. When confronted with the domestic failings of his economic policies, he attempted to disassociate his administration's policies from those of Villeda and at the same time blame Honduras' economic problems on an external source, the Common Market.

The events surrounding the balance of payments issue are an even better example of the impact of domestic politics on an integration issue. Central America's balance of payments problems were due, not to the common external tariff, but to domestic problems: growing social services required by an exploding population, the failure of tax reforms, inefficient revenue administration, and low productivity of the government sector. Costa Rican President Trejos recognized this fact and attempted to secure the Assembly's approval of an austerity program designed to balance the budget. But the Assembly refused, causing Trejos to implement the dual exchange rate; he engineered a crisis in an attempt to force the Common Market members to come up with a regional solution to the balance of payments situation. The result was the San Jose Protocol, which, according to Schmitter, marked a turning point in the integration movement: it signaled an increase in the scope of the integration process.

However, the investigation in Chapter 5 of the domestic political events surrounding the attempt to implement the San Jose Protocol has raised serious doubts about Schmitter's observations. While integration theorists interpreted the San Jose Protocol as a rational policy response by the member governments to common balance of payments problems, from the domestic political perspective, it was another attempt on the part of the politicos to solve their problems at the regional level and thus avoid politically controversial domestic reforms. The presidents of Costa Rica, Guatemala, and El Salvador had recently failed in their attempts to solve their balance of payments problems by raising taxes. For the presidents and the powerful economic elites who opposed the domestic reforms, the San Jose Protocol was a viable alternative to the politically explosive tax reforms.

It is generally held that the border and migration issues were the principal causes of the 1969 war between Honduras and El Salvador. But the discussion in Chapter 7 has concluded that, while the war would not have occurred if these two issues had not existed, the principal causes of the 1969 hostilities were the domestic political problems of the two countries.

Both countries had attempted to use the Common Market to resolve acute domestic political problems. Opposition to Honduran President Lopez had been increasing steadily since the coup of 1963; and in the late 1960s, Lopez began to direct the public's attention outward to Honduras' relations with El Salvador. Besides the border and migration issues, Lopez had managed to convince the majority of the Honduran population that the Common Market was a tool of Salvadoran economic imperialism. Lopez hoped to precipitate a crisis similar to the ones engineered earlier by Costa Rica and Nicaragua, a crisis which would force El Salvador to agree to preferential treatment for Honduras in the Common Market. This would give Lopez the diplomatic victory he needed to quiet his domestic opposition and to negotiate from a position of strength on the border and migration issues. The Honduras manipulation of the migration and border issues got out of hand when Lopez intensified his anti-Salvadoran campaign during the strikes and mass demonstrations of 1968 and 1969. El Salvador became greatly alarmed: a mass return of Salvadoran refugees would aggravate El Salvador's worsening political and economic situation.

Lopez was aware of Salvadoran apprehensions. But he counted on the fact that El Salvador's primary concern would be to keep the Common Market viable. El Salvador had depended on the Common Market to penetrate the markets of its neighbors and thus avoid the necessity of integrating the traditional sector into the modern economy. Thus, like most observers, Lopez thought that the industrial elite and its moderate military allies would give in to Honduran demands in order to protect their vital interest in the Common Market. But Lopez had misjudged the domestic political situation in El Salvador. Sanchez Hernandez, the moderate Salvadoran president, was too weak to prevent an alliance of right-wing military men and the traditional oligarchy from forcing the government to launch an attack against Honduras.

Both countries were (and still are) military governments which lacked genuine popularity. Each country faced a crisis of legitimacy which caused it to manipulate the bilateral problems with its neighbors in an attempt to forge internal unity by rallying the population around the banner of patriotic nationalism. In fact, the ease with which the nationalistic sentiments of the population were aroused seriously challenges Nye's contention that the lack of a strong sense of nationalism in Central America made the integration movement possible. In the conclusion to Chapter 6, this study has described an inarticulate, emotional type of nationalism which had been increasing in scope and magnitude since the end of World War II--the result of the process of political development. The discussion of the evolution of the Salvadoran and Honduran political systems since 1948 has demonstrated that there had been a growing political consciousness among the urban populations of both countries and among a large segment of the rural populations. This growing political awareness caused a large number of citizens to feel that their government was not legitimate. In response, the political leadership attempted to strengthen its position by evoking nationalistic sentiments against an external opponent. This escalation of nationalistic feeling culminated in the Salvadoran attack on Honduras.

The analysis in Chapter 7 of the events of the post-1969 period confirms this study's contention that the balance of payments and balanced growth issues would not have caused the Common Market to collapse. The immediate cause of the Common Market's collapse was the Soccer War and its aftereffects. The bilateral dispute between El Salvador and Honduras was the principal reason for El Salvador's sudden withdrawal of support for the *modus operandi* in December 1970 and Honduras' subsequent decision to leave the Common Market. The chapter has concluded that, because of the increasing political instability and the major political changes taking place in both countries, there is no likelihood of any improvement in the formal relations between El Salvador and Honduras in the near future. This impasse will prove to be the greatest short-term obstacle to the restructuring of the Common Market.

The greatest long-term obstacle to the restructuring of the Common Market is the fact that the political elites are essentially satisfied with the current situation. After the 1969 war, the member governments moved rapidly to establish new trade patterns and relations; and the three neutrals signed bilateral trading agreements with Honduras. These bilateral agreements seriously weakened the tecnicos' attempts to win acceptance of the restructuring program. They were dramatic proof that the politicos valued increased trade--a return to the status quo *ante bellum*--over reconstruction. The member governments have demonstrated that their consistent primary concern has been the maintenance and expansion of free trade and that all other issues have been secondary. Their original goal in 1960 had been to expand trade. The 1975 figure of over $500 million in regional trade, 40 percent above the pre-war high, is dramatic proof that they have succeeded in expanding free trade outside the legal framework of the Common Market. Now that this high volume of free trade has become part of the "status quo" which the political elites are eager to protect, the member governments have become more and more reluctant to sacrifice these advantages for the highly questionable benefits of a restructured market.

In sum, the reason that the Common Market failed to progress to higher levels of integration after 1966, and the reason that the Common Market is not likely to be effectively restructured for the forseeable future, is that the political elites allowed the integration program to progress far enough to achieve their goals but no further. Now that their goals have been met and the benefits can be maintained without any further sacrifices, they seem to find the necessity of restructuring highly questionable.

THE CONFLICT BETWEEN REGIONAL INTEGRATION AND NATIONAL POLITICAL DEVELOPMENT

There is one final area in which the focus on domestic political events has proven to be extremely valuable, and that is in the examination of long-term trends and processes. This study has demonstrated that it is impossible to discuss meaningfully the process of regional integration in Central America without referring to the process of national political development. Economic and regional integration theorists have attempted to analyze the Central American integration movement without taking into account national politics. Gary Wynia points out that, while in Europe detailed studies of individual countries preceded the analysis of integration, in Central America the reverse is true. "It is a curious phenomenon that we know more about Central American regional institutions than about the national politics of the region."[6]

Most theorists acknowledge that political development is the crucial variable which determined the path taken by the integration movement. However, not one observer has attempted to explore in depth the relation between national political development and regional integration. Thus, political development has become "the explanatory variable of last resort."[7]

Hansen acknowledges that Central America's traditional political structure has "obstructed" the regional integration process, but his interest in domestic politics is superficial. He is only concerned with the constraints under which the integration movement is operating in Central America. Political instability, administrative incapacity, and uncoordinated fiscal and industrial policies inhibit the government from implementing sound national and regional development policies. In short, Hansen is only concerned with establishing in Central America the <u>political preconditions</u> necessary to make regional integration a success.[8]

Cochrane likewise is only concerned with the domestic political "obstacles" to regional integration. Employing concepts introduced by Almond and Powell,[9] he says that because the Central American governments are concerned with "nation building," "state building," redistribution of society's resources, and interest aggregation and articulation, they are hostile toward regional integration, because it takes authority away from the national government. Thus, says Cochrane, it is only "natural" that, due to Central America's low level of political development, "politicization," "spill-over," and "externalization" did not work.[10]

Nevertheless, Cochrane has erred in his contention that the politicos were hostile toward the regional integration program because they saw it as a threat to their efforts at national political and economic development. As this study has shown, it is misleading to portray the Central American political leadership as a group of "modernizing elites." Moreover, this study has demonstrated that, far from opposing the integration movement, the politicos actively supported the integration movement because it was a way of avoiding the very domestic political and economic reforms which Cochrane and Hansen hypothesize they were supposed to be attempting. Thus, the attempts of theorists to generalize the Central American case from Almond and Powell's general conceptual framework fail, because these same theorists lack detailed knowledge of Central American political changes and processes.[11]

This study has examined the major national political processes in Central America and their effects on the process of regional integration. The domestic political processes which were determined to have the greatest impact on the integration movement were the emergence and cooptation of marginal political elites and the development of political parties and increasing political opposition.

The actions of the tecnicos could be better understood if it were remembered that they are a domestic political elite first and an "integration mafia" second. The traditional pattern of elite socialization in Central America has been reinforced by the successful cooptation of the two recent marginal elites to emerge in the post-war era, the industrialists and the tecnicos. Like the agricultural exporters who preceded them, the industrialists and then the tecnicos used external assistance as a source of external power with which they could bargain for a position in the political hierarchy. From this perspective, there is nothing unique about either group. This dimension is missed by regional integration theorists, who as a result have misinterpreted the role played by the tecnicos in the integration movement.

The major trend in domestic politics was the growth of organized political opposition in El Salvador, Honduras, and Guatemala. As Chapter 6 has demonstrated, the war between El Salvador and Honduras was sparked by the growing political instability in both countries. In both countries, opposition to the military regimes had increased as each government attempted to undermine its organized political opposition. Honduras' "experiment in democracy" had ended in 1963, when Lopez overthrew the Villeda government, because Villeda's "democratic reformism" had threatened to integrate the traditional sector into the mainstream of political and economic life. From 1963 on, opposition to the Lopez regime grew steadily; and Lopez sought to focus the country's attention on external causes of Honduras' problems, first the Common Market and then El Salvador. El Salvador's experiment with political pluralism had begun in 1964, when the military government attempted to legitimize its dominance by permitting the organization of a formal political opposition. But by 1968, the opposition, the Christian Democrats, had grown so powerful that the military had to forestall what had appeared to be the rational conclusion of the earlier reforms, a working constitutional government with meaningful party competition at the highest level. At the same time, the ruling military-oligarchy coalition had split between the moderate military reformers and the conservative members of the military and oligarchy who opposed even the most modest reform efforts. When Sanchez came to power in 1967, he faced such opposition from the conservatives that he was unable to fulfill his reformist campaign pledges. This failure led to a dramatic series of student and worker strikes and demonstrations, which by mid-1968 caused the Sanchez government, under intense pressure from both left and right, to seize upon the border, migration, and Common Market problems with Honduras in an attempt to rally public opinion behind the regime.

The other aspect of the impact of domestic party development on the integration movement concerned the growth of the Christian Democratic Parties of El Salvador, Guatemala, and Honduras. Chapter 7 has concluded that, ironically, the emergence of a strong Christian Democratic movement in Honduras appears to be changing the hardline attitude of El Salvador and Guatemala toward the restructuring movement. The Christian Democrats have been "robbed" of the presidency of both countries recently--El Salvador in 1972 and 1978 and Guatemala in 1974--and El Salvador and Guatemala are both very much afraid of the potential "demonstration effect" which a successful Honduran Christian Democratic movement would have. Thus, they may be willing to concede to Honduras' demands for preferential treatment in order to strengthen the hand of the essentially conservative Honduran military.

In sum, Cochrane's hypothesis that the process of nation and state building in Central America conflicted with the process of regional integration is faulty. There does not appear to be any conscientious effort at political institutionalization in any country other than Costa Rica. The discussion of the growth and subsequent deterioration of the process of party building and interest articulation in three Central American countries demonstrates that it was not a question of regional integration challenging the politicos' attempts at national political integration which caused the problems of the late 1960s. Rather, the growth of opposition political parties created a serious degree of political instability because the dominant elites--a combination of traditional oligarchy and conservative military--refused to allow the opposition's full participation in the political process. As indicated earlier, one of the major political goals of the dominant elites has been to prevent the integration of the traditional sector into the mainstream of political and economic life; and the growing political pluralism threatened to do just that.

NOTES

1. Haas and Schmitter, "Economic and Differential Patterns," op. cit.

2. Nye,"Regional Integration and Less Developed Countries," pp. 26-9; Cochrane, "The Politics of Regional Integration," pp. 170-8.

3. Cochrane, pp. 173-6; Nye, pp. 27-8.

4. Wynia's study is a partial exception, as is Cohen's.

5. Interview with Wackerbarth.

6. Wynia, "Paradox," p. 331.

7. Ibid., p. 330.

8. Hansen, Central America, pp. 71-81.

9. Gabriel Almond and G. B. Powell, Comparative Politics: A Developmental Approach (Boston: Little Brown and Co., 1966), pp. 34-7.

10. Cochrane, op. cit., pp. 158-61.

11. See also the works of Segal, Nye, Schmitter, and Fagan.

Bibliography

The primary sources of this study are the interviews with government officials of both the United States and Central America who have been involved in the Central American integration movement. The interviews were carried out during the summers of 1974 and 1975 and the spring of 1976.

DOCUMENTS

Banco Central de Costa Rica. Memoria anual: la economic nacional: 1963-70.

Central American Bank for Economic Integration. "Bases para la formulacion de una politica regional en materia de fomento de inversiones," Tegucigalpa, March 1965. Mimeographed.

Congreso Nacional de Honduras. "Medidas para impulsar la produccion nacional y normar el comercio exterior," Decreto numero 97, Diciembre 1970.

Inter-American Development Bank. Economic and Social Progress in Latin America. Washington, D.C. Annuals: 1971-1975.

Organizacion de Estados Americanos/Secretaria. "El esfuerzo interno y las necesidades de financimiento externo para el desarrollo de Guatemala." Washington, D.C.: OAS, 1969.

Secretariat Permanente del Tratado General de Integracion Economica Centroamericana. "El desarrollo integrado de Centroamerica en la presente decada." October 9, 1972. Mimeographed.

SIECA. "Preliminary Draft of the Treaty for the Creation of the Central American Economic and Social Community." December 9, 1974. Informal translation by AID/ROCAP in Guatemala.

SIECA. "Acta de la segunda reunion del Consejo

Economico Centroamericano, El Consejo Monetario y los Ministros de Hacienda de Centroamerica." San Jose, June 1, 1968. Mimeo.

United Nations/Economic Commission for Latin America. "Evaluacion de la integracion economica en Centroamerica." New York: 66:11.G.9, March 1966.

_________. "El Mercado Comun: Centroamerica y sus problemas recientes." Mexico: E/CN.12/CCE/363, March 1971.

_________. "Consideraciones sobre la situacion del empleo en Centroamerica." Mexico: E/CN.12/CCE/365, April 1971.

_________. "The Economic Development of Latin America and its Principal Problems." E/CN.12,1950.

_________. "Towards a Dynamic Development Policy for Latin America." New York: U.N., 1963. E/CN.12/690/Rev. 1.

_________. "The Economic Development of Latin America in the Post-War Period." New York: U.N., 1964. E/CN.12/659/Rev. 1.

_________. "La politica tributaria y el desarrollo economico en Centroamerica." New York: U.N., 1956. E/CN.12/486.

_________. "Procedimientos de libre comercio y equiparacion aranceleria en el mercado comun." New York: U.N., 1960.

_________. "La planificacion en America Latina." Santiago, 1967. E/CN.12/772.

_________. "Report of the Committee on Economic Cooperation." New York: U.N., 1964.

_________. "El programa de integracion economica de Centroamerica y el Tratado de Asociacion Economica suscrito por El Salvador, Guatemala, y Honduras." E/CN.12/CCE/212, May 6, 1960.

_________. "Breve resena de las actividades de las CEPAL en Mexico desde su creacion en 1951 hasta Mayo de 1968." CEPAL/Mex/68/11, April 1968.

_________. "Informe del represente regional de la Junta de Asistencia Tecnica de las Naciones Unidas para Centroamerica." E/CN.12/CCE/330, January 1966.

_________. "Informe del Comite de Cooperacion Economica del Istmo Centroamericano." E/CN.12/CCE/330, January 1966.

UN/Committee on Economic Cooperation in Central America. "Algunos aspectos de la politica comercial Centroamericano." Mexico, 1967. E/CN.12/CCE/SC.1/96.

_______. "La integracion economica de Centroamerica" New York: U.N. 1966. E/CN.12/CCE/33.

_______. "Resoluciones del CCE." Guatemala: SIECA, 1967.

_______. Carreteras, Puertos, y Ferrocarriles de Centroamerica. Santiago, 1965.

UN/FAO Advisory Group for Central American Integration. "Plan perspectivo para el desarrollo y la integracion de la agricultura en Centroamerica." Guatemala: Documento GAFINT 4/72, March 1972.

UN/UNCTAD Report of the Group of Experts. "Current Problems of Economic Integration." TD/D.394, 1973.

U.S. Comptroller General. "Progress and Problems in United States Aid to the Economic Unification of Central America." Washington, D.C.: Government Printing Office, 1970.

United States Congress, Senate Committee on Foreign Relations. "United States and Latin American Policies Affecting Their Economic Relations." Washington, D.C.: G.P.O., 1960.

U.S. Department of State. "The Presidents' Meeting at San Jose," Department of State Bulletin 48, April 8, 1963.

U.S. Department of State/ARA-LA/Cen: E.L. Barber. "Current Situation of the Central American Common Market." April 15, 1974, unpublished.

U.S. Department of State/Airgram. "Latin American Economic Integration." February 1, 1974. Unpublished, unclassified.

U.S. Department of State/AID/ROCAP:Guatemala. "Growth Trends in the C.A.C.M." Capto-Circ A-47, December 1, 1972.

U.S. Department of State/AID. "Economic Data Book: Latin America." No date.

U.S. Department of State/AID/ROCAP. "Economic Integration Treaties of Central America."

U.S. Department of State/ARA-LA/Cen: Barber. "Analysis of the SIECA-UN Report: The Integrated

Development of Central America in the Present Decade." December 14, 1972. Unpublished.

World Bank/IBRD. "The Common Market and its Future: A Report ofthe Industrial Finance Mission to Central America." Washington, D.C., April 20, 1971.

SECONDARY SOURCES

Amaro, Nelson, ed. El reto de desarrollo en Guatemala. Guatemala: Editorial Financiera Guatemalteca, 1970.

Anderson, Charles. Politics and Economic Change in Latin America. Princeton: Van Nostrand, 1967.

Balassa, Bela. The Theory of Economic Integration. Homewood, Ill.: Richard Irwin, Inc, 1961.

________. "Regional Integration and Trade Liberalization in Latin America," Journal of Common Market Studies Vol. X, No. 1, September 1971.

Barrera, Mario and Haas, Ernst. "The Operationalization of Some Variables Related to Regional Integration," International Organization 23, No. 1, Winter 1969.

Billick, James. "Costa Rican Perspectives and the Central American Common Market: A Case Study of International Integration." University of Pittsburgh: Unpublished Ph.D. dissertation, 1969.

Borbon, Jorge. Costa Rica y la integracion economica Centroamericana. San Jose: Asociacion Nacional de Fomento Economico, 1961.

Cable, Vincent. "Problems in the CACM," BOLSA Review Vol. 3, No. 30, June 1969.

________. "The Football War and the CACM," International Affairs 43, October 1969.

Cantouri, Louis and Spiegel, Steven, eds. The International Politics of Regions: A Compararative Approach. Englewood Cliffs: Prentice Hall, 1970.

Carias, Marco Virgilio. Analisis del conflicto entre Honduras y El Salvador. Tegucigalpa, Honduras: Universidad Nacional Autonoma de Honduras, 1969.

Castillo, Carlos. Growth and Integration in Central America. New York: Praeger, 1966.

_______. "New Issues in the CACM," *American Institute for Free Labor Development* 2:4, 1970,

Castrillo Zeledon, Mario. *El regime de libre comercio en Centroamerica*. San Jose, Costa Rica: EDUCA, 1970.

Christou, G. and Wilford W.T. "Trade Intensification in the CACM," *Journal of Inter-American Studies and World Affairs*, May 1973.

Churchill, Anthony. *Road User Charges in Central America*. World Bank Staff Occasional Papers No. 15. Baltimore: Johns Hopkins Press, 1972.

Cline, William. *Potential Effects of Income Redistribution on Economic Growth: Latin American Cases*. New York: Praeger, 1972.

Cochrane, James. "Central American Economic Integration: The Integration Industries Scheme," *Inter-American Economic Affairs* Vol. 19, No. 2, Autumn 1965.

_______. *The Politics of Regional Integration: The Central American Case*. New Orleans: Tulane University Press, 1969.

_______. "U.S. Attitudes Toward Central American Economic Integration," *Inter-American Economic* Affairs Vol. 18, Autumn 1964.

Cockroft, James; Frank,Andre Gunter; Johnson, Dale. *Dependence and Under-development: Latin America's Political Economy*. New York: Doubleday, 1972.

Cohen Orantes, Isaac. *Regional Integration in Central America*. D.C. Heath: Lexington, Mass., 1972.

Cooper, C.A. and Massell, B.F. "Towards a General Theory of Customs Unions for Developing Countries," *Journal of Political Economy* Vol. 73, No. 5.

Cuenca, Abel. *El Salvador: Una democracia cafetelaria*. Mexico: ARR-Centro Editorial, 1962.

Dalponte, Mario. "La mecanica de le integracion," *La Universidad* 3/4, May/August 1968. University of El Salvador.

Dell, Sidney. *A Latin American Common Market?* London: Oxford University Press, 1966.

_______. "Obstacles to Latin American Integration," in R. Hilton, ed. *The Movement Toward Latin American Unity*. New York: Praeger, 1969.

Denham, Robert. "The Role of the U.S. as an External Actor in the Integration of Latin America," Journal of Common Market Studies VII, March 1969.

Fagan, Stuart. Central American Economic Integration: The Politics of Unequal Benefits. Berkeley: Institute of International Studies, University of California, 1970.

Fernandez Shaw, Felix. La integracion de Centroamerica. Madrid: Ediciones Cultura Hispanica, 1965.

Faletto, Enzo and Cardozo, Fernando. Dependencia y desarrollo en America Latina. Mexico: Siglo XXI Editores, 1969.

Flanders, M. June. "Prebisch on Protectionism: An Evaluation," Economic Journal Vol. 74, June 1964.

Fonck, Carlos O'B. "Modernity and Public Policies in the Context of the Peasant Sector: Honduras." Unpublished Ph.D. dissertation: Cornell University, 1972.

Fonseca, Gautama. "Las fuentes del derecho comun Centroamericano," Derecho de la integracion No. 1, October 1967. INTAL: Buenos Aires.

Fuentes Mohr, Alberto. La creacion de un mercado comun. Buenos Aires: INTAL, 1973.

Galindo Pohl, Reynaldo. "Condicionamiento sociopolitico de la integracion," Journal of Inter-American Studies and World Affairs 12:2, April 1970.

Gerstein, Jorge. "El Conflicto entre El Salvador y Honduras," Foro Internacional, Colegio de Mexico, Mexico D.F. 11:4, April/June 1971.

Gonzalez del Valle, Jorge. "Monetary Integration in Central America," Journal of Common Market Studies Vol. VI, No. 1, September 1966.

Gordon, Jerome. "Labor Mobility and Economic Growth in Costa Rica and El Salvador," Economic Development and Cultural Change 17:3, April 1969.

Haas, Ernst and Schmitter, Philippe. The Politics of Economics in Latin American Regionalism. Denver: University ofDenver Monograph, 1965.

________. "Economics and Differential Patterns of Political Integration," International Organization XVIII, Autumn 1964.

Hansen, Roger. Central America: Regional Integration and Economic Development. Washington, D.C.: National Planning Association, 1967.

________. "Regional Integration: Reflections on a Decade of Theoretical Efforts," World Politics 21, January 1969.

Hirschman, Albert. A Bias for Hope. New Haven: Yale University Press, 1971.

Hoy, Don. "A Review of Development Planning in Guatemala," Journal of Inter-American Studies Vol. 12, No. 2, April 1970.

Jaber, Tayseer. "The Relevance of Traditional Integration Theory to the Less Developed Countries," Journal of Common Market Studies Vol. 9, No. 3, March 1971.

Jackson, Nancy. "The Adaptation of Technology in Nicaragua," University of Florida: unpublished Ph.D. dissertation, 1973.

Jalloh, Abdul. "Neo-functionalism and Regional Political Integration in Africa." Yale University, unpublished Ph.D. dissertation, 1970.

Johnson, Harry. Economic Policies Toward Less Developed Countries. Washington, D.C.: Brookings Institution, 1967.

Karnes, Thomas. The Failure of Union. Chapel Hill: University of North Carolina Press, 1961.

Lainez M., Francisco. "Discursos pronunciados en el acto inaugural del primero seminario nacional sobre la integracion economica Centroamericana." Managua: Banco Central, 1965.

Landry, David. "United States Interests in Central America: A Case Study of Policies Toward Integration and Development From 1952 to 1968." Notre Dame, unpublished Ph.D. dissertation, 1972.

Leiva Vivas, Rafael. Un pais en Honduras. Tegucigalpa: Calderon, 1969.

Levine, Meldon. "El sector privado y el mercado comun." Guatemala: Instituto Nacional de Administracion para el Desarrollo, 1968.

Libro Blanco. "El Salvador y su diferendo con Honduras." El Salvador: Imprenta Nacional de El Salvador, 1970.

Lindberg, Leon and Scheingold, Stuart. Regional Integration. Cambridge: Harvard Press, 1971.

Lizano Fait, Eduardo. "Una reflexion acerca de la integracion economica Centroamericana," Revista de la integracion 7, November 1970. Buenos Aires: INTAL.

_______. El mercado comun y la distribucion del ingreso. San Jose: Editorial EDUCA, 1970.

_______. Comentarios sobre la economia nacional. Costa Rica: Universidad "Rodrigo Facio," 1971.

_______. "Problemas actuales de la integracion," UN/TD/B/394, Geneva, 1973.

Lizano, Eduardo and Wilmore, L. N. "Second Thoughts on Central America," Journal of Common Market Studies Vol. 13, No. 3, March 1975.

Lopez, Roberto. "Empresas de accion o capital multinacional en Centroamerica." Guatemala: SIECA, 1972.

Martz, John. Central America. Chapel Hill: University of North Carolina Press, 1959.

Mathis, F. John and Krause, Walter. Latin America and Economic Integration. Iowa City: University of Iowa Press, 1970.

McCall, Louis. "Regional Integration: A Comparison of European and Central American Dynamics." Beverly Hills: Sage Publications, 1976.

McCamant, John. Development Assistance in Central America. New York: Praeger, 1968.

McClelland, Donald. The Central American Common Market. New York: Praeger, 1972.

Monteforte Toledo, Mario. "Los intellectuales y la integracion Centroamericana," Revista Mexicana de Sociologia 29, No. 4, October 1967.

_______. Centroamerica. Mexico City: Universidad Nacional Autonoma de Mexico, 1972.

_______. "La integracion economica y el panorama politico de Centroamerica," La Universidad. Universidad de El Salvador, May/August 1968.

Mora Valverde, Eduardo. "La integracion Centroamericana: un caso de penetracion imperialista," Historia y Sociedad Vol. 15, No. 3, 1969.

Myint, Hla. Economic Theory and the Underdeveloped Countries. London: Oxford University Press, 1971.

Nott, David. "Central America: Common Market Reconstruction Proposals," BOLSA Review, August 1973.

Nugent, Jeffrey. Economic Integration in Central America. Baltimore: Johns Hopkins Press, 1974.

Nye, Joseph. Peace in Parts. Boston: Little, Brown, 1971.

________. "Comparative Regional Integration: Concept and Measurement," International Organization XXII, Autumn 1968.

________. "Patterns and Catalysts in Regional Integration," International Organization XIX, Autumn 1965.

________. "Central American Regional Integration," International Conciliation No. 562, March 1967.

Parker, Franklin. The Central American Republics. London: Oxford University Press, 1964.

Pincus, Joseph. "Interim Adjustment Policy in the CACM," Journal of Inter-American Studies and World Affairs 13:2, April 1971.

Pozas, Ricardo. "Peasant Cooperatives in Honduras," Revista Mexicana de Sociologia, 1967.

Prebisch, Raul. "Commercial Policies in the Underdeveloped Countries," American Economic Review, Papers and Proceedings , May 1959.

________. "Economic Development of Latin America and Some of its Principal Problems," Economic Bulletin for Latin America Vol. 7, No. 1, February 1962.

Ramsett, David. Regional Industrial Development in Central America. New York: Praeger, 1969.

Robinson, E.A.G. The Economic Consequences of the Size of Nations. New York, 1963.

Robleda, Roberto. "La industria del calzado y algunos problemas y perspectivas de desarrollo," Economia Politica, January 1972. Honduras.

Rostow, Walter. The Stages of Economic Growth. Cambridge: Cambridge University Press, 1960.

Rostow, Walter, ed. The Economics of Take-off into Sustained Growth. London: McMillan, 1968.

Sancho, Jose. "El marco institucional del CACM y las perspectivas de un esquema comunitario," Derecha de la Integracion 13, July 1973. Buenos Aires, INTAL.

Saxe-Fernandez, John. "The Central American Defense Council and Pax Americana," in Irving Horowitz, et. al., eds., Latin American Radicalism.

New York: Vintage Books, 1969.

Schiavo-Campo, Salvadore. "Estructura y sustitucion de las importaciones en el MCCA." Guatemala: SIECA, 1972.

Schmitter, Philippe. "Central American Integration: Spillover, Spill-Around, or Encapsulation?" Journal of Common Market Studies IX, No. 1, September 1970.

_______. "Further Notes on Operationalizing Some Variables Related to Integration," International Organization XXIII, Spring 1969.

_______. Autonomy or Dependence as Regional Integration Outcomes. Berkeley, Institute of International Studies: University of California Press, 1972.

_______. "A Revised Theory of Regional Integration," International Organization XXIV, Autumn 1970.

_______. "Three Neo-Functionalist Hypotheses About Regional Integration," International Organization XXIII, Winter 1969.

Segal, Aaron. "The Integration of Developing Countries: Some Thoughts on East Africa and Central America," Journal of Common Market Studies Vol. V, No. 3, March 1967.

Seligson, Mitchell. "Transactions and Community Formation: Fifteen Years of Growth and Stagnation in the CACM," Journal of Common Market Studies Vol. 11, March 1973.

Sol Castellanos, Jorge. "Proceso de la integracion economica Centroamericana," Revista de la integracion Centroamericana 4, April 1972.

Staley, C.E. "Costa Rica and the CACM," Economia Internationale 15, February 1962.

Tobis, David. "The CACM: The Integration of Underdevelopment," NACLA Newsletter, III, Jan. 1970.

Torres-Rivas, Edelberto. Interpretacion del desarrollo social Centroamericano. Costa Rica: EDUCA, 1971.

Villagran Kramer, Francisco. Integracion economica Centroamericana. Guatemala: Editorial Universitaria, 1967.

Weiselfeiz, Jacobo. "El comercio exterior, el mercado comun, y la industrializacion en relacion con el conflicto," Faculty of Humanities, University of El Salvador, 1969.

Wilford, Walter T. "Trade Creation in the CACM," Western Economic Journal , March 1970.

________. "The CACM: Trade Patterns After a Decade of Union," Nebraska Journal of Economics 12, No. 3, Summer 1973.

Willmore, L.N. "Free Trade in Manufacturing among Developing Countries: The Central American Experience," Economic Development and Cultural Change 20, July 1972.

Wionczek, Miguel, ed. Latin American Economic Integration: Experience and Prospects. New York: Praeger, 1966.

Wionczek, Miguel. "La integracion economica Latinoamericana y la inversion privada extranjera," Comercio Exterior XX, September 1970.

________. "The Rise and Decline of Latin American Economic Integration," Journal of Common Market Studies Vol. 9, September 1970.

________. Economic Cooperation in Latin America, Africa, and Asia: A Handbook of Documents. Cambridge: MIT Press, 1969.

Woodruff, William and Olga. "The Illusions About the Role of Integration in Latin America's Future," Inter-American Economic Affairs Vol. 22, Spring 1969.

Wynia, Gary. "Central American Integration: The Paradox of Success," International Organization Vol. XXIV, No. 2, Spring 1970.

________. Politics and Planners. Madison: University of Wisconsin Press, 1972.

Young, John Parke. Central American Monetary Union. Guatemala: AID-ROCAP, 1965.

For Product Safety Concerns and Information please contact our EU
representative GPSR@taylorandfrancis.com
Taylor & Francis Verlag GmbH, Kaufingerstraße 24, 80331 München, Germany

www.ingramcontent.com/pod-product-compliance
Lightning Source LLC
LaVergne TN
LVHW021621091026
849796LV00027B/346
* 9 7 8 0 3 6 7 1 6 7 8 1 3 *